Singing in a Foreign Land

JEWISH CULTURE AND CONTEXTS

Published in association with the
Herbert D. Katz Center for Advanced Judaic Studies
of the University of Pennsylvania

Series editors: Shaul Magid, Francesca Trivellato, Steven Weitzman

A complete list of books in the series is available from the publisher.

SINGING *in a* FOREIGN LAND

Anglo-Jewish Poetry,
1812–1847

KAREN A. WEISMAN

PENN

UNIVERSITY OF PENNSYLVANIA PRESS
PHILADELPHIA

Copyright © 2018 University of Pennsylvania Press
All rights reserved. Except for brief quotations used for purposes of review or scholarly citation, none of this book may be reproduced in any form by any means without written permission from the publisher.

Published by
University of Pennsylvania Press
Philadelphia, Pennsylvania 19104-4112
www.upenn.edu/pennpress

Printed in the United States of America on acid-free paper
1 3 5 7 9 10 8 6 4 2

Library of Congress Cataloging-in-Publication Data
Names: Weisman, Karen A., author.
Title: Singing in a foreign land : Anglo-Jewish poetry, 1812–1847 / Karen A. Weisman.
Other titles: Jewish culture and contexts.
Description: 1st edition. | Philadelphia : University of Pennsylvania Press, [2018] | Series: Jewish culture and contexts | Includes bibliographical references and index.
Identifiers: LCCN 2018002989 | ISBN 9780812250343 (hardcover : alk. paper)
Subjects: LCSH: English poetry—19th century—History and criticism. | English poetry—Jewish authors—History and criticism. | Romanticism—Great Britain. | Judaism and literature—England—History—19th century.
Classification: LCC PR590 .W38 2018 | DDC 821/.7098924—dc23
LC record available at https://lccn.loc.gov/2018002989

For Arthur, and for Aviva and Noah

CONTENTS

Introduction. Hath Not a Jew	1
Chapter 1. Emma Lyon's Spacious Firmament	16
Chapter 2. Mourning, Translation, Pastoral: Hyman Hurwitz	70
Chapter 3. The Early Efforts of Celia and Marion Moss	123
Chapter 4. Grace Aguilar and the Demands of Lyric	167
Coda. Amy Levy's Impossible Modernity	215
Notes	225
Bibliography	235
Index	243
Acknowledgments	249

Singing in a Foreign Land

INTRODUCTION

Hath Not a Jew

> [The Jew] hardly has left, when all is said, a drop of bucolic blood in his veins.
> —Amy Levy, "Jewish Humour" (1886)

Amy Levy's assertion goes to the heart of one of the central tensions of this study: if the Jew hath not a drop of the very blood that defines one of the central features of British literary inheritance, then how do we understand Anglo-Jewish poetry that would situate itself within the canonical domain of British cultural tradition? Indeed, how do early nineteenth-century Anglo-Jewish poets situate themselves as cultural figures within a cultural matrix for which the bucolic is a foundational value term? Hath not a Jew? If you prick him, he will not bleed bucolic blood. Levy's pronouncement is no lament over deprivation; in fact, for Amy Levy, the late-nineteenth century Jewish poet, prose writer, and essayist, the putative rootless cosmopolitanism of nineteenth-century European Jewry is one foundation of Jewish perspicacity. Levy's allusion is not merely Shakespearean. It is not the Jewish merchant she is struggling to understand, but rather the cultural presumptions of Jewish authors in a land whose cultural accents are defined in terms that present them with singular challenges. Her remark is taken from a study of Heinrich Heine, in which she diagnoses the idiosyncratic idiom of Jewish humour, but it clearly bears the weight of her reflection on the modes of Jewish literature more generally in her century. The putative dearth of bucolic blood goes hand in hand with the distinctiveness of the Jewish gaze: "He [the Jew] has been huddled in crowded quarters of towns, forced into close and continual contact with his fellow-creatures; he has learned to watch men's faces; to read men's thoughts; to be always ready for his opportunity."[1] If the authority of the bucolic is not hers to claim, then she will embrace the alertness of the unsettled cosmopolitan: the Jew who has learned to be "always ready," to be vigilant in his interpretive savvy ("to read men's thoughts"), is the Jew who has learned to be safe even while exercising a cultural audacity.

The poetry I engage in this book is confined mainly to the first half of the nineteenth century, a period that precedes Levy. I have cited her in this introduction because the critical distance from her immediate Jewish predecessors and her privileged insight enable her to put her finger directly on the central tensions that engage their work. The Jew without a drop of bucolic blood in his veins is the Jew who, in the Romantic period, defines his subjectivity both against and within British cultural norms. As such, the expressive resources appropriated by Jewish poets define at once a highly qualified forum for self-understanding and a necessary forum for the discovery of a self-alienation. In establishing the dates of this study between 1812, the year of the publication of Emma Lyon's volume of poems, and 1847, the year of Grace Aguilar's death, I am designating an Anglo-Jewish "long Romanticism." Although I naturally read my three later authors (Celia and Marion Moss, and Grace Aguilar) within their particular respective historical contexts, which includes early Victorianism, I argue that they reflectively situate themselves within a Romantic inheritance, especially where they refract the ideals of Romantic nature through Jewish cultural and religious values. Reading Jewish poets as they engage Romantic standards of value also situates the authors before full Jewish emancipation, and before the greater expansion of Jewish immigration in the later part of the century. By the middle of the nineteenth century, there were approximately 60,000 Jews in England. By the end of the century, there were over a quarter of a million.

Anglo-Jewish Romanticism is, in many respects, an extreme version of Romantic self-reflexivity: it tends to engage Romanticism's received orthodoxies with a heightened consciousness of the constructed nature of its claims even as it seeks to establish affiliation with its cultural authority. Jewish poets inherit from the mainstream canon an already ironized and deeply scrutinized literary form. Many of the central questions about Romantic lyric—its vexations with respect to consolation, to the articulation of identity, to the ethics of place, and to the tensions inherent in negotiating the public sphere—take on singular dimensions when studied through Jewish authors. Anglo-Jewish Romantic poetry, then, models a Romanticism that recognizes its own ironic reversals even as it acknowledges its longing to claim a cultural home within it. To ironize the fiction of "home," even in the face of claiming rightful belonging within it, is to present, perhaps, a particularly arch reading of Romanticism. There are, to be sure, several layers of displacement in this dynamic; however, for Anglo-Jewish Romantic poets negotiating Romanticism and regarding their own place within it, the text becomes finally an arbiter of cultural value.

I am staking a claim, then, to a highly self-reflexive Romanticism and an Anglo-Jewish poetry that both cherishes and resists its myths of tranquil restoration within the landscape and within English nationalist aspirations. If some versions of canonical Romanticism constitute the landscape as the forum for a recuperative interiority, then Jewish authors who follow in their wake recognize its profound appeal as well as the perils of its constructed nature, which is as much to say that their love of canonical English poetry meets their recognition of its nostalgic sentimentalism in highly nuanced ways. This dynamic is further complicated by Jewish authors' appreciation that what they love—the very poetry that nurtures them and by which they instantiate their subjectivity—is also a site in which they recognize their distance from its promises. The dislocations engaged by Jewish Romantic poetry do not ultimately undermine its valorization of lyric, which remains a value term in despite of the Romantic currents that insistently qualify its efficacy. Like their mainstream peers, they negotiate lyric inheritance in all of its dynamic tensions without finally abandoning the belief, with Wordsworth, that the poet "hath put his heart to school."

This book, then, studies the uneasy literary inheritance received by early nineteenth-century Anglo-Jewish authors from British cultural and poetic formalist norms. I argue that the most salient features of Jewish expressive identity in this period can be found in the domain of elegiac and pastoral writing, as well as landscape poetry, but that other lyric forms also play a significant role.[2] The evolution of lyric, especially the pastoral and elegy, has always occupied a central role in British literary history. Joined as such forms are with British nationalist aspirations and self-assertions, Romantic lyric especially evolved in complicated ways to take explicit account of the limitations of its rhetorical power and its consolations, particularly where elegy and pastoral are concerned. I argue that such limitations join hands with the age-old enmity between lyric temporality and the narrative extension from which it presents itself as detached. Jewish literary history, both liturgical and secular, has also recognized the vital roles played by lyric forms, especially where a post-exilic consciousness is sustained. Indeed, diasporic Jewish lyric expression is inextricably linked to its historicity insofar as it has historically absorbed, refracted, and reworked poetic traditions from many national literatures and cultural types, lending it a hybridity that tends to issue in a profound self-reflectiveness. In narrowing my focus to lyric poetry by Anglo-Jewish authors of the Romantic period, I throw into relief the challenges to constructing a narrative of stable identity posed by historical, nationalist, religious, and linguistic disruptions. With no secure history binding them to the landscape of British hearth and home, their history becomes a meditation on their historicity, on their urgency to constitute in their writing a stable narrative of identity within England and within the King's English even as they gesture toward the impossibility—and sometimes even the undesirability—of so doing.

Aspects of the complicated dynamic of Jewish expressive identity were recognized by many Romantic authors, some with more sympathetic regard than others. William Hazlitt's posthumously published essay in the *Tatler* of 1831, "The Emancipation of the Jews," reveals a clear understanding of what Amy Levy would later describe as the want of "bucolic blood." Hazlitt observes:

> We shut people up in close confinement and complain that they do not live in the open air. The Jews barter and sell commodities, instead of raising or manufacturing them. But this is the necessary traditional consequence of their former persecution and pillage by all nations. They could not set up a trade when they were hunted every moment from place to place, and while they could count nothing their own but what they could carry with them. They could not devote themselves to the pursuit of agriculture, when they were not allowed to possess a foot of land. You tear people up by the roots and trample on them like noxious weeds, and then make an outcry that they do not take root in the soil like wholesome plants. You drive them like a pest from city to city, from kingdom to kingdom, and then call them vagabonds and aliens.[3]

Hazlitt was writing in response to the Jewish Relief Bill of 1830, which I discuss in more detail below. His diagnosis of the effects of Jews not taking "root in the soil" serves as a crucial reminder of the context for the Jewish relationship to pastoral. Hazlitt recognizes also the vigilance and index of suspicion of which Amy Levy will speak in 1886: "A man has long been in dread of insult for no just cause, and you complain that he grows reserved and suspicious."[4]

Hazlitt's perspective was not merely abstract. Even the "gentle-hearted Charles," the name Coleridge assigned to Charles Lamb in "This Lime-Tree Bower my Prison," exemplifies precisely the kind of perspective Hazlitt derides. In one of the *Essays of Elia* published in the *London Magazine* in 1821, Lamb insists that he has "no disrespect for Jews" in "the abstract." After all, he offers, "they are a piece of stubborn antiquity, compared with which Stonehenge is in its non-age."⁵ Still, their obduracy—another leitmotif in the discussion about Jews in general—does not render them palatable: "But I should not care to be in habits of familiar intercourse with any of that nation." It is their increasing acculturation within English society that seems most to repulse him:

> A Hebrew is nowhere congenial to me. . . . I boldly confess I do not relish the approximation of Jew and Christian which has become so fashionable. The reciprocal endearments have, to me, something hypocritical and unnatural in them. I do not like to see the Church and Synagogue kissing and congeeing in awkward postures of an affected civility. . . . If they can sit with us at table, why do they kick at our cookery? I do not understand these half convertites. . . I like fish or flesh. A moderate Jew is a more confounding piece of anomaly than a wet Quaker. The spirit of the synagogue is essentially *separative*.⁶

The separateness of the spirit of the synagogue, as Lamb would have it, is a recurrent motif in the discourse of both Jews and Christians. For Jews seeking to establish publicly their loyalty to England and its traditions, universalizing Jewish doctrine and ethics became one way of establishing good will; it also became one way of joining Jewish discourse to British values, so much so that, as we shall see in Chapter 4, Grace Aguilar sometimes took on the sobriquet of "Jewish Protestant." But the "essentially separative" spirit of the synagogue need not be entirely pejorative, at least not to many practicing Jews in England. And it is not only the kicking at Christian cookery, by which Lamb intends the observance of such separatist Jewish laws as those pertaining to Kosher food, that is to the point here. The Jewish authors that I study are not seeking to be recognized as ersatz Protestants. They are engaging with the cultural norms of British traditions *as* Jews and trying to establish a ground of lyric expression within them. The primary point of their struggle is not about antisemitism or political advantage; it is about establishing cultural self-representation and authority in the political, social, and cultural world in which they are situated. And establishing such cultural authority becomes also the process of establishing a forum for defining their subjectivity, a formidable task in a world in which they must confront so many self-divisions and self-contradictions.

P. B. Shelley's 1821 drama *Hellas* provides another fine reminder of the stereotypes and stakes of Jewish utterance, ones that are quite different from Lamb's; in seeking relief from inexplicable dreams, the character Mahmud calls for "a Jew" who, precisely because of the multifaceted breadth of his "spirit," is presumed to be a wise interpreter:

> Thou didst say thou knewest
> A Jew, whose spirit is a chronicle
> Of strange and secret and forgotten things.
> I bade thee summon him:—'tis said his tribe
> Dream, and are wise interpreters of dreams.[7] (ll. 132–136)

If Shelley here invokes the image of the Wandering Jew, as many authors did, he is offered as no sentimental traveler. His interpretive authority is recognized by the Sultan in much the way that Amy Levy diagnoses Jewish cosmopolitanism: he can "read men's thoughts" because of the vastness of his spirit's chronicle. The Wandering Jew of Christian tradition, oft adapted by the Romantics as a proxy for the suffering poet, can call upon a vast chronicle of history only because, having taunted Jesus on the way to Golgotha, he has been cursed to wander the world until the Second Coming.[8] For Jewish poets themselves, to possess a spirit full of strange and secret and forgotten things is to be a wise interpreter who would *write* dreams within the heady matrix of multiple cultural and historical confluences. The dream of interpretive authority does not always join hands with a secure self-understanding, however. The vexations of the Anglo-Jewish poet without a drop of bucolic blood in his veins, as Levy would have it, make not only for a wise interpreter, but also for a suspicious one. The cultural conditions of what the Jews of England lack, whatever their position of gratitude to England's sheltering haven, are among the most important idealizations of Romantic ideology: a reliable history in a land whose landscape thereby demands its allegiance. The tensions inherent in this history converge upon the problematics of cultural authority.

The formative tensions of Anglo-Jewish poetry are therefore especially obvious in the engagement with pastoral and in poetry that more generally valorizes external nature. Pastoral, and pastoral nostalgia, conventionally depend on the fiction that it can presuppose stable rootedness and historical continuity within a landscape that stands as a permanent locus of objectivity; this is a framework that the Jews—for much of the nineteenth century still laboring under various civil and political disabilities, still largely regarded by the mainstream as a foreign race, and many only recently arrived in England—could not access. All the same, these Jewish poets actively and self-consciously seek self-definition within the very forum that they also recognize as ultimately alienating. My central claim is that Jewish authors encounter in the course of their writing an alienation from their own expressive resources, even as those very resources define their deepest subjectivity. Where Nature is taken to be the signature of History, many Jewish authors implicitly ask, whose History? And whose Nature? And who possesses the cultural authority to offer the signature? This is a form of self-alienation that is as vexing as it is productive of lyric exploration.

I take as my primary points of reference Emma Lyon, Grace Aguilar, Hyman Hurwitz, and Marion and Celia Moss. The history in England that they enter is marked by a steady progression toward Jewish emancipation from civil and political disabilities. Crucial as this context is, however, the poetry I discuss does not offer itself as a form of agitation on behalf of Jewish relief. The challenges they face are existential, cultural; they are challenges related to but not defined exclusively by statutory discrimination. The history of the Jews in England is certainly a complicated one, and it offers a story that belies present ease. They were expelled from England altogether in 1290, and allowed limited reentry in 1656 under Cromwell. It is indeed true that European Jewish history generally is a story of difficult sojourn, exile, and civil and political disabilities. Certainly the great shattering Spanish exile of 1492, until which time the Jews in Spain had enjoyed an immense flowering of cultural production and power, is part of the mainstream cultural memory. What is perhaps less well understood is that the banishment of the Jews from England in 1290 in fact was the first wholesale expulsion (from an entire country) of its kind in Europe, and that it set an important precedent, one with momentous consequences in history. Some Jews did not survive the 1290 expulsion. What became of those who did survive is not known with certainty. The immediate post-1290 history of the Jews in Europe centers prominently on Spain and Portugal, major centers of Jewish learning and culture that came to bitter ends in the Inquisition. Most Jews in England during the period of the seventeenth-century resettlement were Sephardim, of Spanish or Portuguese extraction. They came seeking safe haven and understood themselves to have largely found it. In the terms of the larger history of expulsion and escape, this was a circularity not lost on many of them.[9] Indeed, in *The Genius of Judaism*, published in 1833, Isaac Disraeli, father of the future prime minister, traces the contemporary Jewish population from those fleeing the Inquisitions: "It was this race which formed the first general settlement of Jews in England; Spanish and Portuguese fugitives from the infernal fires of the Autos da Fe, and the living graves of the Inquisition. Ships freighted with Jewish families and Jewish property landed on the shores of England and Holland. Many escaped without any preparation, to save their lives by a day."[10]

* * *

In Romantic-era England, the entire Jewish population numbered between 12,000 and 15,000.[11] As Jewish numbers increased through the nineteenth century, agitation for relief from the Jewish civil and political disabilities became an increasingly public concern. These included, among other disabilities, an inability to vote or to trade in the City and on the Exchange, exclusion from membership in Parliament, and exclusion from standing for mayor of London. There was some doubt, and some controversy, over whether Jews could own freehold land, a situation not clarified until the 1840s.[12]

Even before the abrogation of these disabilities, however, like their seventeenth-century predecessors, English Jews in the nineteenth century tended, within various qualifications, to recognize England as a land of relative freedom, indeed of political and social refuge. The characteristic stance of English Jews was one of gratitude for safe haven, even if that haven had its thorny protrusions. For Jewish writers, one of those thorns was represented by their exclusion from study and later from fellowship at England's ancient universities, including Oxford and Cambridge, a condition that was not remedied until 1871 with the passage of the Universities Tests Act, which stipulated that persons entering the ancient universities not be required to subscribe to any formula of faith.

The Jewish civil disabilities are by no means the sole defining or even the most important context for Jews in the nineteenth century. Especially in comparison with their coreligionists on the continent, English Jews, as David Vital asserts, "had little to complain of."[13] For England, national Christianity was defined by the Church of England. Penal law had enacted civil disabilities against Protestant Nonconformists and Catholics in the seventeenth century with the goal of ensuring that municipal, civil, or military office be held only by members of the Church of England. In 1828 Parliament easily passed the Sacramental Test Act, which repealed the Test and Corporation Acts for Nonconformists.[14] Catholics received emancipation in 1829 with the passage of the Catholic Relief Act. This left only the Jews still subject to the civil disabilities. Oaths "on the true faith of a Christian" were still mandatory. In the Hansard summary of the debate for May 17, 1830, General Gascoyne is reported as opposing the Jewish Relief Bill precisely by pointing out that no analogy between Catholics or Nonconformists and Jews ought to be entertained: "The Constitution was a Protestant Constitution, and it was necessary for its support and protection that the institutions which made it so should be maintained. If any man had a few years ago asserted that, in the course of two Sessions, that House would repeal the Test and Corporation Acts—remove all the political disabilities of the Roman Catholics—and then entertain the question of relieving the Jews—he apprehended that his friends would have thought him a person it was necessary to keep a tight look after."[15] When the Jewish Relief Bill of 1830 failed to pass Parliament, the Jews, as Michael Clark observes, "were now no longer part of a broad excluded group but a deliberately stigmatized community; the only politically disadvantaged minority in Britain."[16] One of the Jewish community's leaders, Francis Goldsmid, referred to the bill's failure as a "badge of dishonour,"[17] and indeed it is the existential, subjective dilemma posed by such "dishonour" that is most relevant to my study of Anglo-Jewish Romantic poetry.

The invective raised against Jews whenever their statutory rights were addressed tended to be registered as invective against Jews *as* Jews, not simply as persons who subscribe to a faith other than the Church of England. The condition of the Jews in England, that is, was not analogous to that of Nonconformists or Catholics. Indeed, the subject of nationalism for English Jewish subjects was never an elementary affair. An earlier controversy also bears relevance to this study. I refer to the Jewish Naturalization Bill of 1753, the so-called "Jew Bill" that was in fact repealed almost immediately after it was passed. It produced one of the most fiery political clamors of the eighteenth century, and some of its resonances were felt into the nineteenth century. Its tremors were hardly earned, however; as things stood at the time, there was no legal recourse for Parliament to naturalize professing Jews. The Jew Bill sought to change the constitutional requirements that would grant Parliament the right to confer naturalization; this process could only have been granted, however, through a private act of Parliament, an expensive and inevitably rare prospective occurrence.[18] The bill passed, and it erupted into the loudest political and religious clamor of the eighteenth century. It was quickly repealed before ever once being resorted to, and still its tremors raged. Eventually the storm died down, with very little real political fallout.

But the deep terror of the remote possibility of a Jew or two potentially becoming, in some ill-defined future, a British citizen, produced a clamor whose implications, even a century later, could not be entirely forgotten. As Todd Endelman described it, "Opponents of the act resurrected crude medieval libels and made extravagant claims about the consequences of the legislation. Britain would be swamped with unscrupulous brokers, jobbers, and moneylenders, who would use their ill-gotten gains to acquire the estates of ruined landowners. Moreover, because dominion followed property, Jews would control Parliament (which would be renamed the Sanhedrin), convert St. Paul's to a synagogue, circumcise their tenants, and perpetrate countless other anti-Christian crimes."[19] In his book-length study of the Jew Bill, Thomas Perry asks, "Surely a violent political-religious controversy is one of the last things we should expect to find in the tolerant and sleepy 1750s. . . . And what are we to make of the undignified spectacle of Parliament, in the period of the Whig supremacy, scrambling to repeal an act that it had solemnly passed only six months before?"[20] What would wake up the sleepy 1750s is the Jew presenting himself for citizenship. English nationhood struggling to define itself found a ready subject in Jewish aspirations: England depends, among other features, upon national Christianity for self-definition. Its "imagined community," to borrow Benedict Anderson's well-worn phrase, could not include Jews within its circumference. Todd Endelman appropriates Linda Colley's phrase of "forging the nation" to make sense of the clamour. English xenophobia had typically occupied itself with Catholicism and the French; however, "given the ubiquity of centuries-old stereotypes about Jews, it is not surprising that these too were pressed into service at times in defining what was British."[21]

Grace Aguilar also briefly discusses the Jew Bill in her "History of the Jews in England," where she notes in particular that the City of London was vehemently opposed to the Bill and loudly participated in the outcry surrounding it. All the same, her history was published in 1847, and it clearly struggles to find in the vexed history of the Jews in England a telos of final arrival and ultimate sanctuary. It struggles because it clearly cannot do so entirely, looking to America as the locale of presumed greatest emancipation, and ending with a prayerful hope for fuller acceptance. The Jew Bill clamor and the controversy surrounding the failure of the 1830 Jewish Relief Bill help to clarify an important background framework for the context of Anglo-Jewish poets seeking to understand themselves, in part, in terms of an English literary inheritance. These are controversies that powerfully underscore the ways in which the political struggle for Jewish emancipation concurrent with Anglo-Jewish Romanticism is not simply about penal law. In discussing the vexed and sometimes contradictory regard of the Jews in the nineteenth century, Nadia Valman observes that "while Jews were represented as the best possible objects of progressive universalism, they were also seen as anti-citizens, constantly refusing or compromising their right to inclusion."[22] For the poets, the challenge is to define the space from which they speak as a space they rightfully occupy; more important, they must project a voice that defines and sanctions the presumption of their cultural authority.

In "singing the Lord's song in a foreign land," is the story these poets finally tell about themselves a story of the foreign, a story of the Lord, or a story about themselves as singers? I study these poets with reference to all three of these questions; however, the question I believe to be of most pressing concern for scholarship is the latter: in constituting their authority to speak within the very formalist parameters from which they are all the same alienated, the self-regarding aspects of their lyrics sometimes become forms of self-elegy, in which they implicitly and subtly lament their alienation from their own expressive resources. All the same, they ultimately mobilize the resources of elegy, pastoral and nature poetry to establish their cultural authority; paradoxically, then, their lyrics of longing become implicit assertions of strength. Long thought to have never experienced a Haskalah—a Jewish Enlightenment—comparable to the tremendous intellectual secularizing thrusts experienced in Germany, the Anglo-Jewish community in the nineteenth century negotiated their vexed British and Jewish inheritances with a vitality that rises to the challenge of their multiple, and sometimes mutually contradictory, points of reference. Indeed, this is a period in Anglo-Jewish history in which Jews are progressively secularizing. Since they faced many fewer penal barriers than their continental coreligionists, and since they could indeed come into more frequent contact with their neighbors from the majority culture, generally the Jews of England by the middle of the eighteenth century gradually shed many of the Old World accoutrements of dress (they shed long black coats in favour of modern clothes, for example), language of daily discourse (the Ashkenazim spoke English instead of exclusively Yiddish), and educational emphasis (they became increasingly more interested in secular studies).[23] As a result, Hebrew literacy itself began to decline, and Jewish leaders came to understand the importance of English translation of Jewish texts to the cause of Jewish continuity. This is a subject related to the important theme of translation of the Hebrew Bible, which I discuss below and in the first two chapters of this book.

The poets in my study are well versed in both Jewish texts and in mainstream literary history. They fully self-identify as Jews and self-consciously negotiate the tensions inherent in the hyphenated marker of identity, Anglo-Jewish. To study them is to read them within the broader cultural norms to which they respond; as such, I would emphasize again that this is fundamentally a study of a particular dynamic within British Romanticism, one which is incessantly gauging itself against its broader context. Recent scholarship in Romanticism has of course been expanding our understanding of the canon for decades, and the intensity of this endeavour remains at a high pitch. I believe that the time is now right for an in-depth critical analysis of a representative grouping of Anglo-Jewish poets who can be studied in the terms of a singular argument that does not read them exclusively as an example of their historical antecedents. This is not a comprehensive survey; it does establish the fundamental cultural forays achieved by Jewish poets in the period. This is a study, then, unified by authors who understand themselves within both the particulars of Jewish culture, and the general—and complicated—norms of the mainstream.[24] Each of the authors in my study offers variants of my argument. Hurwitz, Aguilar, and Lyon, for example, are each preoccupied with education and with the ethics of cultural transmission and continuity, Jewish and secular; as such, they are uniquely situated to consider the process by which cultural values are internalized. They are also attuned to both the benefits and impediments posed by such internalization. Marion and Celia Moss proceed as if writing verse is their just inheritance *as* Jews and as English women, even as they struggle to define the ground of such an inheritance. Lyon, Aguilar, and the Moss sisters are acutely conscious of the ways in which they represent themselves as women, a condition they negotiate with remarkable subtlety as they engage the inflections of a doubled outsider status conferred by being Jewish and female and educated and intellectually sophisticated. Indeed, gender issues are interwoven throughout this study. Three of the four major chapters are dedicated to women authors, each of whom negotiates her place *as* a woman author in distinctive ways. In many respects, however, being female and Jewish does not simply intensify the trials of alienation. For the Jewish woman poet, the challenges of locating herself within a narrative of Jewish and English cultural continuity are moderated by the prospect of recognizing an affiliation with the distinctiveness of English women of letters; that is, the woman author of the early nineteenth century already negotiates the margins of English culture, and the Jewish woman poet can often recognize their common ground. This ground is not entirely common, of course, but it does represent another source of at least partial affiliation that can be variously claimed by Emma Lyon, Marion and Celia Moss, and Grace Aguilar.

* * *

Emma Lyon, the subject of my first chapter, was the daughter of the renowned Hebrew teacher Solomon Lyon. In her volume of 1812, which is her sole extant volume of poems, she freely translates psalms from the Hebrew to conclude a collection of poems that otherwise sets up a quiet complaint against her exclusion both from access to higher education and from the fiction of rustic simplicity. In so doing, she establishes first her self-understanding as an exile even in a relatively accommodating land, and then claims an alternative cultural authority by showcasing her mastery of the Hebrew and her appropriation of it *as* a Jew to write back to her self-identification as alienated author. Lyon also writes odes, hymns, and other lyrics, and often uses these forms to interrogate her self-positioning as a Jew. Her volume of poetry is of particular interest because of its very self-conscious exploration of lyric form. This is all the more remarkable in light of her concluding psalm translations and its showcasing of her apparent mastery of several complicated literary traditions. I introduce the vexed subject of Hebrew translation in this chapter. As David Ruderman has examined, the debates in the eighteenth and nineteenth centuries over translation into English of the Hebrew Bible amount to a debate over proprietary ownership of the sacred; reliance by Christians on biblical translation by unredeemed Jews, or even upon the Masoretic text, posed threats that were political, ideological, and cultural in consequence. Philological clamors erupted over the typological reading of the Old and New Testaments that were the clear intentions of many Christian translators. This is a debate that goes right to the heart of the cultural authority of Jewish authors. Biblical translation and biblical interpretation were central to Protestant English intellectual life during the Enlightenment, and Christian debate about proper translation often reverted to complaints about Jewish preservation of the Hebrew text.[25] The two main camps of translators, headed by Benjamin Kennicott and John Hutchinson, viewed their work in Christian triumphalist terms. For the Huchinsonians, the "preoccupation with reading the Hebrew text of the Old Testament in the original and extracting from the peculiar readings the Christian 'meaning' of the text was colored throughout by an anti-Jewish animus and a deep resentment of Christian dependence on a Hebrew text shaped and preserved through the centuries by the Jews themselves."[26] The implications for the history of poetry by Jews in England, especially in the Romantic field, is a subject that I explore in this chapter as well as in Chapter 2.

My second chapter focuses primarily on Hyman Hurwitz. In 1817 Hurwitz, who had arrived in England from Poland in the 1770s, published a dirge in Hebrew to commemorate the death of Princess Charlotte (the only child of the Prince Regent). It was chanted in the Great Synagogue in London to the tune of a well-known Hebrew poem associated with the commemorative festival of Tisha B'Av, the day of mourning for the destruction of the Holy Temple in Jerusalem. The dirge is replete with Hebrew allusions and references to biblical and liturgical texts, a show of control over the sacred even in the face of British monarchy. When the translation into English by S. T. Coleridge—denuded of all such allusions—went into public circulation, Hurwitz was a willing participant in its dissemination, an indication of his careful gauging of audience and his conscious effort to assert the authority of his cultural standing. The translation debates of the day form an interesting antecedent. Hurwitz was concerned about the decline of Jewish and Hebrew literacy among his fellow Jews, but he was also clearly alarmed by the misrepresentation of Jewish culture among the mainstream. Though many Jews of the time relied on English translations of sacred texts, many could still read the Hebrew, and among such individuals there was a dawning awareness "that the English Bible was not necessarily an authoritatively Jewish one, and that translation could often distort the original meaning of a text.... In a Jewish community that had virtually translated itself into an English religious and cultural entity, the challenge of a new Christian ascendancy of master translators of the biblical text, along with their new prerogatives claiming exclusive Christian ownership of the text, was felt acutely and painfully by Jewish leaders and educators."[27] This is the context in which Hurwitz, as both Jewish teacher and Jewish poet, finds himself. Hurwitz also wrote an elegy in 1820 for George III, and it too was translated by Coleridge. His work implicitly addresses the challenges posed to Jewish subjectivity both of the Jewish need for English translation and the frustrations of encountering Christian translators of Hebrew texts who presume to correct the putative unenlightened Hebrew of unredeemed Jews. I study these two poems against the backdrop of other Hebrew (and Jewish) elegies for British monarchs, both in the eighteenth and nineteenth centuries. The study of Jews writing elegies for members of the British royal family yields an increasingly clearer picture of the dynamic tensions in the culture.

Celia and Marion Moss, the subjects of my third chapter, jointly published their first and only book of poetry, *Early Efforts*, in 1839, when they were eighteen and sixteen, respectively. For the Mosses, embracing with zeal their English literary inheritance constitutes one aspect of their self-representation, even as the English Jew in their poetry is presented often in the exile's habit, longing for Zion. Such forthrightness, however, is perpetually subjected to ironic reflection; their poetry, which often stages a confidence in the simplicity of their hybrid identities, also pulls the rug out from under their own self-definitions. Entitled, yet self-consciously in exile; mature in insight, yet with a still nascent identity; grateful for safe haven, yet angry at England's history of inhospitality and violence toward the Jews: what we have, finally, is the presentation of a selfhood hovering between various anchors. The Moss sisters' poetry therefore presents a good forum for further exploring and fleshing out the implications of Anglo-Jewish poetry. The admixture of ambivalence and hope, self-effacement and defiance, comprise powerful notes of self-exploration.

In Chapter 4 I take up Grace Aguilar, who, writing closer to mid-century, authored the first English history of the Jews in England written by a Jew. In her poetry she struggled with and against her British Romantic inheritance by explicitly joining rustic themes, ballad stanzas, and lyric effusions to Jewish historical concerns. Her poem about Purim, for example, engages two young girls debating the relative merits of frolicking in the spring scene and reading the Book of Esther; this necessarily recalls Wordsworth's "Dialogue Stanzas," whose central characters debate the relative merits of book learning and natural learning in the midst of impulses from the vernal woods. I mention this example here because it is paradigmatic of Aguilar's careful calibrating of the inheritance she obtrusively considers when presenting herself as a specifically *Jewish* poet in England. Perhaps the most familiar of all the poets in my study, Aguilar wrote poetry and prose for an appreciative and somewhat broader audience than the rest of the poets in my study. She is acutely conscious in her poetry of the vexed relationship between audience expectation and her manipulation of formalist orthodoxies.

This is a study that seeks to understand Anglo-Jewish poetry of the early nineteenth century as lyric utterance in search of a tenable voice. The poets here trouble their own terms of reference as much as they hold tenaciously to their value. I present a poetry, then, of both longing and resistance: a poetry that demands attention both to the terms of its separateness, its unique claims upon culture, and to its principled participation in canonical measures.

CHAPTER I

Emma Lyon's Spacious Firmament

In 1947 Bertrand Bronson, in a well-known critique of Romanticism that sought to valorize the ethics of neoclassical poetic idioms, notoriously asserted that for the Neoclassicals, "generalization was one of the chief ways in which man transcended his private experience and became adult."[1] At the height of the New Criticism, becoming a child, that is, unlettered and unsophisticated, had often been taken as the modus operandi of Romanticism. And champions of Neoclassicism like Bronson sought to salvage the grown-up precursors of the Romantics by reading Romantic particularity as an ethical flaw, as a transgression against the civility of consensus. This complaint about self-interest has resurfaced in sundry ways over the years, though I suspect that few scholars would be willing to grant their affinity with Bronson's literary moral code. The problem of generalization, of course, has never really gone away, even when detached from the quotation that was Bronson's immediate catalyst: "to Generalize is to be an Idiot."[2] Any reading of Romantic lyric is of necessity pulled between the Scylla and Charybdis of generalization and self-interest, but a focus on Anglo-Jewish poetry of the early nineteenth century, as this chapter on Lyon will illustrate, complicates the story again even further. For here we confront the stark realities of how the demands of subjectivity are served by generalization; that is, the self who is read as a foreign race, who is alienated from the history upon which the succors of British hearth and home depend, knows something else about generalization: those who have an uncomplicated relationship with their nation's history, those who are recognized as part of the generalization of the normative human, or the body politic, have their selfhood guaranteed within various stable structures of identity. It is precisely the specter of a stable structure of identity that is vexed by Emma Lyon, a poet who subtly negotiates the tensions of Jewish identity within the already complicated matrix of English cultural inheritance.

A Poet's Apology

Emma Lyon (1788–1870) is certainly one of the earliest Romantic-era Jewish poets. She published only one volume of verse, at the age of twenty-three, in 1812. She was the daughter of a very prominent Hebrew teacher, Solomon Lyon, a teacher who had taught Hebrew at institutions no less august than Cambridge, Oxford, and Eton, but who as a professing Jew could not be given secure employment in any of them. He suffered temporary but prolonged blindness, which was the immediate occasion of Emma publishing her poetry: with fourteen siblings, the family desperately needed money during their father's incapacity, and her volume was sold by subscription at ten shillings six pence a copy. There were over 350 subscribers, virtually all from Oxford, Cambridge, and Eton, and very few of them, in fact, seem to have been Jews. Like virtually all women writers of the time, Jewish and otherwise, she offers a strenuously apologetic preface apologizing for her presumption, proclaiming financial necessity in spite of her modesty as her primary motivation, and generally disclaiming any talent or indeed right to present her verse in the public domain. As a Jewish woman, Emma Lyon's access to formal higher education was severely limited. There is anecdotal evidence that she became well read all the same, and her poetry is obtrusively dense with allusions to canonical ancient and modern English culture, whose authority she putatively cannot appropriate, indeed whose contents her poetry laments not knowing. She was herself a Hebrew teacher, and it is certainly clear that her father would have taught her Hebrew well.[3]

It is not simple presumption, however, for which she apologizes in her volume. The apologetic frame of reference is centered on access, which is as much to say that its focus is on the authority conferred by right of entry—to education, to the fields of learning, to great poetry, to the depths of culture. "It will soon be perceived that my education has been confined, and that nature has not been so munificent towards me, as to supersede the necessity of cultivation."[4] The disclaimer about her talent and, more important, about her cultural authority is offered first in the poetic dedication and then in the preface. The dedication is offered to Her Royal Highness, The Princess Charlotte of Wales, who was the daughter and only heir to the Prince Regent, the future George IV. The dedication enacts a subtle protest, especially in light of the progression of the volume. Charlotte is an important figure for the Jews because, as heir to the throne, granddaughter of a madman, daughter of a banished mother and unpopular, overly controlling father, she was widely regarded as the oppressed figure of the brighter future. Charlotte as royal heir to the throne of England came, through various iconographic media, to be represented as Britannia, but a Britannia with a more expansive and generous largesse, one with authentic empathy for the disenfranchised and the disappointed. The poetic prefatory dedication to Charlotte is, then, particularly suggestive.

> While thought unbending wings thy playful hour,
> Say, lovely Princess! Dares my Muse advance?
> Or hope, mild beaming in thy studious bow'r,
> From thy bright eyes one momentary glance?
> (Lyon, v)

The references to Milton are unmistakable and qualify the apologetic disclaimers: in appropriating the quintessence of Britannia as her feminine Muse, she establishes an identification that works in diverse, indeed mutually contradictory, ways: deferential but still presuming to confer blessing upon the princess, an abject subject invoking protection, she is also the self-declared heir of the author of *Paradise Lost*: "Say, lovely Princess! Dares my Muse advance?" Milton pleads, demands actually, "Sing, Heav'nly Muse" because

> I thence
> Invoke thy aid to my advent'rous song,
> That with no middle flight intends to soar
> Above th'Aonian mount, while it pursues
> Things unattempted yet in prose or rhyme.
> (*Paradise Lost* I. 12–16)[5]

Here is Emma Lyon addressing Charlotte, unhesitating in her appropriation and internalization of the Miltonic poetic line:

> What spirit leads to thy august abode
> My daring, unpremeditated flight?
> All unsolicited my numbers flow'd,
> Soon as thy name allur'd my wond'ring sight.
> (Lyon, v)

In asserting implicitly to whom she would be poetic heir, she establishes the grounds for asserting a literary inheritance. Her avowal of a literary inheritance establishes the ground of her literary authority; the identity she would construct from such an authority, however, knows itself to be partly an assertion of textual finesse.

Rustic Longing

Lyon establishes the importance of the literary inheritance she claims for herself even while situating herself as alienated from it. The poetry comes to establish the inextricable meaning to her subjectivity of that literary negotiation; an implicit mourning is enacted for the very expressive resources that at once centrally define her and from which she is, at least in part, alienated. When she finally signals a readiness to move beyond the apologetics of the disenfranchised and undereducated, a self-fashioning that is always self-consciously performative, the triumph of her authority signals a severing of the ties that bind her to the mainstream literary community in the only way she could have carried it off. I am referring to her translations from the Hebrew Psalms at the end of the book. The volume as a whole follows a narrative progression: there are fifty-seven poems spanning 152 pages, with the concluding nine poems paraphrasing psalms which, I argue, function as consolation for a form of self-mourning. She begins the volume in a sentimental idiom, peopling her poetic landscape with mad women, abstract personifications, and rustic images. Many of her poems reveal self-conscious abjections in verse (for example, "An Ode on the Fear of Criticism," "Sonnet on Hope," "An Ode to Indifference"): unlettered, longing for the inspiration of her muse and yet feeling always the impoverishment of her learning and hence of her literary resources. She asserts her lot in conventionalized rustic terms to describe her unlettered state, but this rusticity is more than just a signal of alienation from high art. It is also a way of claiming while qualifying the pastoral, of identifying with the land even while detached from it, of establishing a connection to the landscape of a land in which, as a Jew, she has no stabilizing history. Her claim to the rustic is a claim that at once announces a way into a cultural authority even as it signals a further alienation from it, from the default forum (rustic because unlettered) that finally cannot possibly have her. Neither leech-gatherer nor wanderer nor learned don, she speaks from the no-man's land of the Jewish cosmopolite, a space with little recognized history in her country. The pastoral for the Romantics was already highly qualified by 1812, of course, and its redemptive powers rigorously ironized by the Romantics themselves. Still, however ironized, place remains a value term, and in the pastoral as inherited in early nineteenth-century England the landscape defines the stable rootedness, the warranty against self-loss in the external world, that defines also pride in British nationalism. The landscape and the land of England are joined in the dream of stability, which becomes a principled dream. Home here means not only hearth but also history. Or rather, hearth depends upon a reflective history.

The landscape as locus of objectivity depends, however, upon a history of stable rootedness, or at least a credible constructive imaginary of stable rootedness, which is one reason why the Protestant poetics of redemption upon which pastoral consolation in the post-Reformation elegy depends is an alienating inheritance for the Jews. The Romantic peripatetic is not the same as the Wandering Jew, is not the same as the exilic cosmopolitan, and the horizon in which they meet signifies in vastly different ways. "Fresh woods and pastures new" is the famous consolatory telos to which Milton's "Lycidas," which in 1637 established the form of the pastoral elegy in England, is propelled. Lyon's "An Ode on Death" tries out a melancholy mood, one very much in line also with Thomas Gray's mid-eighteenth-century "Elegy in a Country Churchyard," but it becomes a meditation on the muse, on poetry, on how this poet can make death a subject fully answerable to her contorted relationship with poetic inheritance, which stands as the contorted relationship with the landscape:

> My muse contemplative delights to stray,
> Where the green sod conceals the mould'ring clay:
> In hallow'd shades she glories to recline,
> And pensive bend before thy sable shrine!
> (Lyon, 17)

The prefatory poem asks, "Forgive the maid that with a rustic smile / Intrudes upon thine ear unpolish'd praise" (vi). A similar dynamic can be found in "Lines Addressed to the University of Cambridge":

> Not unamaz'd my wandering eyes survey'd,
> By me unsung, sweet Cam! Thy classic shade.
> Yet oh! What flow'rets can my Muse provide,

To deck the mansions of her earliest pride?
Far too unletter'd is my rural verse,
Immortal Cam! Thy glories to rehearse.
(Lyon, 83)

Announced on the advertisement of the volume is that Emma Lyon is the daughter of Solomon Lyon, Hebrew teacher. This address to Cam is not from the amazed shepherd swain. It is from the Jewish woman whom they will not let in. The rustic simplicity of pastoral life is no more Emma Lyon's to claim than is the immortal Cam. She has a history in neither, and subtly claims in fact a history of exclusion from both.

Translating and Paraphrasing the Psalms

Of perhaps greater concern for my immediate purposes is the translation debates of the eighteenth and nineteenth centuries, which I outlined in the introduction to this book. The King James Bible was of course the standard source of biblical knowledge for most English subjects, including, at this time, many British Jews. The 1662 Book of Common Prayer (still in use during this period) was also an important source for Anglicans. The torrent of debates raging over the subject of biblical translation during the eighteenth and nineteenth centuries, and its concomitant controversies about proprietary ownership of the word of God, was of central concern to Jewish authors who were perpetually monitoring their own cultural self-positioning. The call for specifically Christian translators and Christian translations of Hebrew texts went hand in hand with increases in Jewish immigration into England. David Ruderman has persuasively argued that Benjamin Kennicott, for example, the renowned eighteenth-century Christian Hebrew scholar who sought to collate all Hebrew manuscripts of the Hebrew Bible in the service of producing a new authoritative edition, implies "that his aggressive search for new manuscripts, his assembling of a large staff of assistants and collators, and the extraordinary fund raising involved in sustaining his project are all motivated by a Christian purpose, to wrest the authority of determining the words of divine revelation from the Jews and to restore them to Christians."[6] David Katz similarly observes that Kennicott was challenging the Jewish monopoly not only on the Hebrew Bible but "on the Hebrew language itself. . . . Kennicott in effect was cutting the Jews out of the inheritance of

Scripture by claiming to have discovered a method of textual criticism which would reveal God's message in its pristine Sinaitic glory."[7]

Lyon's turn to psalm translations for the last nine of her poems introduces a new voice into her volume and a claim to textual authority that is resonant of the larger issue about the status of Jewish textual expertise. Psalm translation by the early modern period, to be sure, was often freer than translation of the Five Books of Moses, for example. Some Christian translators believed that they should adapt the psalms in the service of reproducing the experience of the original for modern times; others refashioned the psalms for their own political or aesthetic ends.[8] It is precisely this freedom that Lyon appropriates for her own particular needs, ones that combine both the publicly acknowledged freedom to adapt with the specialized freedom that she implicitly claims to be conferred by her intimate knowledge of the original Hebrew source. More important, this is knowledge self-consciously arrogated as her rightful inheritance as a Jew. Of the nine psalms she chooses for translation and adaptation, none, as Michael Scrivener has pointed out, are penitential psalms, general hymns, or laments (and more than half of all the biblical psalms are within these three subgenres). Rather, they are bold claims for justice, wisdom psalms, and didactic psalms.[9] She translates freely, boldly announcing, for those in the know—for those, that is, who can read the Hebrew well enough to know her liberties with the text—that she is the real thing, both a real translator, an authentic Jew who knows the original sacred text, and a real poet, presumptuous enough to play with diction and syntax, indeed to alter, when she so chooses, the original altogether to suit her needs. If the forty-eight poems that precede the Psalms are largely sentimental odes and meditations preoccupied with doomed learning and rustic simplicity, then the Psalm translations are prophetic assertions of cultural authority. For here there are no images of rusticity apologizing for its diction, no emphasis at all, in fact, upon the landscape. There were plenty of psalms that might have accomplished an alternative pastoral authority, but the boldness of Lyon's psalmist translations is striking precisely because they transfer cultural authority out of the landscape and into the text.

I would suggest that this holds the clue to the proliferation of personified abstractions and Neoclassical odes in the earlier sections. The poetry of Emma Lyon is poised unevenly between a Neoclassical decorum and an early Romantic aesthetic. Her engagement with odic form (odes to "Autumn," "Melancholy," "Death," "Sympathy," and so on) hovers over a Horatian meditative quiet and a Pindaric dialectic, but the hovering favors the quiet, favors the simpler closure of consensus. The personified abstraction depends for its efficacy on a common acceptance of the meaning of its object of address. It depends upon generalization. Lyon's appropriation of this common Neoclassical form, one that is overlaid with an early Romantic rustic apologetic, itself signals a negotiation of the common problem of consensus for a Jewish woman writer who would participate in a culturally sanctioned ethic. We would do well to recall Bertrand Bronson's claim: "Generalization was one of the chief ways in which man transcended his private experience and became adult." Emma Lyon's generalizations present competing versions of her own subjectivity, or at least prepare for a reading of the Psalms she translates as the consolatory answer to the implicit lamentation over her cultural poverty. The psalm translations complicate the aesthetic of the volume; we cannot but re-read the earlier poems retrospectively and palimpsestically: the quivering address to the British princess is made by the translator of and the emender of David himself. The address to royalty is counterpointed by the address to God, and the disclaimer about speaking to Charlotte from the depths of her rustic soul is ironized by the translator who chooses psalms that do not highlight the pastoral, that showcase instead ethics, justice, and inspired prophecy. In context of the translation debates that vilified the Jews as unredeemed translators of the Hebrew Bible, this palimpsest becomes all the more resonant. Psalm 73 becomes a valuable case in point. The closing lines of the original are as follows (I give the Jewish Publication Society [JPS] 2003 translation). Asaph, the author of this psalm, recoils from his envy of others and concludes,

> Yet I was always with You,
> You held my right hand;
> You guided me by Your counsel
> and led me toward honour.
> Whom else have I in heaven?
> And having You, I want no one on earth.
> My body and mind fail;
> but God is the stay of my mind, my portion forever.
> Those who keep far from You perish;
> You annihilate all who are untrue to You.
> As for me, nearness to God is good;
> I have made the Lord God my refuge,
> that I may recount all Your works. (73:23–28)

The differences in Lyon's translation are instructive:

> Oft have I follow'd all the ways they trod,
> And lost in wonder, ask'd with dubious eye,
> "Where are the righteous judgments of my God?
> Where is the Ruler of the sky?"
> But lo! The justice that dispels the gloom,
> And to his altars bids me lowly trust;
> I see descend the swift avenging doom,
> I see the glories of the just!
> (Lyon, 142)

Lyon does not take up an explicit translation of "having you, I want no one on Earth," though to be sure, the biblical emphasis on the things of this earth being superseded by the faith in God is prominent. I would compare Psalm 73 with one of Lyon's earlier pieces, "Lines to the Muse," which does situate her in a pastoral retreat, does invoke a muse she is not certain she can rightfully claim, and which very strangely charges those who do not respond to the poetic muse with a criminal disposition:

> I sing thy praise: unblest, alas! is he,
> Whom fate relentless alienates from thee!
> Whose soul ne'er tastes the soft melodious rhyme,
> Is form'd from earliest infancy to crime,
> To horrible confusion, deeds of ire,
> and thoughts too dark for the recording lyre.
> But he, blest infant! whom the fates incline
> At thy lov'd voice to thrill with joy divine,
> To heavenly lore and contemplation born,
> Shall hail thee as the sweet approach of morn;
> With innocence shall wing the gladsome hours,
> And trace thy footsteps through the dews and flowers.
> (Lyon, 15–16)

If the muse saves from horrible confusion and deeds of ire, and if Emma Lyon has no cultural authority on which to claim a muse, then the author has a soul in peril. If she can claim a cultural authority, though, the reward, in the logic of this poem, is to trace thy footsteps through the dews and flowers. The right to succor staked in the Psalm is the right of the righteous, the reward of the good, and this is clear in the original Hebrew. In her translation, Lyon dispenses with the lengthy qualifications or even ponderings. This represents a departure from other, older Psalm translations still familiar during the period: Isaac Watts in his famous psalter invokes justice and Christian worship and humility, while Sternhold-Hopkins calls down vengeance against transgressors while remembering the succor of the Lord. Lyon goes right to the heart of transgression: she does not linger on reward, or on the progressive revelation of the vanity of envy. She is startlingly succinct: "I see descend the swift avenging doom, / I see the glories of the just!" She does not have to qualify with any strenuous activity the uses of earthly pleasures. Her consolations are not within the flowers and dews of her Muse. She makes no apologies. She denudes the biblical text of its slow searching. Instead, she pronounces. The pain of cultural poverty is met by a sloughing off of the terms by which general culture is valued. The highest authority on earth is hers. The sacred is her very domain. The ruler of the Sky, in Lyon's translation, recalls the classical Pantheon only to remind that it has no place here—and the "here" pronounced is the Here and Now of textual authority. If the earlier poems present a persona whose expressive resources are a source of alienation, then the psalm translations become the guarantee of expressive authority.

This discussion of Lyon could only lead to further questions: If the cultural authority longed for in the earlier sections defines the consensual point of reference for authority, then what degree of self-canceling, rather than self-affirming, is being staged? Once one accepts that a qualitatively new value system is being put in place to affirm the identity and centrality of Emma Lyon as Poet, once one recognizes that the regrets of the earlier sections are answered in the later psalms, is there still a move that cannot quite let go of that earlier self-constitution? I have been describing an implicit mourning for expressive resources that both define the poet and are denied the poet. But do the psalm translations kill off an earlier self, that is, the one whose unlettered simplicity helped her to fashion common cause with English standards of value? The authority of the psalm translations moves well beyond simple rusticity; they move too beyond the more sophisticated pastoral of Wordsworth. In the dynamic I am describing, the bold Psalm translations come close to killing off the one fashioning of self that granted Emma Lyon community in the great Pantheon of English poets. Neither chronicler of rustic simplicity nor unlettered rustic, this translator of the Psalms is of the disenfranchised foreign race whose cultural authority herein is absolute.

This is an authority that further sets her apart even as it defines and elevates her. We are still meant to read the psalms in the knowledge that their locus of authority is under threat of death; the cry against the criminal mind of the one who does not seek the muse, who is as a result struck by "thoughts too dark for the recording lyre" (15), is the cry of the poet moving toward denial of one poetic system of value. The implicit celebration of her ultimate cultural authority undermines the ethic of rustic simplicity. You don't need pastoral ease to lay bare that which is most permanent and important in human existence (to recall Wordsworth's prescriptions in the 1802 Preface to *Lyrical Ballads*).[10] You need literacy, knowledge, language. If Lyon is elegiac at this point, it is because she must mourn the losses inherent in her refusal to mourn.

The Audacity of the Jewish Poet: Psalm 19

If Psalm 73 proclaims Lyon's cultural authority as much as it announces her authority to read the letters of her faith with unrivalled accuracy, then her paraphrase of Psalm 19 advertises an audacity that also establishes her affiliation with the English literary tradition in which she struggles, in the earlier section of the volume, to define her voice. Psalm 19 is today popularly identified with Joseph Addison's paraphrase, "The Spacious Firmament on High." This version was renowned already in Lyon's day as well. First published in *The Spectator* for August 23, 1712, the poem is preceded by a brief essay on faith, memory, and nature, in which Addison observes that experiences of "feeling" related to the Deity concur with human Reason. He ends his essay by quoting the first three verses of the translation of Psalm 19 from the 1662 Book of Common Prayer, which I quote from the essay:

> The Heavens declare the Glory of God: And the Firmament showeth his handy-work. One Day telleth another: And one Night certifieth another. There is neither speech nor Language: But their voices are heard among them. Their sound is gone out into all Lands: And their words into the Ends of the world.

Addison's version of the psalm was set to music by Franz Joseph Haydn in 1798, furthering its renown throughout Europe. Psalm 19 had been used by Robert Lowth in his discussion of synthetic parallelism,[11] and in the English translation of Lowth's *Lectures Upon the Sacred Poetry of the Hebrews*, published in 1787, his translator (from the Latin) opined of Addison's version: "Mr. Addison's paraphrase of a part of the psalm infinitely excels every translation that I have seen, as well in sublimity as elegance; and is indeed, in my opinion, the most beautiful and perfect specimen of sacred poetry extant in English verse." This note was also reproduced in the 1811 text, *Select Psalms, in Verse, with Critical Remarks by Bishop Lowth and others, illustrative of the Beauties of Sacred Poetry*. Edited by Walter Hutchinson Aston, the volume singles out Addison's translations of two psalms for special praise: "In Addison we find a model for all future translators. His versions of the 19th and 23d Psalms have been the theme of universal praise for near a century, and will remain so, as long as the English language continues to be admired."[12]

For a twenty-three-year-old Lyon to take up Psalm 19 for translation and paraphrase, then, is to immediately signal an inheritance that she fully intends to establish as rightfully her own *as* a Jewish poet and Hebrew translator, even as she equally intends to be recognized publicly within its mainstream historical association. This mainstream, British association includes religious poetry by women as well as specifically psalm translation and psalm paraphrase. Women were not included generally among the translators from Hebrew into English of the authoritative translations of the Hebrew Bible; that task was the privileged domain of men. Translations of the psalms, however, were a different matter. In the early modern period especially, educated women often engaged in translation of religious texts; indeed, they were even positively urged to translate the gospels for the benefit of those who did not have access to original texts, usually in Greek or Latin.[13] Personal lyric or poetic narrative of a personal nature, however, was discouraged for women. The psalms therefore provided a public forum for personal expression not otherwise provided for women. As Margaret Hannay points out, "Psalm translation offered more opportunity for individual meditation, for Christians had long been urged to treat the words of the psalmist as if they were their own, thereby providing women with a more effective persona for public speech than other sacred translations."[14] Many such "translations" were in fact renditions based on other English translations, not on knowledge of the original Hebrew. The now famous psalm renditions of Mary Sidney—based not on the original Hebrew but on other translated models[15]—were not published until 1823, and so too late to be read by Lyon, but the Sidney Psalter did circulate widely in manuscript and is known to have influenced many other authors, including John Donne. It is likely that Lyon had knowledge of the

Sidney Psalter, at least by reputation, and at least as an example of a well-established woman gaining public recognition and honor for both religious and especially literary accomplishment specifically through psalm renditions. Lyon would certainly have been familiar with the many Christian religious hymns written by women in the eighteenth century and the early part of the nineteenth. Some of these were based on biblical psalms, while others were more directly personal expressions of praise of God for having comforted them in their despair. Although, as Susan Gillingham points out, there were far fewer new translations of the psalms in the eighteenth and nineteenth centuries than in the early modern period, older Psalters circulated more easily and were more readily accessible during the later period.[16] These older, early modern Psalters formed a conspicuous part of the literary landscape, and naturally would have reinforced Lyon's decision to establish her literary credentials partly through her psalm paraphrases. And though Lyon has also situated herself in relation to her immediate Romantic precursors, in her own psalm renditions she makes it clear that she is refracting that inheritance through the prism of religious writing generally and psalm rendition from her uniquely Jewish perspective in particular. Recognizing, no doubt, in the early Romantics a mediated religiosity that appropriates biblical language, Lyon's entry into English letters announces a belonging that is also an implicit assertion of her mastery of that tradition and even supersession of it: she stands for knowledge of the Hebrew original and mastery of lyric expression on account of that very knowledge. She does not merely vie for a place in the pantheon. Rather, she presumes to enter it, and she makes implicit corrections to the work of her predecessors. In this, we are reminded that Lyon's efforts to establish her authority within an English mainstream tradition is undergirded by her belonging also to another affiliation, another tradition: that of Hebrew and Jewish sources. This is a complicated dynamic precisely because she is never far from the recognition of her partial estrangement from the expressive resources of mainstream English poetry by which she would nevertheless piecemeal fashion herself; but that fashioning is inflected further by Jewish culture, with which it is sometimes at odds.

Paula Backscheider has persuasively illustrated the importance of the devotional hymn to eighteenth-century Christian women. Paraphrases from the Bible were the most common form of religious poem in the eighteenth century,[17] though other religious verse based on biblical themes also played a role. Women were able to appropriate the personal experiences of biblical figures and work them into their own idioms. This provided sanction for women's ambition as well as for the highly personal, sometimes domestic, writing that would otherwise have been deprecated in women writers. As in their early modern predecessors, eighteenth-century women poets found in the Bible a source for individual expression that was fully sanctioned, indeed even celebrated. "The paraphrases, often in straightforward, dignified language, contrasted with the ornamented language of many classical forms and surely helped move English poetry away from artificiality."[18] Such poetry, then, may be properly understood as one of the important forces in the shaping of English Romanticism, which retained the Neoclassical's investment in sacred themes even while individualizing or secularizing them.

Lyon would have been familiar with and appreciative of this aspect of her literary inheritance as well, but she also must inveigh against it, at least in part. She recognizes its importance to the literary milieu, to be sure, and she is deeply invested in an affiliation with that milieu; all the same, it is a context in which she does not sit entirely comfortably. Most of the women writers who provided a historical context for Lyon's inclusion within the sphere of religious writing and psalm translation were themselves either Christian Dissenters or part of the Church of England establishment. Dissenters and Catholics still adhere to a Christian tradition, of course, even where there are deep doctrinal differences and even civil disabilities with which to contend. Most important, many of them are contending primarily with a dominant male tradition, in which their selection of religious theme is one of the only entry points into the literary sphere. Their self-positioning, in other words, is as poets who are not immediately recognizable as occupying the center of the dominant mainstream of English culture. To enter it through poems of Christian piety and religious devotional lyric is already to recognize a difference from full canonical acceptance. It is not that men did not write religious lyric in the eighteenth century and later; most emphatically they did, and sacred poetry was an important genre in the eighteenth century. Still, sacred devotional lyric does not stand with the upper echelons of canonical high culture. As such, in Lyon's efforts to establish her cultural authority in the realm of lyric, she cannot fully give herself to the community of Christian women poets who carved special entry points of their own into the realm of culture. For one, she cannot situate herself within the tradition of Christian piety. Many of the circulating psalm paraphrases include direct references or allusions to Christ, or depend in other ways on specifically Christian themes or Christian typologies. Beyond even that obvious and pressing impediment to direct affiliation, to establish herself as a part of the dominant culture,

Lyon cannot self-identify with those who write from its margins or from a position of lesser prestige. This is not simple arrogance; it is about the struggle to locate herself properly within a tradition she would claim as her just inheritance, even if she will also, as we have begun to observe, challenge some of the merits of that very tradition. The tradition of women's Christian poetry is not readily available to her as an unambiguous inheritance; moreover, the tradition of any poetry making claims upon the culture from the margins is not the ultimate model for her. She does recognize and implicitly acknowledge the tradition, and it does serve as one precursor that exerts some influence. But it too remains a sign of necessary alienation.

In 1775, the Dissenting writer Anna Letitia Barbauld published a compendium of religious texts entitled *Devotional Pieces, Compiled from the Psalms and the Book of Job*. Described more recently by William McCarthy as having "the appearance of an inchoate, groping attempt toward a liturgy,"[19] the volume includes various headings, including "Moral Psalms," "Psalms of Praise, Penitence and Prayer," and "Occasional and Prophetic Psalms." It serves as one example among many of women of letters in the early Romantic period turning their attention to psalms in the context of Christian evangelism. Barbauld achieved real distinction in her day, notably within the tradition of Dissenting culture, a milieu that might have modeled some indirect encouragement for Lyon. Daniel White goes so far as to assert that "the religious dispositions, political aspirations, economic interests, and literary tastes of Dissenting communities impelled the genesis of Romanticism in England."[20] In 1812, when Lyon published her volume, Dissenters, like Jews, still suffered a number of civil and political disabilities. While still Protestant Christians, and therefore not outside the boundaries of Christian England entirely, Protestant Dissenters still insisted upon an expression of, and education in, religious faith that did not conform to Church of England positions. Again, the encouragement to Lyon would have been indirect, muted, and highly qualified in terms of what it could offer her as a poet and as a religious Jew. Barbauld's religious poetry also includes many hymns. When William Enfield published *Hymns for Public Worship* in 1772, he included five of Barbauld's hymns (anonymous in Enfield's collection).[21]

Hymn II echoes some themes of Psalm 19; I cite here the first five stanzas, which are typical of the hymn:

> Praise to God, immortal praise,
> For the love that crowns our days;

Bounteous source of every joy,
Let thy praise our tongues employ.

For the blessings of the field,
For the stores the gardens yield,
For the vine's exalted juice,
For the generous olive's use:

Flocks that whiten all the plain,
Yellow sheaves of ripen'd grain;
Clouds that drop their fatt'ning dews,
Suns that temperate warmth diffuse:

All that spring with bounteous hand
Scatters o'er the smiling land:
All that liberal autumn pours
From her rich o'erflowing stores:

These to thee, my God, we owe;
Source whence all our blessings flow;
And for these, my soul shall raise
Grateful vows and solemn praise.
(Enfield, 80–81)

Barbauld herself footnotes Habakkuk 3:17 for the first stanza. What is important here is the example of hymnic praise of God that cites biblical precedent for its authority and which, in the case of Enfield's volume of hymns, is offered to the public by a religious figure not securely within the domain of Church of England sanction. Characteristic of Dissenting poetry in general, there are many religious poems in the volume that refer directly to Jesus or that draw on well-established Christian themes and images, many of which reference or allude to the Hebrew Bible. I have cited Barbauld's "Hymn II" to make the point that Lyon herself published her volume, the first by a Jewish woman in England, within a framework that she would have regarded as conferring ambiguous support for her own project; that is, her own work is premised on her knowing that religious poetry by women abounds in her day; that there is a mainstream English readership for poetry of a religious nature which unabashedly praises God; that such proud religious poetry is sometimes written by women, like Barbauld, with deep secular learning and standing; and that it is sometimes written by Christians outside of the Church of England. But if this is the best that Lyon can call upon in England as a source for emulation, then it obviously still falls short. Lyon recognizes the tradition in which she seeks to find a place, but the space for it is one that she must still uniquely carve out and define. She must define an inheritance even as she must recognize the dilution of its meaning to her.

The tradition of paraphrase of the Bible based on other English translations is yet another example of an affiliation she decidedly does not and will not join, even as it certainly forms part of the necessary background to Lyon's writing. In her table of contents, she labels her section of psalms "Paraphrases upon Psalms XIX, XV, XLIX, L, LVIII, LXXXII, LXXIII, LXXVI, XCI." On the first page of the psalms themselves, the title is given as "Paraphrased from David's Psalms." This is clearly a gesture in the direction of the English tradition she inherits, but she soon makes it clear enough that she holds that her paraphrases are based on a more sophisticated understanding, and therefore on a privileged interpretation, of the Hebrew Bible. I would suggest that the title is similar in effect to the disclaimer she offers at the beginning of the volume, in which she dedicates her poems to the Princess of Wales while both apologizing for the presumption and boldly claiming the right to such presumption after all. Lyon knows what would be, by convention, her place. If she is going to enter into the territory of psalm translation, she is going to announce it with the proper gesture to tradition. Lyon thus inherits an English tradition that she refracts. She makes use of it as an anchor to describe at once her difference from it and her right to association within it. If she comes to recognize an alienation from its central meaning, then she will assert such alienation on her own terms. The struggle for Lyon is made all the more complicated by another tradition against which she must define herself, and that is the one of translation by Christian Hebraists. Where they seek to correct the text from the putative errors recorded by the Jews, they also seek to establish themselves as the more capable, as Christians, for the task of genuine understanding. We will visit this question again; for now, it is important to note that Lyon's joining of the English cultural tradition is a vexed movement for her as a Jew and as a woman.

If Addison is the model for all future translators and paraphrasers of Psalm 19, indeed if no less an authority than Lowth's translator recognizes that Addison's version of it "infinitely excels every translation," then Lyon's presumption in offering her own paraphrase is immediately conspicuous. Psalm 19, in fact, is the very first psalm in her collection. If she is trepidatious about presuming to enter the tradition of English psalm paraphrase and translation with so universally lauded an example as her predecessor, then she gives no hint of it. "The spacious firmament on high" (Addison) proclaims the glory of God; the glory of God is declared in the Book of Common Prayer as well as the King James Bible. Addison, in his abbreviated three stanzas, has the heavens proclaiming "their great Original" (4). Lyon's "arched heavens" instead "*instruct*[s] the earth" (italics mine) about "Whose hand stretch'd out the blue expanse." Lyon's is more immediately didactic; heaven first must "instruct," not "proclaim" (as in Addison) or "declare" (as in KJV or BCP). The original Hebrew is מספרים (*mesaprim*), which may be approximately rendered as "tell." For Lyon, we are not given simple license freely to interpret, in facile association, the glory of God from the splendors of nature. We must earn the right to interpret meaning if we are to do so correctly, and we must do so from the basis of learning. The correlative, of course, is that we must earn the right to presume upon translating as well. Lyon's stanzas consist of six pentameter lines, and I quote the first one:

> The arched heavens ere since the birth of time
> Instruct the earth, in characters sublime,
> To read aloft with sudden glance,
> Whose hand stretch'd out the blue expanse;
> Who bade the stars blaze forth from pole to pole,
> And all beneath his high dominion roll.
> (Lyon, 119)

What Lyon implicitly asserts first—for this psalm which in the English tradition has always been read as the psalm about humans "reading" God in His creation—is that we immediately accept the understanding that right reading is the yield of learning; that is, we must not take our interpretive stance with respect to creation for granted. "Ere since the birth of time" the heavens have been instructing, and so we must first be students. We are enjoined to learn how to *translate* the language of the beautiful firmament into a paradigm for understanding the supremacy of God. Lyon's heavens "instruct," and the pupil of such instruction is "the earth," who receives the words of instruction "in characters sublime," so that earth will "read aloft" an understanding of the divinity, "Whose hand stretch'd out the blue expanse."

I have cited above the first few lines of Psalm 19 from BCP as quoted by Addison in his introductory lecture in *The Spectator*. There the firmament that "sheweth his handywork" is a spectacle to be observed by humankind. That humanity hears the declaration aright is presupposed. That the canonical translators have done due diligence with respect to their source texts has also been broadly presupposed in the mainstream community. In Lyon alone is the emphasis on instruction suggestive of a hesitation about legitimate interpretation, or what we may indeed refer to as the adequate translation of the "characters sublime." In Lyon only the heavens instruct the earth *how* to read, and in Lyon the heavens have been doing so since *before* creation. The point here is that the lesson of exegesis is prior to the argument for design as inferred by humans from the splendors of the visible world. Lyon's import about the infinite and eternal instruction of the heavens "ere since the birth of time" is itself an interpolation from the original Hebrew. This is a psalm that is preoccupied with the splendors of visible nature implying the glory of God. Do we infer correctly that which is implied? Do the "characters sublime" form a language we have learned? Lyon will not take for granted what her English predecessors do without demur. In this, we may be reminded of the context of the translation debates that further situate Lyon's efforts. The Christian Hebraists who would likely have been most offensive to Lyon include those claiming that the Jews are untrustworthy translators of the Hebrew Bible. As described earlier, such figures as Benjamin Kennicott imply consistently that the project of retranslating the Hebrew Bible into English is in the service of restoring divine revelation to the place where it belongs and where it is best protected, namely Christianity. This proprietary control is not exclusive to translations that involve discussion of the Messiah, but the controversies are particularly intense in those contexts. Kennicott at one point complains: "And yet there can be no doubt but that the later Jews, where they have found copies reading differently in any passages relating to the Messiah may have sometimes preferr'd that Reading which was the least favourable to the Christian Cause."[22] The daughter of the Hebrew teacher of the would be Christian Hebraists of Eton, Oxford, and Cambridge; the daughter of the Hebrew teacher who barely eked out a living because Jews could neither gain secure employment in such hallowed halls of learning nor be paid decent wages; the daughter who would have gained mastery of the Hebrew language with her mother's milk, as it were, is the daughter of Israel who asserts the primacy of authentic understanding of how to comprehend the sublime characters of the heavens and, by extension, the sublime characters of the Hebrew language whose fraught arena of translation she has entered. And it is indeed a fraught arena; as another example among many, the Christian Hebraist scholar Julius Bate, defending some of John Hutchinson's particular claims about the received Hebrew translation for God and covenant, identifies Jewish scholarship about the Hebrew Bible as the real culprit: "namely, what is before mentioned, the Rules of Grammar and Construction laid down by the apostate Race, to whom the Book of God has been sealed, ever since they sealed the Prophecies with the Blood of the Messiah; and which became sealed among them, from their diabolical Attempts to seal it from Christians."[23] Lyon controls the text in its own language which, we are implicitly reminded, is *her* language, and she offers its rendering (her psalm paraphrases), as well as considered thoughts about how to approach it (her implicit warnings about how to translate the "characters" of divine revelation), in the language of the country in which she lives. She may take on Addison as well as the Book of Common Prayer or the King James Bible or any of the exalted renderings. She does not relinquish her confidence or her audacity because, as the translation unfolds, she makes it clear that she has earned her bold presumptions.

Addison's famous paraphrase is offered in tetrameters of eight lines, and his abbreviated rendering of the psalm is recognizable for its Neoclassical assurance of rational design. I quote the first stanza:

> The spacious firmament on high,
> With all the blue ethereal sky,
> And spangled heavens, a shining frame,
> Their great Original proclaim.
> Th'unwearied sun, from day to day,
> Does his Creator's power display;
> And publishes to every land
> The work of an almighty hand.

I would also like to quote the first several verses of the King James Version, which is similar to that of the Book of Common Prayer:

> The heavens declare the glory of God; and the firmament sheweth his handywork.
> Day unto day uttereth speech, and night unto night sheweth knowledge.
> There is no speech nor language, where their voice is not heard.
> Their line is gone out through all the earth, and their words to the end of the world. In them hath he set a tabernacle for the sun.
> Which is as a bridegroom coming out of his chamber, and rejoiceth as a strong man to run a race. (19:1–5)

Neither Lyon nor Addison includes the image of the bridegroom, which is appropriately rendered in the other versions from the Hebrew חתן (*hatan*). The JPS translation includes a footnote to clarify that the tent for the sun has been placed by God in the heavens. I quote the JPS from verse 4 until the conclusion of verse 7:

> There is no utterance, there are no words, whose sound goes unheard.
> Their voice carries throughout the earth, their words to the end of the world. He placed in them a tent for the sun,
> who is like a groom coming forth from the chamber, like a hero, eager to run his course.
> His rising-place is at one end of heaven, and his circuit reaches the other; nothing escapes his heat.

The bridegroom, then, is the analogy for the sun proceeding from his chamber. Lyon does take up the image of the sun, but she does not retain the original's "bridegroom," and I would suggest that this is because of the oft-cited, familiar associations of Jesus, especially in the Gospel of John, as the bridegroom. Lyon would naturally have wished to avoid not only an association recognizable from the New Testament, but she would also wish to go further in circumventing the typical Christian typological readings that interpret the Hebrew Bible in terms of its imputed predictive New Testament references. Since her psalm paraphrases represent her efforts to harness anew an authority not simply of definitive knowledge of the Hebrew but also of definitive authority for exegetical understanding, she refigures the imagery of sun in rhetoric that strips it of its conventionalized Christian association with Jesus as bridegroom. The omission is obtrusive, even if "bridegroom" is absent from Addison as well who, after all, does describe the sun as displaying "his Creator's power."

It is not until the fourth stanza of Lyon's version that she introduces the sun at all, and then only to assert, surprisingly, that it pales in comparison to his source, which is God:

> Th'enthroned Sun, in his high flaming course,
> A spark compar'd to his almighty source,
> When first his orient beams adorn
> The rosy blush that wakes the morn,
> Through heaven's high bounds proclaims the Lord Supreme,

And writes his name on ev'ry glorious beam.
(Lyon, 120)

For Lyon, the sun is not merely a signifier of God; it is also a mere "*spark compar'd to his almighty source*" and, as such, it is a sign, a language, not equal to its referent. If this psalm has been read as the song of praise for the language of a cherished and beautiful temporal world gloriously signifying its Creator, then Lyon reminds us that the language of temporality takes its place within a dualistic universe that of necessity disconnects it from properly and fully announcing any metaphysical ultimate. The sun is part of the language illustrating the supremacy of God even as it insistently exemplifies the insufficiency of any object in the empirical world to signify the ultimately ineffable Supreme Being. It is also a part of the physical universe, and in its non-symbolic aspect—that is, *as sun*—it is truly beautiful but truly a finite, limited entity. Keeping in mind Lyon's omission altogether of the translation of "bridegroom," it is startling to see how she further manipulates the image: Lyon capitalizes the "S" for "Sun," which is suggestive both of the conventional association of Jesus with "Sun" as well as "Son." But if this conventionalized association occurs to its readers—as surely it must—then it is one also undercut by Lyon at once. She provides her readers unmistakably with the conventional Christian association and recontextualizes it, finally bringing the process back to her overriding concern with exegetical proficiency. "Sun/Son" as divinity is not possible in Lyon's metaphoric rendering. The Sun, a mere spark in comparison to God, an insufficient marker of the "Lord Supreme," adorns sunrise, "The rosy blush." "Sun" does not quite work as metaphoric equivalent, even if it is the best we have as an object of the empirical world to stand for our projected belief. We will see that Lyon insists implicitly upon reading the Sun, however personified, *as* sun, as empirical object, even as object that we invest with symbolic significance, but a symbolic significance that reminds us always of our powers of interpreting natural phenomena. For here Lyon joins Addison in acknowledging that the "spacious firmament" (Addison) can "proclaim": "Through heaven's high bounds proclaims the Lord Supreme," meaning that it is the "rosy blush," the exquisite sunset, that "proclaims" God's supremacy. Recall that for Addison, the "spangled heavens" are a "shining frame," who "Their great Original proclaim." The King James Bible and the Book of Common Prayer have the heavens "*declare*" the glory of God, while the "firmament *sheweth* his handywork." In Addison, the sun itself "Does his Creator's power display." Lyon joins the vocabulary of Addison to the insistence upon her specifically Jewish reading of such proclamations and declarations. The Sun "adorn[s]" the sunrise; the reflected hues that we see from earth are what, in Lyon, "proclaims the Lord Supreme, / And writes his name on ev'ry glorious beam," just as, in Lyon's first stanza, the heavens "instruct the earth" "To read aloft." If at this point Lyon is willing to allow anything to "proclaim" God, then it is because she has established clear ground for the complicated dynamics of "reading" divine signs from the perspective of interpretive authority. There is some question about the antecedent of "his" in the final line of Lyon's fourth stanza, "And writes his name on ev'ry glorious beam." The object of the sentence is properly the "sun," not the Lord. If the Sun, the "mere spark compar'd to God," is the name written on every sunbeam (rather than the name of God being written on every sunbeam), then this is consistent with the first stanza; the heavens instruct the earth in how to read the language of inference. The Sun writes his name on the sunbeams, a great allure to humans who "read aloft." God is ultimately untranslatable, but the desires of humans are profound and the beauty of the world is perceptible.

Lyon is attentive to the psalm's consideration of hearing as well as seeing. In Lyon this becomes yet another meditation on the ineffability of God even as it becomes a marker of her own eloquence in establishing the ground of her multivalent literary inheritance. The Jewish liturgical tradition is replete with praise for God that asserts all the same the insufficiency of human speech and human praise in declaring the character of God. The *Kaddish*, read in daily prayer (not only, of course, during times of mourning), asserts not only the insufficiency of speech but the belief that God is beyond any blessing, song, praise or consolation that are uttered in this temporal world. Lyon interpolates a stanza that emphasizes that her understanding of this psalm is a function of her understanding of the complicated dynamic she negotiates among the traditions (Jewish, English literary, Christian Hebraist) she inherits:

> What swelling anthem can his praise resound,
> Like this grand concert of th' etherial round?
> What dulcet symphonies can boast
> The music of the glittering host?
> What instrumental harmony afford
> Such measur'd cadence, and divine accord?
> (Lyon, 120)

The "grand concert of th' etherial round" alludes not only to the music of the spheres but also to the famous rendition by Haydn of Addison's version of

Psalm 19. But the praise functions also to remind us of Lyon's alternative theme in this paraphrase, which is that human translation is partial, incomplete. This is the case for linguistic translation as well as the translation of temporal markers into signs of divine providence. Swelling anthems are not equal to the "concert of th' etherial round"; "dulcet symphonies" cannot boast music like that of "the glittering host"; "instrumental harmony" cannot be equal to "divine accord." If the glory of the world proclaims/declares the existence of God, then it is a proclamation that resists translation into human language—any human language, including Hebrew. The temporal world itself is a pale shadow of the divine—the sun is a mere "spark compar'd to his almighty source," but the need to make hermeneutical sense of it is shared by Jews, Christians, and non-believers alike. The struggle to assert mastery over the text that putatively defines meaning in the universe, then, is a struggle of life and death. The artistry of our human efforts fall even further from the mark.

Or do they? The third stanza insists upon Nature's eloquence:

All Nature's finger eloquently shows
His wond'rous might in every wind that blows;
His pow'r the beams of day declare,
Still evening, and the midnight air;
The clouds that darken his majestic feet,
Shout it with voices audible and sweet.
(Lyon, 120)

Nature is eloquent, more eloquent, to be sure, than human artifice. But the eloquence of nature here does not rely on visual cues. We have moved from the visual to the audible, from sight to sound. Nature "shows" God's might in the blowing wind, an example of synesthesia worthy of Shelley. The air is eloquent; the clouds that "darken" the "majestic feet" of Nature still "Shout" God's wond'rous might "with voices audible and sweet." When Nature is invisible in the dark, so Lyon's paraphrase would have it, the inference to the existence of God is still available.

Lyon here is certainly alluding to the imagery of sound in the original Hebrew, which is likewise taken up by the other examples to which I have been comparing it. However, the above stanza is an interpolation that essentially clarifies, or rather corrects, the sense conveyed in the King James and Book of Common Prayer's translation. The Book of Common Prayer offers the following for verses 2 to 4 (I have already quoted these lines from both the KJV and BCP above): "One day telleth another: and one night certifieth another. / There is neither speech nor language: but their voices are heard among them. / Their sound is gone out into all lands: and their words into the ends of the world." Here is the Hebrew: יום ליום, יביע אומר; ולילה ללילה, יחוה–דעת/ אין–אמר, ואין דברים: בלי, נשמע קולם. JPS translates the lines as follows: "Day to day makes utterance, night to night speaks out. / There is no utterance, there are no words, whose sound goes unheard." If the Psalm writer imagines a voice emanating from the heavens, Lyon in the stanza about Nature's eloquence clarifies that the voice is not, in fact, an effect of reasonable deduction nor an evangelical call to all the peoples of the world. If the heavens have something to say, as it were, it must be because we are human interpreters whose understanding is unclouded even when "clouds that darken" Nature obscure the natural world. In this, Lyon is being especially bold with respect to her tacit response to Addison: Addison too gestures toward the imagery of sound even as he concludes his version by insisting boldly upon the artifice of the fantasy that we can hear a "real voice," and an even bolder declaration that the recognition that it is fantasy does not undermine the reasonableness of his rejoicing in God:

> What though in solemn silence all
> Move round this dark terrestrial ball;
> What though no real voice or sound
> Amidst their radiant orbs be found;
> In reason's ear they all rejoice,
> And utter forth a glorious voice,
> For ever singing as they shine,
> "The hand that made us is divine."

Thomas Paine in *The Age of Reason* (1794) quotes the entire Addison version in his chapter "Concerning God, and the Lights Cast on his Existence and Attributes by the Bible." He appropriates Addison's paraphrase to illustrate his thesis about God as first cause. After citing the poem, he immediately asserts: "What more does man want to know, than that the hand or power that made these things is divine, is omnipotent? Let him believe this, with the force it is impossible to repel if he permits his reason to act, and his rule of moral life will follow of course."[24] For Paine as for Addison, the operative term is "reason," and it is in "*reason's* ear" that what is "no real voice" at all nevertheless "utter[s] forth a glorious voice" attesting to divine creation. Lyon does not revert to an eighteenth-century optimism over reason's triumphs so much as she joins it to the implicit assertion of her own authoritative knowledge of how to understand the word of God, its language and its meaning. If reason is to exercise itself upon the contemplation of God, then the language being contemplated must first be reasonably comprehended. What Lyon has inherited by 1812, the year of the publication of her volume, is an English literary establishment that seeks the liberating specter of meaning in nature that is both reflective and immanent. If it is for her to translate the real significance of Psalm 19 for her age, then she indeed will inherit that mantle, too. In this, she is the obverse of Coleridge's "pensive Sara," who in "The Eolian Harp" is taken aback by her husband's joyance in nature that strikes against the heart of her Christian orthodoxy. I would posit some subtle Coleridgean influence on Lyon, especially the poet's exclamation about sound in the still air, an image that Lyon may well have deliberately appropriated:

> Methinks, it should have been impossible
> Not to love all things in a world so fill'd;
> Where the breeze warbles, and the mute still air
> Is Music slumbering on her instrument. (ll. 30–33)[25]

Coleridge is attentive to his wife's disapproval, and I cite it here because Lyon is fashioning herself as the daughter of Israel (not "Meek Daughter" of Christ) who does indeed bid other translators to walk humbly with their God, but who knows that her own tenacity is not Sara Coleridge's meekness, but rather the poet's temerity:

> But thy more serious eye a mild reproof
> Darts, O beloved Woman! Nor such thoughts
> Dim and unhallow'd dost thou not reject,
> And biddest me walk humbly with my God.
> Meek Daughter in the family of Christ! (ll. 50–53)

Nature is loud with meaning for Coleridge. It is loud with meaning for the psalmist, and it is loud with meaning for Lyon as paraphraser/translator. As a woman, she stakes her claim to inhabiting a voice that conveys vision: not Sara's disapproving conservatism, but Coleridge's visionary boldness is one model for her. What one understands oneself to have heard becomes the defining question of Lyon's rendition. Coleridge presents himself as having attended to an "animated nature" "That trembles into thought, as o'er them sweeps, / Plastic and vast, one intellectual breeze, / At once the Soul of each, and God of all" (44–48). Psalm 19 is preoccupied with voice, with the silent language of nature in signifying divine providence. For Addison, we recall, the sun "publishes" God's grandeur. We are being reassured about the relationship between God and Nature, perhaps, but Lyon wants reassurance first about human interpretation, a subject that resonates clearly with the theme of human interpretation in the context of the very translation debates that surround her.

Both the Book of Common Prayer and the King James Bible make use of the word "converting" for what the JPS translates as "renewing": "The law of the Lord is an undefiled law, converting the soul: the testimony of the Lord is sure, and giveth wisdom unto the simple" (BCP, 19:7). Given the conditions of early nineteenth-century England, "converting" would have been a freighted term for Lyon to transport.[26] The closest she comes to engaging with the lines is her eighth stanza:

> The fear of thee, great God! Inspires the good
> To make thy law their intellectual food;
> It is this sacred voice of truth
> That guides old age and infant youth;
> (Lyon, 121)

The law of the Lord does not, in Lyon, "convert"; it "guides," "inspires," and nourishes ("To make thy law their intellectual food").

This is a dynamic of which we are reminded repeatedly. In so reminding us, Lyon incorporates more of the original psalm:

> O how, great Ruler of the earth and sky!
> Thy lovely works allure the gazer's eye!
> O happiest of the sons of men,
> Who view thee with celestial ken;
> Who tread undeviating thy heavenly ways,
> Pure, holy, just, and lavish in thy praise!
> (Lyon, 121)

Our eye is allured; we are gazers after all, viewers, offerers of praise. The happiest of men are the ones who know how to view God's works, which is with "celestial ken," knowledge of how to interpret, read, the signs in the sky and on the earth. This psalm most recognizable in English translation as "The Spacious Firmament on High" becomes, in Lyon's hands, increasingly about how to read. We are gazers who become allured. In this, the psalm acknowledges the long history of its rendering as the psalm of praise for a nature voluble in its beauty and thereby reflective of God as Creator. But Lyon then remarks that the "happiest" are those who gaze with a particular kind of knowledge. As such, it is those happiest of gazers/interpreters who are "pure, holy, just."

Lyon presents herself as among the happy interpreters, one of those among the pure, holy and just. In presenting herself as the authoritative reader, then, she is also entering the Christian literary tradition via a different entrance than is commonly designated. English literary history is dependent on biblical translation to the extent that even in high Romanticism, the iambic cadences of the Bible in the King James translation are ever apparent, and the vast reservoir of allusions, of course, leads perpetually to the Bible. Lyon here advertises again her affiliation with Milton, her insistence that even a Jewish woman in early nineteenth-century England can inherit the mantle of *Paradise Lost*. In Book V, Milton records the prayer of thanksgiving of Adam and Eve in language that certainly recalls Psalm 19, and which Lyon no doubt also recognizes as among her precursor texts.

> These are thy glorious works, Parent of good,
> Almighty, thine this universal frame,
> Thus wondrous fair; thyself how wondrous then!
> Unspeakable, who sit'st above these heavens
> To us invisible or dimly seen
> In these thy lowest works, yet these declare
> Thy goodness beyond thought, and power divine:
> Speak ye who best call tell, ye sons of light,
> Angels, for ye behold him, and with songs
> And choral symphonies, day without night,
> Circle his throne rejoicing, ye in Heav'n,
> On Earth join all ye creatures to extol
> Him first, him last, him midst, and without end.
> (*Paradise Lost* V.153–165)

Line 165 is soon to be cited by Wordsworth in the Simplon Passage of Book VI of *The Prelude*, but Milton's source of allusion for line 165 is from the New

Testament, Revelation 1:8: "I am Alpha and Omega, the beginning and the ending, saith the Lord, which is, and which was, and which is to come, the Almighty." Lyon follows first her own authority, but she is also gesturing to Milton's interpretation of Psalm 19, especially the injunction of Adam and Eve to the angels, "Speak ye who *best* can tell." The creatures of earth are all to extol "Him first, him last, him midst, and without end," the latter phrase referring in fact to the requirement of perpetual praise. Lyon does not appropriate Milton's allusion to Revelation, and neither is her call for universal praise without qualification. Praise is due, to be sure, and praise is honorable. Praise of God, however, is a function of gratitude for what one apprehends as among His attributes. If Lyon's primary motive is to read Psalm 19 as a cautionary lesson about how to translate the works and words of God, then even universal praise of God runs the risk of mistranslation. Milton's prelapsarian Adam and Eve are confident that the "glorious works"—nature—are the work of God, the "Parent of good," even as they also know that God is "To us invisible or dimly seen / In these thy lowest works." For Lyon, the sun was a mere spark, but it is after all the best we have to infer the existence of "the Lord Supreme." When Milton's Adam and Eve enjoin the angels to sing God's praise, they do so by first acknowledging that the angels are in a better position to do so, "for ye behold him." It is in such context that they are told to "speak."

Lyon is most attentive, then, to the original language of the psalm as it reflects the process of communication. It is not that the other translations and paraphrases entirely neglect this aspect of Psalm 19; rather, Lyon takes it up as the raison d'être of her paraphrase, and inflects it with her particular concerns. It is important that she chooses this particular psalm as the first of her paraphrases. It concludes with the lines (I cite the JPS translation): "May the words of my mouth and the prayer of my heart be acceptable to You, O Lord, my rock and my redeemer" (19:15). The phrase "May the words of my mouth" is of central importance in Jewish liturgical practice, as it is recited every day in the *Shemoneh Esrei*, or *Amidah*, the central Jewish daily prayer.[27] As such, these are words that are intimately familiar to practicing Jews. Both BCP and KJV provide reasonably faithful renderings of these lines in Psalm 19. Lyon's boldness is at its apex, perhaps, when she takes up these lines for translation in her paraphrase. For she chooses *not* to translate them verbatim, but rather to step out of her posture as David's psalmist and to speak in her own voice. Her final stanza transforms the prayer "May the words of my mouth" into a prayer that still asks for acceptable speech, but speech understood within the various vexed terms of Lyon's paraphrase/translation:

> O Thou, who erst on David's holiest lyre,
> Didst dart thy sacred vehemence of fire,
> Come, teach me to reveal thy ways,
> And scatter round a dazzling blaze;
> Unfolding bright, inspir'd with silent awe,
> Th' unclouded prospect of thy heavenly law!
> (Lyon, 122)

She now speaks not in the voice of the biblical psalmist, but as the present-day inheritor of David. Lyon in her closing stanza addresses God directly and asks for the very same guidance that directed David's holiest lyre. She may be a translator writing paraphrases of David's Psalms, but she claims the mantle of lyricist supreme, an authority superseding all those to whom she had alluded in the course of Psalm 19. Milton and Addison, the Book of Common Prayer and the King James Bible: these are but earthly models whose inheritance she gladly refracts. Her teacher, so she now asserts, is God Himself, and she prays for the selfsame "vehemence of fire" that God "Didst dart" on David's lyre. If Lyon has amply demonstrated that she can control the text in its own language before translating it into English, then here, in her final prayer, she asks to be "inspir'd with *silent* awe," a remarkable juxtaposition with her calling down the inspiration to "scatter round a dazzling blaze." Lyon, the poet who would inherit David's poetic mantle and be tutored by God Himself, knows that "silence" is the first precondition to authentic lyrical exaltation of the divine. She does not take for granted the ability to praise nor, for that matter, the ability to translate, neither language nor the attributes of God. An alert and knowing silence is what guards against the "clouding" that distorts our comprehension of God beyond the natural distortions already inherent in human existence. Within the modesty of her holding such knowledge, she is still able to assert her authority, which is certainly religious but above all poetic: she prays to unfold "Th' unclouded prospect of thy [God's] heavenly law!" After a poem that has consistently alluded to the clouding of apprehension of the divine as the ultimate peril in mastery of the psalms, the prayer to reveal an "unclouded prospect" of God's law should strike one as astounding. Will Lyon come closer to unclouded transmission than any other poet?

The final stanza of Lyon's Psalm 19 is the poet's rendition of "May the words of my mouth and the prayer of my heart be acceptable to You, O Lord, my rock and my redeemer" (JPS 19:15). The word לבי, translated as "my heart," from the noun לב (*lev*), usually "heart," can take other meanings in biblical Hebrew. It is sometimes used in place of "throat," as in Ecclesiastes 5:1: "Keep your mouth from being rash, and let not *your throat* [לבך; the same word for 'your heart'] be quick to bring forth speech before God."²⁸ When Lyon concludes her rendition of Psalm 19 by praying to God directly for instruction in how to reveal His ways, she is alluding also to the organ of speech as signified in the Hebrew, and as related, intertextually, to Ecclesiastes. Ecclesiastes' injunction to keep one's mouth from being rash, as an intertext here, reminds us again of the translation debates, of the context against which Lyon sets herself—that is, the struggle by Christian Hebraists to wrest control, as they tended to see it, of the Hebrew Bible from the Jews. Lyon has established a palimpsest in which heart, throat, and speech together bind the two prayers (from Psalm 19 and from Ecclesiastes 5) that Lyon's words be acceptable to God, especially given the biblical warning not to be rash in speech. The determination of what constitutes rash or acceptable speech is a matter of interpretation, and in the context of Lyon's paraphrases, that interpretation is partly a function of the informed reading that leads to knowledgeable translation.

Psalm 49

When Bishop Robert Lowth published his translation into English, in 1778, of the book of Isaiah, he dedicated it to the king of England, who is thanked for his patronage of the project, which is to the "universal benefit of the Christian Church."²⁹ David Ruderman describes the status of the offering: "Wrapped in the aura of both national patriotism and Christian piety, the bishop's crusade on behalf of a new Christian text of the Old Testament, both artistically and religiously superior to the older version taken from the Jews, was no small matter to be taken lightly." Ruderman goes on to call it Lowth's "declaration of independence" from the Jews. When Emma Lyon takes up Psalm 49 for paraphrase/translation, she interpolates the word "royalty" into the text where it is not there in the original Hebrew nor in any of the other currently available renditions. I quote the first stanzas of the JPS translation first:

Hear this, all you peoples; give ear, all inhabitants of the world,
men of all estates, rich and poor alike. My mouth utters wisdom,
my speech is full of insight. I will turn my attention to a theme, set
forth my lesson to the music of a lyre. (49:1–5)

Here are the first two stanzas of Lyon's rendition:

Awake, arise, ye circling nations, hear!
O Universe, give audience to my lay!
Let royalty attend with list'ning ear,
And bow submiss to truth's imperial sway.

Heaven's holy Spirit breathes upon my lyre,
And cheers the fainting courage of my soul;
The truths I sing no mortal tongues inspire,
From heaven's high fount the sacred numbers roll.
(Lyon, 125)

The voice of Lyon's psalmist does not stop at addressing all the inhabitants of the world, as does the original. She diverges from the text specifically to address royalty, indeed to demand that "royalty attend with list'ning ear." Moreover, royalty is "commanded" to "bow submiss to truth's imperial sway," a demand cloaked, perhaps, in the garb of the psalmist, but clearly here drawn from Lyon herself. It is one thing, perhaps, to insist that royalty listen, another to demand that they bow down to the truth, especially if it is the poet—a young Jewish woman—who is doing the demanding and translating the proper ground of truth. Lyon is demanding that royalty bow down to *her* rendition of the truth, since this is her psalm paraphrase and it is uniquely Lyon who interpolates royalty as the proper audience for hearing the truth. Where Lowth translates a part of the Bible (Isaiah) and dedicates it to the king with thanks for his patronage, Lyon in Psalm 49 obtrusively reminds her reader that there is a power that supersedes the British royal line, and it is one that sanctions the boldness of her insistence that they "bow submiss."

This entire volume, we will recall, is dedicated to the Princess Charlotte, and if Lyon presumes to invoke Charlotte's name as one sign of entry into the privileged domain of English national life, then her elegy for Princess Amelia printed in the earlier section of the volume, "On the Death of Her Royal Highness, The Princess Amelia," also confirms her self-presentation as deeply participant in the most privileged sphere of country and literature. The poem in honor of Amelia does not present the poet as the abject supplicant familiar from the earlier address to Charlotte. As an elegy, it appropriates the conventional act of bidding the weeping family be silent, for the consolation of release from earthly misery—"The bitter ling'ring agonies of death"—and her eternal rest is disturbed by the spectacle of plaintive crying. Though the imperative is conventional, the case of young Emma Lyon lecturing the royal family, king and queen included, to leave off their tears is still notable for its daring:

> Though sadness glooms not in the realms of light,
> Where all her pangs are heal'd with heavenly balm!
> Should sweet Amelia bend her blissful sight
> Our tears alone may violate her calm.
> (Lyon, 87)

Can a woman, a Jew, the daughter of a poor man, scold the royal line, even in the relative safety of poetic convention? Psalm 49, like Psalm 73, recalls the poems in the earlier part of the volume and rewrites their import by offering a palimpsestic reading of them. The lowly girl may tremble at the thought of such temerity, but the inheritor of David does not hesitate. The elegy for Princess Amelia is somewhere in between these two diametrically opposed positions. Princess Amelia died in 1810 after prolonged illness. The fifteenth child of King George III, she was known to be the king's favorite child, and her death is said to have exacerbated his illness.[30] In her elegy, before Lyon reverts to the conventional consolation that leads to the proscription against mourning, she joins the lamentation and asserts her grief:

> My pensive Muse would o'er thy royal bier,
> Fair Princess! Breathe affliction's pitying sigh;
> Would deck thy hearse with many a flowing tear,
> As smiling angels waft thee to the sky.
> (Lyon, 86)

Decking the hearse is one of the common conventions of pastoral elegy. Here Lyon would deck the hearse not with flowers but with "flowing tear," because even her muse is pensive. If her posture of familiarity is permissible because conventional, it still stands as a public assertion of acknowledged association with the deceased, as elegies tend to do. Mourning another presupposes some iteration of connection, if not outright affiliation. To mourn publicly itself advertises the right to mourn, meaning that it advertises the connection constituted by the elegy itself. Sometimes that affiliation takes the form of self-identification with the mourned subject, sometimes merely an identification that relies more on nationalist or other expressly public forums. Whatever the focus, the presentation of the poet's self as a mourning subject requires some source of identification, a recognition of a right to mourn within the inherited genre of elegy and to do so publicly. It is such affiliation that gives sanction to the outpouring of grief, which Lyon here displays as a deep existential wound to herself, compromising even her muse. The association asserted in the paraphrase of Psalm 49, however, is a step well beyond such postures. The Hebrew psalms indeed are replete with warnings even to royalty, but the original Hebrew Psalm 49 offers its warnings about vanity to a more general audience. In Lyon's rendition, the royal family is reminded not only to attend, but to attend with listening ear, suggesting that the poet has good grounds to worry that royalty does not "attend" very well without the requisite emphatic prompting. As in Psalm 19, Psalm 49 also offers a play on the Hebrew word לב (*lev*), which, as in common usage, JPS, KJV, and BCP translate as "heart." Lyon departs from direct translation, but I would suggest that the second quatrain, quoted above, is her answer to what JPS offers as "My mouth utters wisdom, / my speech is full of insight." BCP (similar in KJV) translates it as follows: "My mouth shall speak of wisdom: and my heart shall muse of understanding." *Lev* in biblical Hebrew, as we have already seen, is sometimes also used to denote "throat," the organ of speech. For a psalm that chastises royalty, Lyon has again chosen one that would emphasize the virtuosity of the mechanisms of speech, as well as the conscious choices about what one says. "No mortal tongues inspire" the truths she sings, asserts the second stanza, for the poetry that is herein being rendered consists of "sacred numbers." In altering the opening of the psalm to include "royalty" among the audience commanded to "bow submiss," Lyon is bringing her readers closer to the conscious recognition that they are reading a contemporary renderer, one with her own voice, and one who seizes an authority that few other authors of Psalm paraphrases are able to perform. I would suggest that she is bringing her audience "closer" only to the recognition of Lyon's self-reflexive gestures, because she also appropriates the authority of King David the psalmist to speak in the language of rightful audacity. She also makes use of the cloak of David's voice to engage in rhetorical gestures that would otherwise transgress overmuch the boundaries of decorum that determine the propriety of utterance.

"Heaven's holy Spirit breathes upon my lyre," and as such, the *sound* that it makes must be heeded. She does not fail to point out that the "courage of [her] soul" is "fainting," but only to advise that she understands the potential transgression of propriety performed by her paraphrase and the specific liberties that she takes with it. Were it not for the sanction of heaven itself, that is, were it not for her capacity to translate ably the word of God, her courage would fail her.

But courage does not fail Lyon in the psalm paraphrases, even if she fashions herself in the earlier poems of the volume as failing in courage, ambition, and learning. Her earlier "Ode on Ambition" acknowledges the genuine value of ambition, even wistfully recounts its fruits. In the end, however, she disclaims her hold on it. Ambition, so she demurs, does not belong to her. Addressing the personified Ambition directly, she concludes:

> Then ruffle no more the calm stream of my breast,
> Nor draw from my bosom a sigh;
> Go, blazon the warrior erecting his crest,
> And send the quick flash from his eye.
>
> All-glowing with thee will he range o'er the plain,
> All perils undauntedly brave;
> But, dazzling Ambition! Thy trophies are vain
> To the bosom that sighs for the grave!
> (Lyon, 95)

We are not told why this speaker sighs *in extremis* for the grave, especially not after the expansive catalogue of the benefits of ambition. This is a speaker who seems to pine for the glories that she eventually discounts in the above conclusion. The opening quatrain announces a sort of nostalgia for that which she refuses:

> How glorious the breast that in life's early morn,
> Ambition! Enkindles thy flame;
> Who pants for thy trophies, and longs to adorn
> His youth with the splendour of fame!
> (Lyon, 94)

Does she pant, long, or burn ("Enkindles") for the fruits of ambition? As a poem that begins as an encomium to ambition, it certainly prepares its readers to anticipate a self-reflection that would join the speaker's own efforts to the praise of her subject matter. This expectation is initially reinforced when she notes that ambition is not restricted to the burnishing of the warrior's success; ambition also "wide opens the field / To Genius, the blaze of the mind" (95). However, the poem is also aggressively self-reflexive: its establishing of readerly expectations is plainly staged. It is only *as if* she prepares her readers to anticipate her indulgence in the sweet fruits of ambition, and it is only *as if* we are disappointed when we read that she purports to disclaim such glories altogether. The play on reader response is flagrantly staged, because the reader also knows that no woman, especially no Jewish woman in early nineteenth-century England, would explicitly claim the mantle of ambition directly and without qualification. If Lyon plays along at subverting our expectations of the poem's logical conclusion, that is, if she plays along at having us anticipate a more presumptuous voice, then it is only because we know, in this first section of the volume (before the presentation of the psalms), that poetic propriety within her particular circumstances dictates that she conclude by resigning any claim to ambition at all. The self-contradiction is surely intentional, just as her dedication of the entire volume to Princess Charlotte is both presumptuous and framed within her self-presentation as abject speaker. The playing with expectations and poetic propriety undermines many of its own subversions: we know that she must represent herself as abject; we know that she is in fact implicitly foregrounding her learning, her mastery of literary form, and that she is staking a claim to justly inheriting the fruits of English literary history. When we finally move to the psalms, as we have seen, she implicitly asserts that her audacity is now earned. The poem about ambition, then, carries real significance in presenting her balance between acknowledging the decorum that she must observe and acknowledging the ambition that all the same she possesses.

If we consider further Lyon's appropriation of the sensibility poems of, for example, Charlotte Smith, that balancing act becomes all the more striking. Smith provides a model for a woman poet whose prominence is not defined by religious writing, but whose manifold sorrows belong to the sphere of female experience: an unhappy marriage, the birth of twelve children, and the horror of mourning dead children. Though Smith entered the literary world in part to earn money, and though she earned greater sums from publishing prose fiction, she continued writing poetry because she understood that lyric would serve as the most solid ground of her entry into literary high culture. Indeed, Smith's influence on British Romantic poetry was still felt keenly during Lyon's day. By 1811, the year before the publication of Lyon's volume of poetry, Smith's *Elegiac*

Sonnets had reached its tenth edition, and the *Critical Review*, recognizing that she had revived the sonnet form, enthused that "her sonnets are assuredly the most popular in the language, and deservedly so."[31] In Sonnet XXXII of the *Elegiac Sonnets*, Smith addresses "melancholy." The melancholy signified by the "mournful melodies" of nature are precisely those which "fleet before the poet's eyes." Smith's final address to melancholy in the poem offers a helpful reminder that Lyon's posture of sorrow is also the posture of fine-tuned poetic sensibility found prominently in Smith:

> O Melancholy!—such thy magic power,
> That to the soul these dreams are often sweet,
> And soothe the pensive visionary mind! (p. 34)[32]

Smith's melancholy soothes; Lyon's ambition ruffles the calm stream of her breast. Both poets are working within the rhetorical space assigned to women, even as Lyon's is also the space of a deeper dislocation, one with very little precedent for recognizing the reasonable place of the voice of a Jewish woman in England.

Certainly Lyon's poem, especially the earlier stanzas, also recall Milton, whose presence in Lyon's sole volume is steady and unmistakable, another sign of her choosing an illustrious inheritance. In the "Ode on Ambition," she is recalling "Lycidas," and the "Lycidas" speaker's meditation on the ambition of fame, which I cite here:

> Fame is the spur that the clear spirit doth raise
> (That last infirmity of noble mind)
> To scorn delights, and live laborious days;
> But the fair guerdon when we hope to find,
> And think to burst out into sudden blaze,
> Comes the blind Fury with th'abhorrèd shears,
> And slits the thin-spun life. (ll. 70–76)[33]

The second stanza of Lyon's ode furthers recognition of the Miltonic allusion:

> Impatient of sloth, where thy banners are spread,
> And thy heroes triumphantly shown,
> He mourns, while the laurels high wave on their head,

At the silence that covers his own.
(Lyon, 94)

The speaker's transition to the concluding stanzas insists that she does not "covet" the yield of ambition. Both the insistence that she does not covet the renown as well as the gloomy conclusion that she sighs for the grave participate in a tradition of women's sensibility even as the Miltonic allusions subtly critique that tradition. Pining for the grave is somewhat less conspicuous an aspect of that tradition than is the disclaiming of ambition. Lyon, after all, does not present herself as a woman suffering loss of husband, child, or love, or suffering catastrophic disaster, situations recognized in many women poets of sensibility. Like Charlotte Smith, Lyon does indulge in the noticing of "life's rough blast," from which she claims, in "An Ode to Honour," that she is "Still unsubdu'd." In "An Ode to Indifference," she apostrophizes ambition's diametrical opposite, asking her "To tranquillize my heart," and proclaiming that "at thy calm shrine / I'd bow, though happiness were mine" (59, 60). But why paint herself as longing specifically for the grave in the ode on ambition?

Lyon's publicly declared ambition, like that of most women writing during this period, is of necessity curtailed, at least for unrestricted common view. Where could she possibly go, then, with an encomium to ambition? A mere refusal to join its inviting procession could not have answered the real insecurities faced by its poet. As a woman and as a Jew in early nineteenth-century England, her recognition of the glorious benefits of ambition of necessity recall Milton's illustrious example precisely because they of necessity recall the inaccessibility of its corridors. Lyon's speaker is assuredly not the speaker of Milton's "Lycidas," who harnesses ambition to write the poem, and whose exalted verse sanctions the bold hope articulated early in the poem: "So may some gentle muse / With lucky words favour my destin'd urn" (ll. 19–20). There is a vicious circle in which Lyon catches herself: foregrounding an unmistakable ambition in her poems itself is both a kind of self-canceling even as it stands as a form of self-assertion. Fame, to adapt the Miltonic allusion from "Lycidas," is one of the most egregious infirmities of female mind. It hastens the "abhorr'd shears" that slit the thin spun life in the sense that it brackets the woman poet out of tradition and therefore out of stable ground on which to stand with her poetic powers.

Lyon's Psalm 49 also draws on Milton, even as its ultimate authority is the Hebrew Bible:

> Amid your pleasant palaces and groves,
> Where wealth and grandeur pour the golden tide,
> Already sere! The greedy stranger roves,
> And spurns your trophies with exulting pride.
>
> But ye, the sport of every flatt'ring praise,
> Intent alone on luxury and food,
> Live on, oblivious of the heavenly rays,
> And all remembrance of the fair and good.
>
> Prone like the brute bent downward to the earth,
> Ye blot the bright intelligence of man;
> Ye roam unmindful of celestial birth,
> Nor stretch one thought beyond this narrow span.
> (Lyon, 127)

In Book I of *Paradise Lost*, Milton's Satan lies "prone on the flood" (195), recalled in Lyon's "Prone like the brute bent downward to the earth." Satan, like Lyon's indulged sinners, is surely the ultimate "sport of every flatt'ring praise." The allusion is all the more startling given Lyon's reference to "pleasant palaces." This, like the earlier address to "royalty," is Lyon's own interpolation, not in the original Hebrew, and not in any of the popular translations or paraphrases. The scold of royalty now scolds while alluding to Milton. The Hebrew Bible is joined to Lyon's refraction of English literary history to produce a poetry that represents a resolute Jewish woman who is an English poet and authoritative reader of the Hebrew Bible. From this she presumes to derive her license to address, indeed to admonish, royalty. Where Robert Lowth asserts his authority by dedicating his English translation of Isaiah to the king of England, Lyon dedicates herself, in her translated psalms, to reinforcing her understanding of a textual finesse whose real, spiritual power presumes to supersede that of the monarch.

The Health of the Monarch: Psalm 72

There is an extensive tradition in Jewish history of praying in the synagogue for the health and strength of the government and monarch in whatever land Jews find themselves, a tradition that dates back to Jeremiah 29:7, in which the prophet advises in the name of God, "And seek the welfare of the city to which I have exiled you and pray to the Lord in its behalf; for in its prosperity you shall prosper" (JPS). The tradition in England, as in most countries, cites the monarch by name, as well as his immediate family, as the following excerpt from David Levi's 1782 *A Succinct Account of the Rites and Ceremonies of the Jews* attests: "He shall bless, and preserve, guard and assist, exalt, and highly aggrandize, our most gracious sovereign lord, King George the third, our most gracious Queen Charlotte, his Royal Highness George Prince of Wales, and all the Royal Family, may the supreme King of Kings, through his infinite mercy, grant them life, and preserve and deliver them from all manner of troubles and danger."[34] It is within the idioms of this tradition that Lyon paraphrases Psalm 72, a prayer for the king, in which her other references throughout the volume to the royal family surely resonate. Psalm 72 is also a prayer for justice, imploring God to protect and to guide the king. In Lyon's rendering, he is figured as worthy of this benefit because "still to thee he loves to bend, / With awful reverence prone" (137). The latter is an interpolation, implicit praise by Lyon in context of a volume which elsewhere witnesses her serving as scold, preceptor and interpreter even to the royal line. The original Hebrew of Psalm 72 does not make the case for the king on the strength of any such claim of the earthly potentate knowing his place. Indeed, Lyon's rendering serves both as implicit chastisement—know that to be worthy, the king *ought* still to acknowledge and obey God—and praise for a monarchy that provides relative safety to, but not full freedom for, those who worship God in ways outside of Church of England practice. The implicit praise, then, is grudging, just as Lyon's conclusion emphatically affirms the hierarchy of God before king:

> Then lift, ye nations, lift the voice,
> Sound, blessed be th' Eternal's name,
> Who makes your glowing tongues rejoice
> To crown a Monarch's fame.
> (Lyon, 139)

The final verses of the KJV are as follows:

> Blessed be the Lord God, the God of Israel, who only doeth wondrous things. And blessed be his glorious name for ever: and let the whole earth be filled with his glory; Amen, and Amen. The prayers of David the son of Jesse are ended. (72:18–20)

The KJV in these verses follows the Hebrew original relatively faithfully. Lyon's paraphrase emphasizes "the voice": "Then lift, ye nations." The conjunctive adverb "Then" emphasizes that the yield of recognizing the desired characteristics of the king's justice is voice, sound, the liturgy for God, not king: "Then lift, ye nations, lift the voice, / Sound, blessed be th' Eternal's name." The standard translated versions as well as the original Hebrew do indeed announce the requirement to bless God's name; Lyon's version, however, concludes with voice, sound, and "glowing tongues" as the primary point of reference. The poet praises the king and praises God for directing the acknowledgment of temporal power. The emphasis thereby also underlines the fact that praise of the monarch is directed by God: "Who makes your glowing tongues rejoice / To crown a Monarch's fame." Again and again in Lyon's psalm paraphrases, we are confronted with a psalmic voice that is acutely aware of its own powers and its own responsibilities. It is also aware of its own efforts to transcend the limitations of fractured inheritance. In this stanza that concludes the paraphrase of Psalm 72, the poet claims the authority of God to praise not only the deity, but God as the One "who *makes*" the now "glowing tongues" sing and thereby spread the "Monarch's fame." The fame of the monarch, in other words, is dependent on the poets who correctly read the will of God.

Voice and Hearing: Psalm 58

It is therefore unsurprising that Lyon chooses also Psalm 58 for paraphrase, a psalm of vengeance in which David asks not only for protection from his many enemies but also for acts of revenge against those enemies. This does bring to the fore one of the central points of tension in Jewish and Christian exegesis, one that particularly pervades English literary history: the view that the Hebrew Bible, especially when conceived as the Old Testament, is the book of justice and vengeance, in contrast to the New Testament, proclaiming the dispensation from vengeance in mercy and love. This is a misunderstanding that haunts literary analysis to this day, and it is certainly one that plays a prominent role in Christian understanding of Judaism in Lyon's day. Judaism proscribes revenge and demands loving one's neighbor as oneself in Leviticus 19; this is not to suggest, of course, that the Hebrew Bible does not also illustrate prayers and longings for revenge. When God instructs that "Vengeance is mine," the point is that human beings are not entrusted to execute violent revenge on their own personal terms. Still, psalms like Psalm 58 remain as interpretive difficulties in both the Jewish and Christian traditions. In her paraphrase/translation, Lyon emphasizes the importance of voice, and the importance of recognizing false words. She gives these aspects more emphasis than is apparent in the original or in the other popular paraphrases. She also deletes altogether one of the more graphic images. Where the Hebrew original asserts, "The righteous man will rejoice when he sees revenge; he will bathe his feet in the blood of the wicked" (JPS), Lyon substitutes "loud hosannas" for the bloody feet that signify the rejoicing of the vindicated:

> Then shall blaze out the triumph of the just;
> Then shall the loud hosannas charm
> The God that stretch'd the giants in the dust,
> With strong invulnerable arm.
> (Lyon, 135)

KJV and BCP translate the image of the righteous rejoicing by bathing his feet in the blood of the wicked. Issac Watts in his metrical paraphrase leaves it out; Sternhold-Hopkins and the Scottish Psalter leave it in. Watts gives "Warning to Magistrates" as his subtitle, a sensible choice given that the primary psalm opens by asking: "O mighty ones, do you really decree what is just? Do you judge mankind with equity?" (58:1, JPS).

Lyon does not read Psalm 58 as directed to magistrates only. She renders it instead as the psalm of justice in the service of voice, of just expression. Her poem contains eight quatrains, whereas the Hebrew text contains twelve verses, if counting by the JPS translation (ten if counting by BCP, eleven if counting by KJV). I cite the first three quatrains of Lyon's rendition:

> Still can ye glory that, with one accord
> Bright truth inspires your souls with awe;
> And live profess'd adorers of the Lord,
> Familiar with his heavenly law?
>
> Yes! Ye have words of innocence at will,
> And lips sweet-flowing smooth as oil;
> But guile and falsehood all their bane distil
> Deep in your hearts' corrupted soil.

> E'en from the womb your infant tongues rejoice
> To suck the serpent's venom'd juice;
> Expert to learn the music of the voice,
> That sounds to flatter and seduce.
> (Lyon, 134)

I cite here the opening lines of the JPS translation:

> O mighty ones, do you really decree what is just? Do you judge mankind with equity? In your minds you devise wrongdoing in the land; with your hands you deal out lawlessness. The wicked are defiant from birth; the liars go astray from the womb. Their venom is like that of a snake, a deaf viper that stops its ears so as not to hear the voice of charmers or the expert mutterer of spells. (58:1–6)

The original Hebrew psalm clearly already contains the ominous warnings about voice and hearing. The translation of the Hebrew לב (*lev*, usually "heart") again comes into play here: JPS translates בלב (*b'lev*) as "In your minds": "In your minds you devise wrongdoing in the land." KJV translates *b'lev* using the more conventional "heart": "Yea, in heart ye work wickedness"; BCP also translates using "heart": "Yea, ye imagine mischief in your heart upon the earth." We cannot know with certainty how Lyon herself would have translated the phrase, but we have seen earlier that she deliberately plays on the multiple possibilities for *lev*, and that she is responsive to the possibilities for creating meaning from such ambiguity. Earlier we observed Lyon's play on *lev* as both "heart" and "throat," or the organ of speech. *Lev* can also signify "spirit" or "mind," a possibility the JPS translation picks up. In Lyon's second stanza, she conflates heart and speech for her paraphrase, emphasizing that the primary concern for her rendering is proper speech, proper hearing, and proper interpretation. If she has had to appropriate a complicated psalm of revenge to further the thematic preoccupations of the psalm section, it is not a task from which she shrinks. In fact, her so doing heightens the sense of just how much is at stake in the work of interpretation that leads to and proceeds from translation; and how much is at stake in the very act of articulation. Apprehension of the divine may be beyond mortal ken, and the divine itself may well be ineffable; but human beings live in a world of human activity that here is defined principally by the ethics of speech. Such codes of ethical speech are central to Jewish interpretation and to Jewish rabbinical thought. Violations of the codes of speech are considered by the Talmud to be grave sins; this is an aspect repeatedly emphasized in the Jewish liturgy, and Lyon would have been intimately familiar with the many reminders in Jewish ritual life of the emphasis placed on proper speech.[35] In the grave *vidui,* for example, the liturgical, communal confession of sins that occurs on Yom Kippur, the Day of Atonement, to cite one example among many, forty-three sins are counted. Of these—sins that are confessed in congregation—fully eleven involve speech.[36] In Lyon's decision to appropriate Psalm 58 for paraphrase, she is boldly acknowledging the biblical precedent in which David bears witness to the slander of others. Lyon is interested not merely in considering the effects of slander; she is attentive to hermeneutical misconstrual as well. Lyon refracts her literary inheritance through a web of intensive and profound Jewish scholarly and liturgical meditations on the ethics of utterance, which is as much to say that her paraphrases/translations of the psalm reflect the depth of the burden of her responsibility. She bears this responsibility as an obligation of proper speech even as she manages it as a responsibility to understand the implications of speech in others.

The first task of her Psalm 58 is to recognize the real presence of real evil in the world, manifested in the unsavory image of evil present even in the infancy of the wicked. JPS translates, "The wicked are defiant from birth; the liars go astray from the womb." KJV has "The wicked are estranged from the womb: they go astray as soon as they be born speaking lies," and BCP offers, "The ungodly are froward, even from their mother's womb: as soon as they are born, they go astray, and speak lies." Lyon's paraphrase (the third stanza quoted above) is more graphic: "infant tongues rejoice / To suck the serpent's venom'd juice." For Lyon, the wicked are "Expert to learn the music of the voice, / That sounds to flatter and seduce." But they also have (in the second stanza) "words of innocence at will, / And lips sweet-flowing smooth as oil." They also, moving further down the poem, "undermine the ground / With plots of slander and deceit." Slander and deceit are among the gravest sins in Jewish law, comparable to murder and idolatry. With such prefatory explanation, Lyon's psalm finally moves to the call for revenge. I cite first the JPS translation of the relevant verses, however, so that my reader will be able to note the point of contrast to Lyon when her verses are read immediately after:

O God, smash their teeth in their mouth; shatter the fangs of lions,
O Lord; let them melt, let them vanish like water; let Him aim His
arrows that they be cut down; like a snail that melts away as it

moves; like a woman's stillbirth, may they never see the sun! Before the thorns grow into a bramble, may He whirl them away alive in fury. (58:7–10)

And here is Lyon:

> But oh, great God! From all their caverns deep
> Drag out this lion's murd'rous brood;
> Dash down the teeth that mangle all thy sheep,
> Snatch from their jaws the guiltless food!
>
> Arise! And timely interpose thy shield,
> Flashing with horror and dismay,
> Drive the pale fugitives from field to field,
> And melt their violence away.
> (Lyon, 135)

For Lyon, it is their *violence* that is being melted away, unlike the original Hebrew's imploring to "let *them* melt."

The emphasis on "teeth" evident in the original, and rendered by Lyon as well as the other translators, might be profitably compared with the parable of the four sons in the Passover Haggadah, the book that recounts the story of the liberation of the Israelites from Egypt and includes the rituals attendant with such remembrance. In the parable, the wicked son asks for the meaning of the laws of Passover that God commanded "to you." Because he asks about such laws as pertaining to others and not to himself, he is to be sharply reproved, in ways that are translated variously as "set his teeth on edge" or "hit in the teeth," for in his implicit self-removal from the Jewish collective, accomplished through an act of speech—the misuse of a pronoun—he violates a central principle of faith.[37] Lyon would have read this parable every Passover with her family. It emphasizes again the central importance of speech, and the grave consequences of errors in speech; more important, it emphasizes the relationship between speech and the obligation for each Jew to see himself or herself as part of the Jewish peoplehood, as a member of the collective who was personally enslaved in, and liberated by God from, Egypt. This is the foundational narrative of Judaism, which is why speech that performs a disconnection from it is iniquitous. On account of the wicked son's culpable replacement of a single pronoun (what are these laws to *you*, instead of *me* or *us*), not only is he to be reproved "in the teeth"; it is noted also that had he been enslaved in Egypt, he would not have been redeemed but remained in bondage. Speech functions as the sign of collective affiliation, and the stakes of failing in speech are among the most consequential.

The original Psalm 58 applies itself primarily to the enemies of Israel, the enemies of David who, historically, threatened him on all sides. Still, Lyon's interpretation focuses on enemies who are so defined by their speech. The wicked are identified at first by what their "infant *tongues*" perform; the plots of the wicked are defined by "slander and deceit." Lyon's is a powerful and disturbing poem, as the primary Psalm 58 is indeed disturbing in its original. But in Lyon, her terms of reference identify her primarily as the speaker within a collective who understands the power of voice. If it is surprising that she alludes to a sort of enemy from within (the wicked son of Passover), then that too is because of the way in which he misspeaks. It functions as a warning she issues to herself as well.

When the violence of the wicked is melted away, to appropriate Lyon's language, the triumph of the just is signified in the terms of the alternative sounds that they make, ones that are collective, triumphant, and that conclude in praise of God:

> Then shall blaze out the triumph of the just;
> Then shall the loud hosannas charm
> The God that stretch'd the giants in the dust,
> With strong invulnerable arm.
>
> Then all shall magnify his glorious name,
> And without end exulting own,
> Jehovah guides this universal frame,
> And justice dwells upon his throne.
> (Lyon, 135–136)

Here is the JPS translation of the original psalm's final verses:

> The righteous man will rejoice when he sees revenge; he will bathe his feet in the blood of the wicked. Men will say, "There is, then, a reward for the righteous; there is, indeed, divine justice on earth." (58:11–12)

I have noted that Lyon does not take up the image of bathing feet in the blood of the wicked. Her own conclusion again magnifies the significance of voice, both in the loud hosannas of relief and the exultation that advertises God's "name" and God's "justice." This is an angry poem, but its call for revenge is much tamer, much less bloody, than the biblical original. Her paraphrase of the Hebrew subdues the language for poetic consumption in early nineteenth-century England.

Such self-possession as demonstrated by Lyon in her handling of Psalm 58 is again counterpointed by the earlier section of the volume. In "Revenge: An Ode," Lyon refers to revenge itself as the "stern tyrant" who acts against nature and against "all human laws." If the poet presents herself as capable of vengeful thoughts in this earlier section of the volume, she need only imagine that revenge might dig its own grave:

> Deep in the forest dig thy grave,
> Where never bloom'd one roseate flow'r;
> For ah! Thy presence frights the brave,
> Thou Demon of the lonely hour!
>
> Oh pause! And stop thy dark career,
> Suspend awhile thy lightning eye;
> For hark, a voice would charm thine ear,
> As gentle as the tender sigh.
>
> Ah turn! The heavenly Goddess view,
> Forgiveness! Heed her placid call;
> As guiltless as the morning dew—
> Relent, she cries, and prostrate fall.
> (Lyon, 115)

In this earlier section of the volume, a cautious Lyon fashions herself, for the most part, as demure, timid, diffident, and careful not to offend her audience. It is in keeping with this self-representation that she presents herself in this poem as terrified of the Demon Revenge and longing for the recognizably Christian virtue, forgiveness, to counter its effects. Forgiveness, to be sure, counts as a Jewish virtue as well, but we do well to compare Lyon's approach to the revenge fantasy of Psalm 58 with her approach to the subject of the Demon Revenge in the earlier poem. Again we are presented with a dichotomy: the diffident poetess/Jewess, and the tenacious and proud Jew standing her ground. The Jew who stands her ground is the one who engages the poetry of the Hebrew Bible.

Prophetic Chastisement

Lyon would have had other good reasons to address the subject of voice with so much vehemence. Set against the context of Christian misunderstanding of Jewish culture is, further, the establishment of Christian missions in England to convert the Jews. These increased in number as Jewish immigration became more prominent, but they had always played a role in Christian interaction with the Jews of England. The first organization that listed conversion of the Jews as its sole function was established in 1809. The London Society for the Promotion of Christianity among the Jews experienced rapid growth and became only one among many such societies. As Todd Endelman points out, "The London Society for Promoting Christianity among the Jews, then, was not an isolated effort of a handful of fanatics, but a small part of a wide-scale undertaking to revitalize religious life in England."[38] Christian support for emancipation of the Jews was often tied to the belief that the Jews could yet be converted with conviction, a belief that was held with especial tenacity among philo-semites, the Christian conversionists who held the "carrot not the stick" approach to their conversionist efforts. As such, the London Society established a popular "Temporary Relief Fund" to support destitute Jews, and, as Endelman points out further, "The Society continued to provide lectures to the Jews, expanded its free school, and established various workshops (a basket manufactory, a printing shop, a candlewick manufactory) to provide jobs for converts." Lectures, printing shops, free schools, and all for the uses of converting Jews to Christianity: this is the environment in which Lyon must position herself with respect to the uses and abuses of communication, and of interpretation that is based on communication. Much is at stake in the manipulations of language. In the case of the Christian conversionist missions to the Jews, Jewish survival itself is at stake. For individual Jews, the merest change in self-positioning—the wicked son's ill-fated question recounted during Passover, for example—becomes more than just a rhetorical gaffe. Semantics are of the soul. When the Christian missions go to work to convert the Jews with the allures of printing shops, schools and distribution of New Testaments, language becomes the battleground of belief and of belonging. It is important in this context to recall that during this period Jews still did not enjoy full civil and political rights. Official protests from Jewish quarters against the widespread conversionist efforts were few and far between.

One individual who was indeed willing to protest was David Levi, described by David Ruderman as a "one man anti-defamation league."[39] Levi, a shoemaker by trade, was also a scholar who took exception to prominent conversionist claims by public intellectuals, and who was also involved in various scholarly exertions against what he saw as the misguided and patronizing efforts of the Christian Hebraists. Between 1787 and 1789, Levi was engaged in a polemical exchange in print with Dr. Joseph Priestley, who had written *Letters to the Jews; inviting them to an amicable discussion of the evidences of Christianity*, and then a Part II, *Occasioned by Mr. David Levi's reply to the former letters*. As Michael Scrivener explains, "Levi responded to Priestley in the first place against the received wisdom of the Jewish community whose posture was cautious. . . . The Jewish community blamed Levi for risking persecution of Jews by debating publicly with a prominent Christian."[40] Near the very beginning of Levi's first letter, he explains why so few Jews have joined the discussion:

> For as you have invited our nation to an amicable discussion of the evidences of Christianity, I shall endeavour to answer what you have advanced in behalf of your doctrine, as far as the extent of my abilities, and the little time I have to spare from my other avocations, will permit, as most of our learned men, (as I am informed) have declined the invitation; and that, as I understand, for two reasons: first, on account of the aversion which the elders of our community have towards any of their body entering into religious disputes, for fear, that any thing advanced by them, might be construed as reflecting on, or tending towards disturbing the national religion, as by law established.[41]

"As by law established" may well remind us of the perceived precariousness of the Jews when engaged in speech of any kind directed to disagreement with the mainstream. Lyon's embedding of her own concerns within the fabric of her Psalm paraphrases is not merely female diffidence. Words, response to words, the function of the organ of speech: these are the hallmarks of survival. For David Levi, whose work was almost certainly known in the Lyon household, words are not only the hallmark of survival; they can also lead to real political trouble.

Psalm 50

Is Lyon attempting to avoid the trouble inherent in religious audacity when rendering Psalm 50? This is the psalm in which God Himself is given voice, in which He chastises the nations in His own fury. Lyon transforms the speaking voice into her own, a task that is either strikingly audacious or restrained and modest. For the poet's manipulation of and transformation of voice means that she is either taking upon herself the word of God, or rather refusing to presume to speak *as* God. The first stanza of Lyon's paraphrase of Psalm 50 accords well with the original Hebrew text before she finally introduces a transformation:

> Heaven's matchless King with dreadful ire
> Descends upon the wings of fire;
> The lightning flashes in his path,
> His thund'rous voice denounces wrath!
> He comes, he comes! With furious sweep,
> And frights the fountains of the deep!
> (Lyon, 129)

The first verses of the KJV translation will suffice as evidence that Lyon's beginning follows fairly closely on standard translations and interpretations:

> The mighty God, even the Lord, hath spoken, and called the earth from the rising of the sun unto the going down thereof. Out of Zion, the perfection of beauty, God hath shined. Our God shall come, and shall not keep silence: a fire shall devour before him, and it shall be very tempestuous round about him. He shall call to the heavens from above, and to the earth, that he may judge his people. (50:1–4)

The subsequent stanzas of the primary psalm are given to God's own putative words. I cite the KJV again:

> Gather my saints together unto me; those that have made a covenant with me by sacrifice. And the heavens shall declare his righteousness: for God is judge himself. Selah. Hear, O my people, and I will speak; O Israel, and will testify against thee: I am God, even thy God. (50:5–7)

This is the point of the psalm at which Lyon appropriates the putative words of God. She does not render them in the third person; that is, she does not describe the words of God as attributed to Him in the third person. Rather, there is very much an authorial presence speaking, and it is clearly intended to be understood as the voice of the poet. This poet issues many of the same warnings and instructions as pronounced by God in the original Hebrew. In this rendering, however, the poet presumes to describe God's justification for anger, and so speaks as if in the voice of inspired prophecy. The second and third stanzas establish the authority of the poet's voice:

> O ye, who o'er his host preside,
> Priests of the Lord, his people's guide!
> Go, separate th'unholy train
> Of spirits variable and vain;
> Eject them from th'untainted seed
> That shudder at a foul misdeed.
>
> Not blood in sacrifices spilt
> Can wash away the stains of guilt;
> Where malice, fraud, and guile abound,
> Not large wine-offerings pour'd around
> Can e'er the great JEHOVAH charm,
> Or check the thunder of his arm.
> (Lyon, 129–130)

Both KJV and BCP translate as "saints" what Lyon renders as "Priests of the Lord," clearly avoiding the Christian association with "saints." Lyon here is offering a prophetic reminder to her audience about ethical conduct. In so doing, she is obtrusively offering her readers a reminder about the status of the poet whom they are reading. In the Jewish tradition, women as well as men could serve as prophets, Miriam, the sister of Moses, being the most familiar example. A prophet does not simply pronounce, nor is his or her role confined to telling the future; a prophet is charged with conveying God's message to the people. As such, it was desirable that the role be filled by an individual of high ethical standing and sagacious wisdom.[42] The role of prophet is an elevated one, a characterization that was often appropriated in English literary history, especially English Romanticism, to signify the ultimate authority of the speaking voice in the historical world. The splendor of the prophet's voice is not merely lyrical; it is inspired and authoritative precisely because of its divine inspiration. The ideal prophet according to Maimonides may well be an instrument of chastisement, but the prophet him/herself should not be angry.[43]

Given such characterization, Lyon's appropriation of the role of prophet for herself in Psalm 50 qualifies the modesty of her refusal to speak *as* God. Her voice is the voice of the most authoritative lyricist, which is why she appropriates the role of prophet for Psalm 50 instead of "translating" the voice of God. If she is too diffident for the latter, then it is only because the former is the real prize of the Romantic poet struggling to find a rightful place within English letters. The role of prophet also enables Lyon to include implicitly the general community as well as the established nobility, including royalty, within the circle that she censures in the name of God. Historically, the prophet was tasked with chastising kings as well as the people; the claim to be inspired by God Himself was the crucial license enabling such bold speech, especially to powerful kings. Lyon begins her rendition of Psalm 50 with the words, "Heaven's matchless King," as if to remind us not only that she speaks as inspired by the divine, but also that she speaks against evil in the world knowing that temporal potentates—including those in England—are no match for the divine. This is especially important given the presumption of her pronouncements of royal affiliation throughout the volume, even when clothed in the voice of diffidence. It is also important in light of the real historical poets who haunt the pages of Lyon's volume as both standards against whom she defines herself and in light of whom she is *ipso facto* alienated, at least by conventional standards of British literary inheritance.

The voice—indeed the voices—that she adopts in the later section assert an authority that would transcend that of her English poetic peers. In the earlier "Ode to Genius," Lyon invokes Genius in ways that recall the Romantic preoccupation with prophecy even as it instructs its audience that true Genius is a scarce commodity. Certainly she does not presume in this poem to possess it, but she does indeed presume to plead for its powers. Genius is immediately hailed as an "All glorious power," but the first stanza also describes her as "Yet seldom visiting an earthly guest!" (8). We will recall that in "Ode on Ambition," Lyon resigns any claim on ambition; in "Ode to Genius," she does ask that Genius "make my soul thy transitory shrine." Further, she specifies that the Genius she has in mind is the one who could "guide my fancy when it seeks the Muse" (9). Lyon's may well be a voice of diffidence in the early section of the volume, but her "Ode to Genius" does belie her timidity, especially the closing two stanzas:

> Lead to the bow'rs where haunt thy heavenly train,
> And I will distant watch their mystic tread;
> From their rich harvest glean the scatter'd grain,
> To weave a band fantastic for my head.
>
> By me unenvied, flattering crowds may throng,
> Where Poets trace the never-varying round;
> If thou, bright genius! Animate my song,
> My name shall live, with endless glory crown'd.
> (Lyon, 9)

Lyon is alluding to Charlotte Smith's *Elegiac Sonnets*, in particular Sonnet 1. I quote the first eight lines:

> The partial Muse has from my earliest hours
> Smiled on the rugged path I'm doom'd to tread,
> And still with sportive hand has snatch'd wild flowers,
> To weave fantastic garlands for my head:
> But far, far happier is the lot of those
> Who never learn'd her dear delusive art;
> Which, while it decks the head with many a rose,
> Reserves the thorn to fester in the heart.
> (Smith, 13)

The final line of Lyon's penultimate stanza—"To weave a band fantastic for my head"—is surely recalling Smith's line 4, "To weave fantastic garlands for my head," and both are resonant of Petrarchan forms and of Proverbs 4:9: "She shall give to thine head an ornament of grace: a crown of glory shall she deliver to thee" (KJV). By this point the imagery of garlands to signify poetic prowess is conventional, but the reference to Smith's identification of the garlands of poetry with the "dear delusive art" that provides no solace to the sorrowing poet is striking. Lyon indeed recalls Smith in the "Ode on Ambition" when she concludes by lamenting that ambition's "trophies are vain / To the bosom that sighs for the grave!" (95), but the "Ode to Genius," which in fact appears even earlier in the volume, foreshadows the bolder self-fashioning of the later sections. This is not yet the full blossoming of the assertion of her powers in the psalm renditions. Lyon here is solicitous of a "Genius" she does not yet presume to possess. The ode apostrophizes genius in the hope that it will guide her fancy, and then finally enable her to "*distant* watch" the "mystic tread" of the "bow'rs where haunt thy heavenly train." She is not there yet, but she allows herself the presumption of the prayer. This is a presumption that would supersede even Charlotte Smith's poetic triumphs: where Smith's partial muse cannot remove the thorn festering in the poet's heart, Lyon's call for genius imagines a world where she is free. And not only free: this is a poem in which the first hint of an ambition not only to join literary history, but to achieve mastery within it, is announced. After all, she calls for preeminence that is not necessarily recognized by the standards of taste of the day: "By me unenvied, flattering crowds may throng, / Where Poets trace the never-varying round." This is an extraordinary statement from the Emma Lyon of Part I of the collection, the Emma Lyon disclaiming ambition, education, talent, or even the right to anger. Lyon would not envy the flattering crowds who offer praise to inferior poetry tracing "the never-varying round."

If there is one characteristic of this volume of poems, it is precisely the variation in its self-positioning. In "Ode to Genius," however, it is more a matter of degree than of kind. Here she anticipates the assertions even of Psalm 50; she is not yet the sagacious prophet scolding the populace, scolding royalty, scolding those who do not know how to modulate their voice. She is instead the young poet who signals that for now, she has no choice but to fashion a voice in which she can be heard within the strictures of propriety allotted to her.

CHAPTER 2

Mourning, Translation, Pastoral: Hyman Hurwitz

> Cobbett's objection to the Jews is that they don't plough: he would ask who could produce a Jew who ever dug, who ever went to plough? It is only very lately that Jews have been permitted to hold land: how were they to learn to plough? The only piece of earth that Jews of former years were permitted to possess was a burying-ground: and this little farm the Jews dug and trenched, after all the approved principles of the drill-husbandry.
>
> —"Cobbett and the Jews," *New Monthly Magazine and Literary Journal* (1833)

Jewish poetics is particularly sensitive to the demands of elegiac poetry, in which the binding of the generations joins with the immediate needs of commemoration to form part of the palimpsest of culture. The inherent problematics of elegy are so deeply a part of its generic transmission that its audacity is virtually always taken for granted.[1] Historically, the questions have never not been asked: can elegy really console? Can it maintain decorum? Can it guard against a collapse into narcissistic self-regard? Can resurrecting the dead in language sidestep the maudlin or the grandiose? More than any other poetic kind, elegy knows itself to be self-subverting. Indeed, the very epistemological anxiety of the critical engagement with elegy itself underwrites its generic, aesthetic, and moral history. In "Adonais," Shelley knows that the poet who stands in mourning with animated Nature is one "who in another's fate now wept his own" (l.300).[2] Even Milton's "Lycidas" finds room to remark that the spur of fame is "that last infirmity of noble mind" (l.71).[3] When pastoral is factored into the equation of literary mourning, as in the pastoral elegy, the stakes are inevitably raised, for here we have the appropriation of the landscape serving the ends of a poet turned, at least for the moment, both radically inward and radically outward, which is as much to say that the pastoral often finds the poet in his grief struggling against his fragmentation from an empirical world whose details are obtrusively foregrounded. One correlate of the question about its ethical tenuousness is a question of direct relevance to Anglo-Jewish poets who would take up elegiac poetry, especially in its English literary inheritance. By the time we arrive at Romanticism, pastoral elegy is already recognized by its own practitioners as a burdened form. I would suggest that Jewish poets enter this particular tradition engaging with what they recognize as already subtly ironized by their poetic contemporaries. A Jew in England writing elegy tends to be a Jew interrogating his or her own formalist procedures, even if remaining committed to them. This attention is not simply about the self-regarding aspects of the genre. Rather, one question that implicitly emerges concerns the challenge of what is at stake when we demarcate such meta-poetics as a culpability. In our own time, we have the confession of Geoffrey Hill in "September Song," one of the most oft-cited Holocaust poems: "I have made / an elegy for myself it / is true."[4] Why need the inexorability of self-interest be a confession, and why must it sit so ill with us?

Elegy in both the British and American traditions has become a site of tension over the conflicting demands of self-interest, aesthetic mastery, and memorializing the dead. The contemporary inflection of such anxiety as it has come down to us finds a singular watershed in Romanticism; Jewish elegists, in particular of the nineteenth century, respond to the long history of culpability over the elegy in remarkable ways. I argue that Anglo-Jewish poets of the nineteenth century take up the challenges of elegy by turning its vexations back upon itself and upon its mainstream readers; that is, they address their poems to the very anxieties generated by elegy and worry the assumptions about its ethical culpability.

In "Peele Castle," which provides an important contrastive point of reference here, Wordsworth describes the processes of his changed aesthetic, asserting finally that it is an aesthetic change that provides the ultimate marker of the "deep distress" that "hath humanized [his] soul" (l.36).[5] Here, the elegy finds a ground of sanction only because it records a radical change in aesthetic orientation, and hence throws into relief the instability of the poetic process. Wordsworth is brought, in the course of grieving for his brother, to a moment of repentance and transformation for what he now sees had been a flawed aesthetic choice. Where he would have once imagined himself correcting Beaumont's landscape painting by transforming it into a scene of serenity, he would now paint its sublime dangers. He now would paint it differently; he now says it differently, because distress has corrected him. But the correction itself still proceeds from the greater self-knowledge that grief supplies, or more precisely and more importantly, that grief and the struggle over its aesthetic containment supply. A culpable aesthetic is replaced by another guilty one, for "Peele Castle" still famously contains the marks of its author's discernment of the relationship between his "leisure for fiction" (Samuel Johnson's famous complaint against Milton's elegy) and the integrity of his grief.[6] It showcases, too, a reluctance to address the dead and a sense of failure over having addressed his own selfhood. He may well conclude, finally, by welcoming the abstractions of fortitude and "patient cheer" (l.57), but he has worked his way into the solace of those personifications by working through the implications for his aesthetic choices. If "Peele Castle" is about the relationship between grief and the aesthetic, then it is also about our recognition of that uneasy dynamic. What the nineteenth-century Anglo-Jewish authors do is transform the moment of elegy's culpability and render it, in part, as a lament for the impossibility of their own expressive resources. In such recognition of the limits of language emerge moments, paradoxically, of their greatest strength and their most powerful cultural authority. The elegies to which I turn my attention in this chapter seek a way of engaging the aesthetics of elegy on its own inherited terms of ironic refraction.

Royal Elegies: The Death of Princess Charlotte and the Monarchical Sacred

On November 6, 1817, Princess Charlotte Augusta, the only child of the Prince Regent and his estranged wife, Caroline, died from childbirth after delivering a still-born son, thus bringing to a close the line of succession from George IV. This is the Princess Charlotte who had been the object of Emma Lyon's dedication in her volume of poems. Charlotte had been married only about a year, to Prince Leopold of Saxe-Coburg, who adored her. Her unexpected death set off a national frenzy of mourning not dissimilar to that which followed the death, close to two centuries later, of Diana, Princess of

Wales. The Regency period of England was rife with factionalism and political and economic instability. Charlotte, ill-treated child of an irresponsible father and banished mother and granddaughter of a madman, had won the public's affection precisely because she could be perceived as something of an outsider: a sad but true royal, essentially motherless, an incorruptible princess adored by the nation yet treated with political suspicion even by her father, England's reigning regent. On Charlotte the nation had fixed its image of potential for a recuperated royalty. In short, she became a figure for majestic Britannia through various iconic representations within various media. This figuring of Charlotte as Britannia under siege from within her own family was solidified in 1814 when she defied the efforts of her father, the regent, to marry her off to the hereditary Prince William of Orange. The Prince of Orange would have wanted Charlotte to leave England for part of the year, every year, and this she would not do, even though, in fact, she had come to love him. The nationalist fervor this aroused, especially when it was remembered again at the time of her death three years later, was remarkable. Charlotte became the image of the nation's hopes, vanquished, one who turned from love so that she would not have to turn from England, one whose love of England precluded self-exile, however brief. Ultimately, the price of refusing exile was marriage to another and death a short time later from childbirth. The consolatory stanzas of virtually every poem that poured forth from the public offered the prayer that Britannia might shine now from above, or from within our hearts (a little bit of the radiance of royalty within us all).

Stephen Behrendt has done a remarkable job of cataloguing and discussing the various responses to Charlotte's death in his *Royal Mourning and Regency Culture: Elegies and Memorials of Princess Charlotte.*[7] One poem he does not take up in that excellent volume is a dirge written on the occasion of Charlotte's death by Hyman Hurwitz.[8] Hurwitz, an erudite scholar deeply learned in Jewish and Hebrew texts and well educated in secular studies, was the first professor of Hebrew in University College, London, a post he assumed in 1828. He was a close friend of Samuel Taylor Coleridge, who had written in support of his election to the professorship. Born in Poland in the 1770s, Hurwitz came to England about 1800. He is the author of *Hebrew Tales*, a compilation of midrashic stories explicating aspects of Jewish life; a Hebrew grammar; and various essays and poems. Hurwitz's dirge for Charlotte, in Hebrew, was chanted in the Great Synagogue at St. James's Place, Aldgate, on the day of her funeral, and later translated into English by Coleridge.[9] In the synagogue it was set to a tune famously used during the annual services held on Tisha B'Av, the ninth day of the

Hebrew month of Av, a day of fasting and lamentation.[10] The poem's choric refrain is most familiar as part of a renowned medieval Hebrew poem, "Eli Tzion Ve'areha" (of disputed authorship), which in Hebrew quotes Joel 1:8: "Lament—like a maiden [girded] with sackcloth for the husband of her youth" (JPS). This poem, a canonical part of the liturgy for Tisha B'Av, is a dirge primarily for the destruction of the Holy Temples of Jerusalem. Tisha B'Av is a profoundly grave festival of mourning for the exilic condition of the Jews. On the ninth of Av, both the first and second Temples of Jerusalem were destroyed, in 586 BCE and 70 CE, respectively. But other events of significance are conventionally commemorated on the ninth of Av as well, including the expulsion of the Jews from England in 1290 and from Spain in 1492. In the former instance, Jews were required to leave by November 1; however, Edward I issued the Edict of Expulsion on July 18, which corresponded in the Hebrew calendar to the ninth of Av. For our purposes, it is important to note that the notorious York Massacre of 1190, 100 years before the Jews were expelled from England, took place not on but a few months before Tisha B'Av, and two well-known elegies on those who perished there, one written by Joseph of Chartres, are frequently recited during the Tisha B'Av services, among other elegies that address Jewish tragedies. The York Massacre forms part of the history of the Crusades: many Jews, holed up inside York Tower, took their own lives rather than succumb to the enemy. Those who did not participate in the self-slaughter were captured and killed. A memorial of the massacre at York Tower stands there today. (I return to the subject of the York Massacre at greater length in the chapter on the Moss sisters.) Much of the synagogue service on Tisha B'Av is recited in mourning fashion while sitting on the ground. In the Ashkenazi service, the elegy "Eli Tzion Ve'areha" is usually chanted after the congregation rises to its feet.

What could writing a dirge in Hebrew, first chanted in the Great Synagogue to the tune of a renowned Tisha B'Av elegy mourning the destruction of the Jerusalem Temples and the exilic wandering of the Jews, have to do with Princess Charlotte, or with the complicated Jewish response to the British monarchy? Having Coleridge translate it opens further questions, since the signature of his translation stands as the signature of high culture, a mark of the cultural authority of Hurwitz's original. Still, the English translation also stands as a mark of one discontinuity with the medieval Hebrew poem and the Jewish poetic tradition that it represents. The numerous elegies for Princess Charlotte, like the elegies for all historically notable figures, seek to establish the authority of a connection to the deceased. Hurwitz's elegy goes beyond a mere claim to personal authority, since he speaks also as the mouthpiece of his community: the Jews of England stand in relation to a member of the monarchy that legitimizes a communal lament, one that is not out of place within a canonized Hebraic liturgy. The poem is called "Israel's Lament," though the Hebrew gives it more precisely as "Yeshurun's Lament." I quote the first stanza in Hebrew, and followed by its translation by Coleridge:

אלי ישרון ובניה!
כמו אשה בחבליה
וכבתולה, חגורת–שק
עלי בעל נעוריה.

Mourn, Israel! Sons of Israel, mourn!
Give utt'rance to the inward throe!
As wails, of her first Love forlorn,
The Virgin clad in robes of woe.[11]

The stanza in Hebrew is a rendering of the medieval poem, virtually a direct quotation:[12]

אלי ציון ועריה, כמו אשה בציריה
וכבתולה חגורת–שק, על–בעל נעוריה.

Abraham Rosenfeld provides the following translation: "Let Zion and her cities lament like a woman in the pangs of birth, and like a young woman girded with sackcloth (in mourning) for the husband of her youth." This first stanza becomes the refrain of the medieval poem, as it becomes the refrain of Hurwitz's. Both are also citations of Joel 1:8. Coleridge's Hebrew was good enough for him to know what he was doing, rendering "virgin" as an entirely unveiled reference to the Virgin Mary, transforming Charlotte into some amalgam of both mother of Christ and Christ himself, a reference obviously not present in Hurwitz's Hebrew. The translation of the Hebrew term for virgin is, of course, one of the central points of reference in debates about translation of the Hebrew Bible. On such translations, the meaning of virgin birth, and therefore the divinity of Jesus, depend.[13] Further, there is nothing in Coleridge's translation that could have provided any clues to the striking similarity of the Hebrew to the medieval lament.

Hurwitz's sanction for, perhaps even his participation in, the English rendering is particularly striking. The two lived in close enough physical proximity to one another that virtually no correspondence about the translation took place, but the poem with translation did circulate publicly in a face-en-face edition. Hurwitz remained Coleridge's Hebrew teacher while Coleridge remained Hurwitz's strong public supporter, a fact that became particularly important when Hurwitz was proposed as the first chair in Hebrew literature at University College, London. Nowhere in the public domain would the Tisha B'Av references, or the quotations of and references to the medieval Hebrew lament, nor any of the other Tisha B'Av allusions, have been obviously accessible to the general public. It is not exactly that this is being figured as the secret language of the Jews, but it bears the mark of a knowing whispering, a confiding among those who know of the radical disjunction effected by translation, effected by the transplantation of a cultural idiom: what and how the Jews mourn in verse is ultimately unfathomable, especially in England, even within an elegy for an English public figure—indeed, even within an elegy that boldly claims the authority of such an address.

This point opens onto the vexed subject of translation. As I have made clear in the introduction and the chapter on Emma Lyon, translation of the Hebrew Bible and of Hebrew rabbinic texts was a topic of intense debate during this period. For our purposes in reading this particular poem, most important is the controversy over translation of the Hebrew as a matter of proprietary ownership of the sacred. And the proprietary claim to the monarchical sacred, of the sanctity of the royal lineage, is here set in apposition to the ferment of Hebrew translation. By what right does a Jew from Poland, known to complain (however courteously) about the misrepresentation of the Hebrew committed by philologically challenged Christian scholars and divines, presume now on the sanctity of holy ground, where holy ground is the burial place of a British princess who stands not only for the Church of England but, in her particularity, for the glory of Britannia? I restate this question below, because it assumes inflections that go to the heart of the British pastoral.

Hurwitz's poem, especially in Coleridge's translation, emphasizes the universality not only of the grief inspired by the death of the princess but also the common ground of the response it provokes; that is, the Jews may well have a coded subtext, but the world will see their liturgically inspired grief as part of a Judaism that is amenable to universalizing its morality. Early on, Coleridge's translation offers a plea for universality that is reasonably faithful to the original:

Mourn for the universal Woe
With solemn dirge and faultr'ing tongue:
For England's Lady is laid low,
So dear, so lovely, and so young!

Here is the Hebrew:

עלי עלטה, אשר עטה
פני תבל וישביה;
במות פרינצעס שארלטה,
בטרם מלאת ימיה.

The translation does not make contact with the Hebrew's allusion to the strange vision of Abraham in Genesis 15, nor to Hurwitz's allusion to Psalm 24. It does, however, translate Hurwitz's transliteration of Princess Charlotte as "England's Lady." Hurwitz uses a Yiddish form for the transliteration of Charlotte's name, as he does in another stanza for the transliteration of Prince Leopold. But the universality is being claimed even as the particularity of Hurwitz's self-positioning as Hebrew-literate European Jewish scholar who yet participates in the glory of Britannia is being flagrantly staged. The most egregious aspect of this staging, however, is for those who could read the Hebrew and follow the allusions—educated, Hebrew-literate Jews and Christians, usually scholarly clerics, of the sort who could participate in the translation debates (remembering that many of those translation debates assumed nasty and anti-Jewish polemics).

The phrase in this stanza that Coleridge renders as "universal woe" is *alata*. That is the very word used in Genesis 15, in which Abraham is promised progeny and land by God, during the course of which God proclaims to Abraham:

> "Know well that your offspring shall be strangers in a land not theirs, and they shall be enslaved and oppressed four hundred years, but I will execute judgement on the nation they shall serve, and in the end they shall go free with great wealth. As for you, you shall go to your fathers in peace; You shall be buried at a ripe old age. And they shall return here in the fourth generation, for the iniquity of the Amorites is not yet complete." When the sun set and it was very dark [*alata*], there appeared a smoking oven, and a flaming torch which passed between those pieces. On that day the Lord made a

covenant with Abram, saying, "To your offspring I assign this land, from the river of Egypt to the great river." (Genesis 15:13–18)[14]

By asserting a rightful claim to mourn for Charlotte, Hurwitz is insisting upon his rightful claim as subject in a land not entirely his, to be sure; but the leveling in which he is interested makes of the universal woe a meditation upon self-interest.

The biblical allusion both secures Abraham's future and reminds him of the precariousness of place; that is, even after escaping the confines where the Israelites are strangers in a land not theirs, they will inevitably be on the run again: they will return "here" in the fourth generation because "the iniquity of the Amorites is not yet complete." For whom does a land become a landscape, and for whom are its implicit nationalist aspirations framed? Those who are designated "strangers" in a land (remember that the Jews in nineteenth-century England were still generally considered a foreign race), those who are dwelling in the locale of their historical expulsion, cannot engage in the transformation from dwelling place to pastoral scene.

Hurwitz, writing at the moment of the far end of the pastoral elegy in England, and alluding to a Jewish liturgical tradition whose incorporation of landscape imagery is well established, goes to almost extreme lengths to qualify his association with the pastoral or the bucolic in England. There is one stanza that allows entry of some tree imagery, but it is primarily in the service of the blossoms on Charlotte's Tree of Life, which are now transplanted in the Garden of Eden, rendered by Coleridge as Paradise. This is a hint of nature that, if anything, calls attention to this elegy's exclusion of conventional English nature imagery. I say *English* nature imagery because there is what I would call an allusive counterpoint occurring in the dirge in which the pastoral of the biblical psalms is invoked. What Coleridge renders as "Mourn for the universal Woe / With solemn dirge and fault'ring tongue," the Hebrew gives as

עלי עלטה, אשר עטה
פני תבל וישביה

It would more correctly translate as "Mourn for the darkness that is upon the world and its inhabitants." The wording for the latter is virtually a direct quotation of Psalm 24, "The earth is the Lord's and all that it holds, the world and its inhabitants. For He founded it upon the ocean, set it on the netherstreams" (1–2). The first stanza of Psalm 24 in the Hebrew is as follows:

ליהוה, הארץ ומלואה
תבל וישבי בה:
כי הוא, על ימים יסדה; ועל נהרות, יכוננה:

Hurwitz goes to extreme lengths in detaching himself from the fully public indulgence of the private and Jewish communal meaning of his expression of grief, in favor of a universalizing that, all the same, he can only be forced to qualify. Making of any monarch a personified abstraction requires, in the grand tradition of neoclassical generalization, a consensual ground of recognition of the meaning of that abstraction. Charlotte as Britannia, which is clearly invoked in the poem, signifies in radically different ways for readers of Hurwitz's original Hebrew than for readers confined exclusively to Coleridge's translation. Perhaps of even greater significance to one meaning of the poem, readers of Coleridge's translation encounter their own felt exclusion from a Hebrew authority, the ultimate guarantee of a severance from a sanctity, an original language whose most famous book (the Bible) in fact defines the nation and the Church of England. The turn from the British inheritance of pastoral is obtrusively offered in line with the larger argument I offer in this book, namely, that the Jewish history of exile and the deeply vexed Jewish history in England make for an alienation from the expressive resources of the pastoral and bucolic traditions in poetry, even, and especially, when those traditions are claimed by Jewish authors. This is a more prominent concern in the nineteenth century because, by this period in English literary history, the communal redemptions offered by the pastoral are already under threat, and nostalgia for their worth has already set in. The stable rootedness in land, the stable landscape that can provide security against the threat of self-loss in the empirical world for Wordsworth, for example, becomes for Jewish poets the sign of an alienation from their very own expressive resources. We have encountered this dynamic, in somewhat different form, in Lyon: Romantic nature, whether received as consciously ironized or not, figures for Jewish authors both a longing for inclusion and the sign of a persistent alienation: the Romantic wanderer and the Romantic peripatetic may well have been read in terms of an overly sentimental nostalgia by this point, but Hurwitz's response takes into account both the problematic nature of the Romantic inheritance and his acknowledgment that the Jew in Romantic England is disconnected from the very inheritance he would refract. The self-alienation that is the yield of such self-contradiction relies precisely on the inaccessibility to Jewish poets of a principled claim to the redemptions putatively inherent in the history of the English landscape, the pastoral nostalgia that Wordsworth himself may well partly ironize, but which becomes the dislocated specter the Jews can only mourn.

Must it become such a relentlessly dislocated specter, however? Not necessarily or so simply if they write in Hebrew: for Hurwitz, Hebrew is the one expressive resource that at once connects with sacred history and guarantees his alienation from rootedness in the soil of his domain; that is, his mastery *as* a Jewish Hebrew teacher of the Hebrew Bible is at once the sign of an authority and of his disconnection from the long historical reach of British cultural inheritance. The foundation of his Hebrew elegy transplants, as it were, the pastoral from native soil to inherited language—the Jew may have little connection to the British pastoral because of his fragmented history, but he claims an authoritative right to an authentic and original biblical pastoral from which even the British monarchy is alienated. Hurwitz's coded allusions to his ultimate cultural authority, which is the authority of unmediated (untranslated) access to the Hebrew Bible, is the long-reaching linguistic authority that finally needs no prop in the landscape.

The lament for Charlotte proceeds abstractly, but being located within the tradition of Jewish elegies chanted on Tisha B'Av, Israel's lament becomes both Israel's lament for Charlotte and Israel's claim to entitlement within Charlotte's land. It does not neglect the realization that it must also be Israel's lament for its very alienation, both from the expressive resources of Charlotte's land and from its full self-constitution. The famous dirge by Joseph of Chartres on the 1190 Massacre of the York Jews is often included in the liturgy for the Tisha B'Av services. It begins with an address to God: "O God! Other lords besides thee have ruled over us, the raging waters have almost consumed us." And at approximately its midpoint comes the most telling outpouring: "Let there be no dew or rain on the land of the isle, from the day your king was crowned, woe to you, O land! O daughter of my people, arise from its midst and go forth. . . . Let there be no dew or rain on the land of the isle"—טל אל ואל מטר על הארץ האי. As one of the few Tisha B'Av elegies directed specifically to a historical atrocity committed by the *English* against the Jews, it forms part of the background for Hurwitz's appropriation of Tisha B'Av liturgy for his dirge. The Joseph of Chartres elegy takes up the grief and the outrage of the Jews in medieval England. With its baptismal and pastoral references, it cries out against England's self-definition. Like that of Joseph of Chartres, Hurwitz's elegy takes up England's self-definition and makes of his exclusion from it a claim upon his own authority.

I close with two of the stranger stanzas of the Charlotte dirge:

While Grief in song shall seek repose,
    We will take up a Mourning yearly:
To wail the Blow that crush'd the Rose
    So dearly priz'd and lov'd so dearly.

Long as the Fount of Song o'erflows,
    Will I the yearly dirge renew:
Mourn for the firstling of the Rose,
    That snapt the stem on which it grew.

בכל שנה, נישא קינה,
ובלב דוי, נצעק הוי,
עלי שושנה, אשר נקטפה
בטרם צאת פרחיה.–

ואהימה, ימים ימימה,
ברוח צר, ומספד מר,
על הציץ, אשר קצץ
ושת מות בקרביה.

Was the *yahrzeit*[15] for Princess Charlotte to be observed by the Jews? It is the custom of Jews to observe special prayers for the anniversary of a loved one's death, of course, but more to the immediate point here, it is the liturgical practice of Tisha B'Av to mourn the anniversaries of the destruction and exile of the Jews through history. The first quoted stanza, with its reference to שושנה (lily or rose), alludes quietly in Hebrew to the Song of Songs, whose pastoral is the forum for erotic longing, long interpreted by the rabbis as a figure of longing for Jerusalem: "My beloved has gone down to his garden, to the beds of spices, to browse in the gardens and to pick lilies" (6:2). The second above-quoted stanza alludes emphatically to a Tisha B'Av elegy whose choric refrain is quoted virtually exactly in the first line of Hurwitz's Hebrew, and which Abraham Rosenfeld translates as "Indeed I will moan from year to year." The second stanza of this elegy is highly resonant: "Mournful is my heart, consolation has ceased completely, and my pain is utterly different from every other pain."[16]

The pain of this exile is utterly different from the pain to Hurwitz of the loss of Princess Charlotte. In this, the dirge memorializes loss and suffering that is at once detached from Charlotte, yet utterly defined, by indirection, by her. Israel's lament becomes a poem that hails an Anglo-Jewish textual authority.

Ambivalent Elegies

The subtlety of Hurwitz's negotiation of the public sphere and of Jewish community was extended further on the occasion of the death of George III in 1820. "The Tears of a Grateful People" was produced as a pamphlet for distribution at the Great Synagogue. The full title is "*The Tears of a Grateful People: A Hebrew Dirge & Hymn, Chaunted in the Great Synagogue, St. James's Place, Aldgate, on the Day of the Funeral of His Late Most Sacred Majesty King George III of Blessed Memory.* By Hyman Hurwitz, of Highgate. Translated into English Verse, by a Friend."[17] The pamphlet was printed as a face-en-face with Hebrew and English, and it is virtually certain that the translating "friend" was again Coleridge. Since this pamphlet was not printed for publication and possibly not even for distribution beyond the service,[18] the position of the reader is somewhat easier to determine: in "Israel's Lament," the disjunction between the primary original Hebrew and the English translation is, in part, a function of Hurwitz's acute consciousness of the varying readers of his elegy, some of whom are beyond the synagogue congregation, and their varying degrees of facility with the Hebrew language, ranging widely from nil to full competence. In the 1820 elegy, the readership is strictly circumscribed, even as the poem negotiates variations within that strictly circumscribed community. The lament for George III presents additional stark differences. Princess Charlotte had been adored by the populace, and the outpouring of grief at her untimely death had been massive. She was young and an apt repository for the hopes and the recuperative fantasies of the people. Regard for George III was a more complicated affair, and there was by no means universal admiration for him.

There was, however, a clear precedent, indeed a clear expectation, that the Jews express their loyalty to the Crown *as* Jews. This precedent includes a long history of celebration at the coronation, and mourning upon the death, of the monarch. The tradition can be traced back virtually as long as Jews have been residing in England. In some earlier instances, the welcoming representations of the Jews to the new monarchs had been rebuffed, notably the pre-expulsion efforts of the Jews to congratulate King Richard I in 1189. The very effort provoked a pogrom, the details of which vary according to the chronicler providing the account.[19] Since the 1656 Resettlement, Jews continued to recognize the importance of publicly illustrating their unwavering allegiance to England and to its rulers, and they have generally been met with more hospitality than was the case in Richard I's time. Indeed, since the Resettlement, the Jews even observe the commemorative days and fast days commanded by the Crown for services in Church of England places of worship; they do so by adapting the standard synagogue service to meet the national communal needs of commemoration, mourning, or thanksgiving for success in battle, whatever the case may be. Jewish prayers and poems composed specifically for the monarch or the state of the nation are usually composed in Hebrew, sometimes with an appended English translation, but not always. For those Jews who could not understand the Hebrew in such instances, the need for translation was not usually very pressing; the practice of expressing loyalty to the Crown even in the synagogue had been sufficiently conventionalized, and so a general confidence about appropriate expressions of loyalty on behalf of English Jewry could be readily presupposed. What makes Hurwitz's case different is that the English translations he sanctions offer a divergence from the Hebrew that itself constitutes a text; that is, the very points of difference between his Hebrew original and the translation themselves constitute a text about Hurwitz's very subtle conceptual negotiations of the place and state of the Jews in his contemporary England. He writes with the conscious anticipation of a translation and the conscious realization of who will and will not comprehend the Hebrew original. Such discernment is central to his poetry. And it is precisely because the precedent of Hebrew verse for English monarchs already does exist that he can inflect the genre to serve his purposes.

Hebrew verse to celebrate accessions to the English throne is not confined exclusively to Jews. Academic exercises were in place at Oxford and Cambridge to congratulate new monarchs in various languages, and the small contingent of Christian Hebraists participated in them. In "Hebrew Loyalty under the First Four Georges," I. Abrahams opines that many of these academic exercises were of inferior quality, excepting poems by Lowth, Kennicott, and a handful of others.[20] Hebrew *could* sometimes be used by such academics in crafty ways, however, as a claim to superior learning or enhanced understanding. This is well demonstrated by the Rev. Henry Dimock, who, besides other posts of distinction, occupied the role of Chaplain to the Archbishop of Canterbury. Dimock's "Hebrew Odes" range over several subjects, from thanksgiving odes for the recovery of King George in 1789, to "An Elegiac Dialogue, sacred to the memory of Miss Moore, only daughter of the Archbishop of Canterbury, who died, Jun 6, 1797, after a very short illness, aged 17." Dimock first printed the poem in Hebrew without translation, "to prevent any additional trouble to his Grace and family . . . as it was improper to revive the memory of this sad event so soon."[21] The Archbishop clearly could not read Hebrew. This implication is made emphatically clear in Dimock's "sympathetic" announcement about his efforts to spare the Archbishop further pain by refusing to translate it into English until 1798. Where such a father is an Archbishop, however, the assertion easily reads as moderately condescending. The ode would not offer comfort to a man who could not read it. And if we are to infer that the poem is a mere academic exercise, then it is unlikely to reopen the grievous wound in any event. Instead, the note seems poised to establish Hebrew as a super-specialized language that can all the same be employed, at times, for cross-purposes. In this instance, it advertises mastery of an ancient and biblical tongue; to be sure, the implicit assertion of superior religious mastery and learning is not identical to Hurwitz's; however, it is important in this context to note that Hebrew language mastery was regarded as a highly privileged skill by the educated Christian elite of the ancient universities, even while such mastery was confined to a select few. To be able to read and write in the language of the first Bible was recognized as a particularized refinement, whatever the attitude to the Jews at that moment in history. This is why, as I have noted in the previous chapter, the father of Emma Lyon was in demand as a teacher of Hebrew at the ancient universities but was unable, as a Jew, to obtain secure employment in any of them.

In 1894 Elkan Adler, son of the renowned chief rabbi of the British Empire Nathan Adler (chief rabbi from 1845 to 1890), published an article about the Hebrew elegies written for English monarchs by Joseph Ben Jacob Abendanon in the late seventeenth and early eighteenth centuries.[22] Abendanon's life provides a fine illustration of the Wandering Jew, as it were, who finally finds stability in England: born in Belgrade to the rabbi of Belgrade, he traveled to Bohemia and then to Kremsyr, Prague, and Amsterdam.[23] He is thought to have arrived in London near the end of the seventeenth century and to have become a Hebrew teacher.[24] Abendanon clearly absorbed the ethos of his coreligionists in England, since he penned two Hebrew elegies on the death of Queen Mary in 1694, one on William III, who died in 1702, and one on the son of Queen Anne (who was heir to the throne), who died in 1700.

That a newly arrived and much-traveled European Jew should so quickly absorb the posture of loyal gratitude to the English Crown as exhibited by the Jews of England is a fine marker of the community's general public bearing with respect to the nation. The concept of loyal gratitude, however, is ingeniously qualified. These elegies are paradigmatic of the complex attitude of English Jewry to the throne as early as the late seventeenth and early eighteenth centuries: not only public gratitude, as articulated in the synagogues, but also presumptively private meditations extol the virtues of the putatively sheltering British monarchy. Such gratitude does not presume to erase the memory of past ills, persecutions, or the expulsion of 1290; neither does it presume to deflect attention from the civil and political disabilities still suffered upon the Jews of England. It does, however, insist upon the Jews as loyal subjects in despite of the necessary qualifications, and who, *as* loyal subjects, do what the whole of the learned nation does at the accession or death of a member of the royal family: they celebrate or grieve, publicly and sometimes even privately, in discourse suitable to the event and to their learning. Hurwitz's lament for Charlotte is "*Israel's Lament*," and the lament for George III is "The Tears of a Grateful *People*": the circumscribed nation of Israel residing in England identifies itself with and as part of the nation of England, even as it draws attention to its particularity. To be part of that whole is not to relinquish one's designation as a distinctive people; it is to redefine the meaning of Jewish nationhood within English national identity. The life events of the monarch provide unique opportunities to claim affiliation, even if such affiliation is subtly qualified in the poetry by indirection, ironic reversals, and Jewish and Hebrew citation that mark the affiliation of the Jews with England as fraught with multiple competing claims. The Jews and a very few Christian Hebraists write poems in Hebrew, and in both instances the effect is a claim upon a specialized and privileged knowledge, one with deep resonances of biblical understanding. Such understanding makes contact with the very prerogative to comprehend the word of God. For Jewish authors so writing, it often further becomes an assertion of their cultural identity within the language of their religious and ethnic identity. The posture of gratitude may well contain shades of irony, though I would contend that Hyman Hurwitz is the one who takes that possibility of ironic reflection and makes of it something entirely unique and remarkable for the magnitude of its concentrations.

In Abendanon's elegy for Queen Mary, the full Hebrew text of which is reproduced in Adler's paper, we see already the signs of a veneration in verse that partly pulls itself back, and moves to a recognition of the self-reflective position of the Jew in England extolling the English Crown. He begins with an introduction, in Hebrew, that Adler translates as follows:

> If you perchance should ask,
> Of whom this mournful task:
> Behold an Hebrew born,
> I that so sorely mourn.[25]

The title of the poem, קינה מרה (*qina mara*), "A Bitter Dirge," puns on Mary's name: the Hebrew for bitter is *mara*, which supplies the title for the dirge. *Mara* is also absorbed into Miriam, the Hebrew name for Mary, and the poem's central metaphor, by which Queen Mary is implicitly compared with the biblical Miriam, the sister of Moses. The introduction to the poem has already emphasized the author's Jewish identity; it is "an Hebrew born" who so sorely mourns. It is therefore emphatically within the Hebrew biblical understanding that a Hebrew poem situates an elegy for an English queen. Like Hurwitz, Abendanon borrows from Hebrew liturgy:

מלך כל הארץ הכל יוצר
הוא ממית ומחיה צדיק דינו

Adler renders the lines as follows: "The King, whose word creation fills, / He spake, who makes alive and kills." In the Hebrew, the second line, the words Adler translates as "causes death and gives life" are taken from 1 Samuel 2:6 and are also intimately familiar to Jews from the *Amidah* prayer, the central text of the daily Jewish prayer services. In 1 Samuel, the JPS translation into English is "The Lord deals death and gives life." The full line in the *Amidah* is "The Lord [King] deals death and gives life and causes salvation to arise." The prayer, which I have discussed briefly in the chapter on Lyon and discuss again later in this chapter, is an ancient prayer that in fact contains several biblical quotations. As the core of the Jewish liturgical service, the *Amidah* is generally understood as facilitating a deep engagement with God, for which no external interruptions should be permitted during its recitation. Since Jews are to recite the prayer without interruption, it demands extreme concentration and intentness. In this context, it takes on further relevance: the prayer is divided into three sections, the first of which begins with praise of God, and this is where the quotation in question derives. The second and third parts of the *Amidah* are, respectively, petitions and prayers of thanks.[26] Abendanon does not seem to be incorporating Mary into the structure of Hebrew liturgical prayer so much as he is obtrusively making of an elegy to an earthly potentate a reminder about where the Jews stand: they acknowledge the secular ruler in their specific aspects as Jews, even as they emphasize the radical division between the secular order and Jewish religious existence. Of course, as head of the Church of England, the Crown's position as defender of the faith qualifies the meaning of the division between secular and religious. The kings and queens of England do not give life, though they sometimes cause death. Praise of the English monarch may not stand as an acceptable "interruption" of the *Amidah*, though an elegy to the English monarch may well recall the Jew to his or her obligations to the "king who causes death and gives life." Abendanon's poem in fact makes several implicit—though entirely discernible—distinctions between the "King" who is God, cited explicitly at the beginning of the dirge, and the "king" who is now the bereaved widower of Queen Mary. I cite Adler's translation of the concluding stanza:

> Oh King of Glory, mercy's Lord!
> Comfort our king, bereft, alone,
> Exalt his kingdom, raise his throne,
> In Eden, Miriam! Thy reward!

We have seen this dynamic in the Hurwitz poem: the valorization of the monarchy is offered hand-in-hand with its own counterpoints, which complicate the surface meaning. To be sure, the conventional Christian extolling of the monarchy celebrates royal power and indeed the entire royal family in biblical terms as well. "God Save our King" puts the power of God unambiguously before the power of any earthly potentate, and the king's reign is traditionally contextualized by the presumption of biblical precedent, even biblical inheritance. It is "Zadok the Priest," after all, that Handel composed for the coronation of George II in 1727,[27] which refers to the anointing of King Solomon as described in 1 Kings (employing the English of the King James Bible). This remains the "coronation anthem" for the English throne to this day. Abendanon quotes the Hebrew that is absorbed into the most important of the Jewish daily prayers, however, and so even his prayer that God the King should comfort King William II clearly signals that the historic joining of the English throne to biblical authority is herein being engaged by a Hebrew-literate Jew who acknowledges specific Jewish liturgy as well as the Hebrew Bible. This is not the Hebrew of Christian Hebraists or the mere language of convenience by someone who may not have had full mastery of the English tongue. Abendanon's Hebrew codes the language of Jewish liturgy. It is an elegy that serves more than one function: it marks the passing of the monarch of the land in which the poet lives, and it asserts the Jew's rightful belonging and rightful inheritance of English nationalist aspirations *as* a Jew.

The poem also complicates the question of what a Jew in England is entitled to say. The first stanza imagines God asking Miriam, as a lily in the garden, to be taken from the camp. The image clearly recalls the image of Miriam the sister of Moses being punished with a skin disease, for which she must suffer exile from the Israelites' camp in the desert for one week. On account of her condition, Moses prays to God and asks for his sister to be healed. It is in this prayer that the word "*El*" is used alone for the first time for the name of God. Of greater significance is that Miriam in punished for having spoken harshly of Moses. She is punished for the sin known to Jews as *leshon hara*, a subject that is implicit in some of Emma Lyon's poems as well. *Leshon hara* translates literally as "the evil tongue," but it refers more broadly to gossip, slander, or inappropriate speech. *Leshon hara* is a central concept in Judaism, one that has produced important and compelling commentaries in the Jewish canon about slander, testimony, and speech.[28] The experience of Miriam's quarantine in the desert is foundational to the Jewish interpretation of the concept; further, any reference to Miriam's skin affliction would immediately signify, to any Jew with even minimal Judaic learning, the rabbinic interpolations about *leshon hara*. Elkan Adler suggests that the allusion to Miriam's punishment in the poem "savours of the Jacobin impoliteness which saw in the date and details of the Queen's death a judgment on her for her unfilial conduct to her father, James the Second" (143). All the same, Miriam of the poem is imagined "In Eden," receiving her just "reward," an idea consistent with the fate of the biblical Miriam, whose sin was expiated and who is regarded as one of the important prophets of Judaism. Abendanon has grounded the dirge for Mary in a Hebrew source that, for Jewish readers, signals a distinctly Jewish foundational concept. The allusion to *leshon hara* functions as a reminder about the monumental importance of speech and its implications. It generalizes in political terms as well. In an English world in which Jews have no political rights, are a generally despised minority, and still face resentment over the toleration of the practice of their religion, the self-regulating of the Jews' speech is a necessity.

The year in which the Jews were readmitted to England, 1656, after all, is also the year in which the Quaker James Naylor, having been convicted of blasphemy (for allegedly impersonating Christ by riding into Bristol on a donkey with his followers declaring, "Holy, holy, holy"), drew the attention of those who were becoming increasingly uncomfortable with the expanding religious toleration extended by the Protectorate. He was tried and found guilty of "horrid blasphemy" under the Blasphemy Act of 1650, and sentenced to "be whipped through the streets by the hangman, exposed in the pillory, have his tongue bored through with a red-hot iron and to have the letter 'B' for blasphemer branded on his forehead."[29] Abendanon's elegy for Mary was written a mere thirty-eight years after this event, a mere thirty-eight years after the readmission of the Jews to England. Care with praise of the monarch, care against *leshon hara* of any sort, and care with articulating one's position as a Jew are not merely theoretical excrcises. When William Cobbett in parliament takes up his position against the emancipation of the Jews, a subject to which Hurwitz responds in a pamphlet of 1833, he brings up the very subject of blasphemy as a category that, in and of itself, ought, so he argues, to defeat any claim for the emancipation of the Jews. I return at greater length to Cobbett's speech and its effect on Hurwitz. For now, it is important to note that Cobbett appeals directly to the English blasphemy laws when considering the preposterousness of having a Jew potentially sit on the bench. I cite a small portion of his speech from the Hansard record:

> But let the hon. Gentleman, I say, tell me what would be our position with a Jew Judge upon the Bench—a blasphemer by profession—one who calls Jesus Christ an impostor? What would the hon. Member do with this Judge stuck up there, to try a man for blasphemy? He is himself a blasphemer. . . . As to the fanatics who petition about the matter, they have not considered it—they know not what they say, nor what they pray for. They can never have reflected that the House cannot grant the prayer of this petition, without saying that nothing is blasphemy.[30]

I am not arguing that the legal definition of blasphemy was a primary anxiety among the Jews of England. Cobbett's speech is an index of the ease with which Jewish difference is vulnerable to misprisions so immense that even such extravagance as Cobbett's hostile "misunderstanding" could gain hearing in the House of Parliament. The English law of blasphemy is the extreme example of how much trouble a subject could visit upon him or herself in the act of speech. As in Lyon's poetry, voice and the organ of speech are indeed preoccupations of Anglo-Jewish poets, and they signify in multiple, and multiply complicated, ways. Writing more than a century before Cobbett's parliamentary speech, Abendanon is already attuned to the monumental significance of Jewish voice in a Christian world, and to the public understanding and refraction of Jewish voice in a Christian world. It is a motif that is engaged through the generations of English Jewish writers, and Hurwitz inherits the caution as much as he inherits English elegy.

Abendanon's Hebrew elegy for William III is more accomplished poetry than the one for Mary discussed above. Indeed, Elkan Adler praises it by remarking, "It almost seems as though the author had read Milton and profited by his reading."[31] The Hebrew is written in quatrains, and the language is indeed majestic. If Abendanon had read Milton, though, it would have been to reverse the pastoral impetus of "Lycidas." The poem begins with the suggestion that the natural world is being invoked. The first line in Hebrew—על ההרים אשה בכי בקול סערה וסופה—is rendered by Adler as follows: "O'er hills our voice we raised in weeping sore."[32] That is the full extent, however, of the nature imagery. "O'er hills." Which hills? Whose hills? And where in the rest of the poem did they go? Pastoral elegy is not the domain of the Jews in England, not for Abendanon, and not, as we have seen, for Hurwitz writing a century later. The entire reference is simply abandoned, as if to emphasize that it is just as well to move the poem forward otherwise. The poem goes on to praise William III for his tenacity in standing up for truth and the good of his people. Abendanon announces that in Paradise, William is recognized as foremost among the virtuous monarchs. His strength and wisdom had been conferred by God Himself, a necessity, it seems, to establish his pride of place among the kings now residing in Paradise. An English Jew, that is, asserts that the king of England must be "head" among the kings of the afterlife. Abendanon does not seem to intend the bathos. This is an elegy of beautiful language but somewhat prosaic sentiments. Its significance lies in the very fact of its penning by a Jew residing in England who clearly recognizes the duty to declare allegiance even while subtly acknowledging that such allegiance is never straightforward. Like Hurwitz, Abendanon's poetry throws into sharp relief the Jews' need to establish a right of affiliation with English national pride, even while it is an affiliation established *as* definably Jewish. Where English national pride is also equated with national Christianity, however, a specifically Jewish right of affiliation becomes, paradoxically, a signature of self-division. These are the very tensions that define Hurwitz's efforts to write Hebrew elegies.

George III presents a particularly challenging subject for elegy. His reign was marked by political controversies and divisions, and he is today most commonly commemorated as the king who provoked the strong language about royal "absolute tyranny" in the American Declaration of Independence. Throughout his long reign, which began in 1760, his reputation fluctuated tremendously. Under George III, indeed the American colonies were "lost," though he was also criticized for having opposed independence for the thirteen colonies. He was often accused of abusing monarchical power and violating constitutional propriety. As a staunch believer in the Church of England as one of the central, defining features of English nationhood, he was opposed to emancipation for Jews, Nonconformists, and Catholics. The Regency began in 1810 when George became incapacitated by ill health and mental instability.[33] At his death he was blind, deaf, and entirely powerless. Despite the king's resistance to emancipation for non-Anglicans, his House did enjoy cordial—if politically expedient—relations with Jewish representatives. In 1801, the Great Synagogue of London was visited by the king's brother, the Duke of Gloucester, and in 1809 it was visited by two sons of George III, the Dukes of Cambridge and Cumberland,[34] a visit that provoked great ceremony and excitement in the synagogue. The delicate balancing act for Hurwitz at the time of George's death was political as well as existential: the deference to George III as part of the prayer service was expected and expedient, but the acculturation of the English Jewish man of letters would have prescribed a cultural conviction as well. Hurwitz, that is, is not simply trying to prove a point about the expectations and loyalty of the Jews in England; he is situating the very subjectivity of the Jewish poet within the sphere of English cultural inheritance, for which elegiac commemoration of the monarch is the presumed natural activity. He is also vividly aware of the tensions posed by such parameters, and this is where much of the dynamic interest of the poem resides.

Romantic England indeed produced many elegies for George III, but the general consensus was decidedly different from the one provoked by the death of Princess Charlotte. Famously, Percy Bysshe Shelley vilifies George before his death, in his sonnet "England in 1819," for which the sins of George and the royal court stand for the deplorable state of the nation:

An old, mad, blind, despised, and dying King,
Princes, the dregs of their dull race, who flow
Through public scorn,—mud from a muddy spring
(ll. 1–3)

The poet laureate Robert Southey, on the other hand, wrote the expected sycophantic response at the king's death, entitled "A Vision of Judgement," in which he imagines George elevated to heaven. It famously provoked Byron's "The Vision of Judgment," which parodies both Southey's sycophancy and King George. Though both were published after Hurwitz's elegy was written, Byron's response is paradigmatic of an alternative and angry reading of the king, one which clarifies further the divisive context of literary commentaries about the king:

> He died! his death made no great stir on earth:
> His burial made some pomp; there was profusion
> Of velvet—gilding—brass—and no great dearth
> Of aught but tears—save those shed by collusion:
> For these things may be bought at their true worth;
> Of elegy there was the due infusion—
> Bought also; and the torches, cloaks and banners,
> Heralds, and relics of old Gothic manners,
> Formed a sepulchral melodrame.
> (ll. 65–73)

Byron does not doubt the necessity of the "due infusion" of "elegy," nor the pomp and ceremony in evidence at the funeral. It is, after all, a part of the national inheritance to mourn the king. Later in the poem, Byron's mockery extends to a brief consideration of those whose inheritance of national mourning just might signify in different ways:

> I know this is unpopular; I know
> 'Tis blasphemous; I know one may be damned
> For hoping no one else may e'er be so;
> I know my catechism; I know we're crammed
> With the best doctrines till we quite o'erflow;
> I know that all save England's Church have shammed,
> And that the other twice two hundred churches
> And synagogues have made a *damned* bad purchase.
> (ll. 105–112)[35]

Hurwitz cannot presume on such territory, neither by disposition nor conviction. He is no satirist; he is, however, a writer who recognizes that embracing and presuming to inherit national culture is also to inherit a marker of alienation. Byron may mock that "I know that all save England's Church have shammed," but Hurwitz knows it as part of the spirit of the age against which—and within which—he must define himself.

"The Tears of a Grateful People" engages its readers with a peculiar form of intimacy: like the elegy to Charlotte of 1817, it is laden with specifically Jewish and Hebrew Bible references accessible only to those fully familiar with both the Hebrew language and the Hebrew Bible. Coleridge translates it into an English that does virtually nothing to signal its biblical allusions and explicit references, at times diverging notably from the original Hebrew. Since this text was not published, and probably not intended to circulate beyond the synagogue, it functions as a sort of personal exercise for Hurwitz as well as an intimate communication with some of the participants in the synagogue sanctuary, a heartfelt revisiting of many of the thematic preoccupations engaged in both the elegy for Charlotte and in many of his prose works. It also deepens them. The question of audience becomes all the more complicated, however, because as an elegy confined to the synagogue assemblage, its bifurcated reading establishes a focus on the varying degrees of Hebrew competence, and of knowledge of Jewish references, within the Jewish community itself. As a Hebrew teacher and erudite Jewish scholar of Hebrew and rabbinic texts, Hurwitz's persistent concern is that the "Grateful People," the Jews, be seen not only as "grateful" in the eyes of the dominant mainstream, but that these English Jews, these "grateful people" who, though "grateful" for the established norms, are still recognizably a "people," be equal to the designation of distinct peoplehood: let them be not merely a group dispersed throughout England, but a distinctive people circumscribed first and foremost by their learning. This is a potentially vexed wish for a Jew who is equally attuned to the mainstream English suspicion about the Jews' loyalty to England. For Hurwitz, that is, the Jews of England must learn Hebrew, must learn the Hebrew Bible and its commentaries, and ought to learn something of rabbinic sources even as they demonstrate their acculturation within the English nation, even as they demonstrate a capacity to illustrate the compatibility of Jewish identity with English norms. In the introduction, I cited Charles Lamb's complaint that the spirit of the synagogue is essentially separative. For Hurwitz, that is precisely the point, though it is a point taken under the sign of sympathy; Jewish separateness is for Hurwitz a principled position and a pedagogical ethic, but it need not be incompatible with the values held by the majority culture. If this sounds like special pleading, it also sounds like the condition of Jewish diasporic life in one of its most familiar aspects.

Translating Against Assimilation

By the early nineteenth century, a progressively smaller proportion of Jews were mastering Hebrew and Jewish texts. The lament for George III is, in part, Hurwitz's subtle lament precisely for the diminution of Jewish learning among his own coreligionists even as it stands as a declaration of Jewish affiliation with the grandest inheritance of England. The Jews, that is, still must learn how to be a people apart, retaining their distinctiveness even as they stand as a people gratefully within the mainstream of England. For Hurwitz, the elegy for the king enables him to participate as a Jew in a well-established mainstream cultural tradition (the poetic lament for the monarch) and to foreground the singularity of Jewish inheritance of an English nationalist tradition (publicly declared loyalty to the monarch).

Hurwitz is implicitly addressing an aspect of Jewish life that presents additional challenges to his own self-fashioning as mouthpiece for the Anglo-Jewish community: the effects of assimilation and acculturation of Jews in the eighteenth and early nineteenth centuries in Europe and England. Jews of all classes were increasingly interested in participating in the dominant culture. This march toward modernity, which was by no means smooth or straightforward, often went hand in hand with a dilution of Jewish religious observance and learning. As Todd Endelman points out in *The Jews of Georgian England*, many Jews, both rich and poor, who emigrated to England from Holland, Germany, and Poland during the eighteenth and early nineteenth centuries, had already been exposed to European cultural life.[36] The Sephardim, many of whom had come from Spain, Portugal, or southwestern France, were especially well positioned to absorb English culture because they had already been immersed in European non-Jewish cultural life. Of those who did not choose outright conversion to Christianity in England, the abandonment of the traditional ways of their ancestors was not necessarily intended as a rejection of their Jewishness; it was merely an effort to not stand entirely apart. Still, "the traditional worship service and Hebrew education were too central to Jewish identity to be thrown out altogether, so they were modified and adapted to English conditions."[37] Such adaptations enabled acculturated Jews to maintain their Jewish identity, but Anglo-Jewish life was also marked by a progressive dilution of Jewish learning that led some Jewish commentators to worry about the preservation of Jewish religious identity and Jewish continuity. Jews became progressively less invested in teaching their children Hebrew, or in educating them in the traditional rabbinic texts.

David Levi, whom I have discussed briefly in the chapter about Lyon, worried enough about Jewish access to traditional Jewish texts and learning that in the preface to his first book, the 1782 *A Succinct Account of the Rites and Ceremonies of the Jews*, he clarifies that his text is intended as much for the Jews as for the Christians:

> This work was undertaken for the benefit and instruction of two sorts of readers; viz. The Jew, and the Christian; to the former, very little need be offered by way of Preface to such a work; the nature of which is so obvious, and its utility so apparent: for although, the rites and ceremonies of the Jews, are all set forth in Hebrew, yet, as it hath pleased Divine Providence, to appoint our Lot in a Country, where the Hebrew is not used as a common Language, and there but imperfectly understood by many; it must certainly then, be very acceptable to those, who are natives of England, to receive a Clear, Impartial, and Distinct Account, of their Religious Tenets in English.[38]

Levi is calling on translation into English as a skill intended to ensure the survival and continuity of Jewish ritual practice. More than that, he is describing a scenario in which the Jews would be able to receive an account of the very "tenets" of their religion only as translated into English. As David Ruderman observes, David Levi believed that "Judaism could survive in England only in translation, only if its eternal message could be converted into a language accessible to non-Jews and to Jews whose primary tongue was English."[39]

For Hurwitz, then, the subject of translation is not merely about the privileged discernment of the Jews. It is also about the threat to such privilege, that is, the threat of a denuded Jewish literacy even as it tenaciously insists upon the importance of the English acculturation of the Jews. If these are mutually contradictory positions, it is not a source of tension from which Hurwitz shrinks. The Jews who stand apart are, for him, the Jews who can also stand within Jewish culture. The Jews who are less able to recognize themselves as a people apart are the Jews he would perforce educate. These are among the tensions of modern Jewish culture that all of the authors in this study address in one way or another.

The balancing act that Hurwitz performs is not always stable, to be sure. In the earlier "Israel's Lament," he establishes what amounts to an inside circle of those who comprehend fully, and he does not distinguish between those Jews with facility in Hebrew and Jewish learning and those Jews without such learning. In the elegy for George III, the distinction has shifted: between those who know and recognize the Hebrew and those who do not, with the audience constituted this time exclusively by Jews. This is the unique context in which Hurwitz also pays attention to the larger context of Christian England. Indeed, like "Israel's Lament," the poem is situated within Hurwitz's Jewish vision of the cultural authority that may be tacitly claimed by the Jews of England.

The poem, a discursive translation, and the translation of Coleridge are available in the Bollingen Collected Coleridge, edited by J. C. C. Mays (which I have cited earlier), and it is to this text I refer. I also make use of the editor's English discursive translation, and I note those instances in which I disagree with the translation presented by the editor.[40] The poem begins with an immediate declaration of bereavement, one so grievous that it seems to presuppose, rather than plead for, the Jewish *right* to such mourning. I quote Mays's discursive translation:

> Oppressed with grief, sorrow, and distress,
> my heart is in anguish, my bones shudder.
> My desires are broken off and scattered;
> and my spirit within me is in turmoil like a tempest.

Coleridge's rendition captures the urgency of the outpouring of grief, but he represents a much more self-reflexive poetic stance:

> Oppress'd, confused with grief and pain,
> And inly shrinking from the blow,
> In vain I seek the dirgeful strain:
> The wonted words refuse to flow.

In the Hebrew original, Hurwitz is immediately oppressed, but despite the turmoil of his spirit, he is engaged fully in the articulation of mourning. Coleridge renders grief at what is for him its most pathological pitch: a torment so overbearing that it precludes, or at least compromises, the poet's expressive capacity. In this, Coleridge gives further emphasis to Hurwitz's self-reflexivity, a hallmark by the Romantic age of elegiac poetry; in a move that emphatically situates the Hebrew poetry within the strains of Romantic elegy, both poets represent the author in the very process of writing. Coleridge's

"In vain I seek the dirgeful strain" echoes primarily not biblical poetics but Coleridgean lyric. His own "Dejection: an Ode" is explicit self-lament for the diminution of his own creative powers and the paralysis occasioned by his despair:

> A grief without a pang, void, dark, and drear,
> A stifled, drowsy, unimpassioned grief,
> Which finds no natural outlet, no relief,
> In word, or sigh, or tear—
> (ll. 21–24)

Assuming that there was discussion between the two friends, the self-reflexive opening in the Coleridge version is highly intriguing, as it suggests a deep understanding of Hurwitz's dilemma: speaking on behalf of the Jewish community, where the Jewish community itself does not present a uniform presence in learning or knowledge, and apostrophizing a king whose record with the Jews is far from pristine, Coleridge opens Hurwitz's poem by announcing a challenge to the effort of his own writing. It is not the same challenge as represented in Coleridge's "Dejection Ode," but the public announcement portrays it as the added torment of the mourner grieving a deeply intimate loss: the explicit theme of the first stanza in the Coleridge translation is that the grief over the loss of George III is so great that it defies expression, that it has nearly paralyzed the writer himself. In both versions, the opening stanza makes it emphatically clear that an attachment of the Jews to the monarchy, to normative England, and to high English culture may be assumed. For Coleridge's "The wonted words refuse to flow," we have Hurwitz's "and my spirit within me is in turmoil like a tempest." Hurwitz's tempest *is* the poem, but Coleridge seems to understand, as Hurwitz implicitly encodes, that the poet's words do not flow with facile clarity. Certainly Coleridge's translation refuses to let the words flow in close mimetic rendering; certainly the words reached for belong to the "dirgeful strain," but in truth no Jew had reason to gnash his teeth in mourning despair over the loss of George III. The claim is so clearly extravagant that it can only signify at once the rhetorical mobilization of hyperbole as well as the felt need for such special pleading in praise of the monarch.

The Hebrew of the first stanza quotes two words directly from Psalm 55, ליבי יחיל (*libi yachil*), which Mays translates as "my heart is in anguish." If the reference is to serve as an allusion to the psalm from which it derives, then the context complicates the mourning for the king as well as the regard for the audience of Jewish mourners inside the synagogue. In Psalm 55, King David cries out against his enemies. Probably referring to Absalom's rebellion, the pain of David is made far worse by the recognition that he suffers not from conventional enemies, but from supposed peers:

> It is not an enemy who reviles me
> —I could bear that;
> it is not my foe who vaunts himself against me
> —I could hide from him;
> but it is you, my equal,
> my companion, my friend;
> sweet was our fellowship;
> we walked together in God's house.
> (Ps. 55:13–15)

There were many challenges within to the reign of George III, among which was the disagreement between the king and Prime Minister William Pitt over religious policy, especially George's conviction that he must uphold Protestantism in England.[41] The implication of an enemy from within, however, and the recognition that "my equal, my companion, my friend" is the source of the most wounding grief, resonates more powerfully with the experience of the Jews in England. David's lament in Psalm 55, the very one quoted in Hurwitz's original Hebrew in the very first stanza of the poem, is a lament for the divisiveness within his own people, an assertion of the lack of safety within his own ground. As a source for allusive reference in Hurwitz's poem, this is an implicit lament that can be read in two ways: there is divisiveness within his own people the Jews; alternatively, within the nation of England there is divisiveness, characterized here chiefly by the stance of the English with regard to the Jews. The allusion is available only to readers of the Hebrew who recognize the specific citation of the psalm, which would not have included everyone in the synagogue congregation. It functions both as a subtle qualification to the grief over George, who was no advocate for the emancipation of the Jews within his own kingdom, as well as a subtle qualification of the community of Jews who are being invoked, at least superficially, as a hegemonic mass. The whole people of Israel lament in one grief-stricken voice over the death of King George III of England, defender of the (Christian) faith? Hurwitz putatively speaks on behalf of English Jewry, as his poem's title and form of address make clear; his "spirit is in turmoil like a tempest" as the mouthpiece of the Grateful People who weep their tears of mourning for the king. Hurwitz also appropriates the voice of King David, and of other Hebrew biblical figures throughout his Hebrew text; the David who laments the enemies within becomes for a time the mouthpiece of the lamenting nation of Israel. It is not King George whose enemies are being railed against; King David is no proxy for King George. It is the mourner himself who appropriates the biblical cry of David. In the allusive intertextual puzzle presented by Hurwitz in the Hebrew exclusively, King David stands not for King George III but for the Jews who mourn him. In this, Hurwitz represents absolute unity and absolute historical continuity within the people Israel, even as it is evident that those restricted, by reason of the paucity of their Jewish and Hebrew education, to the English side of the page do not fathom the full meaning of his utterance. It is as if Hurwitz is addressing one aspect of his thematic preoccupations to one part only of the Jewish community—those who comprehend the Hebrew—and inserting an implicit critique of their—and his—coreligionists who do not, because they cannot, understand. This does not make of the Hebrew-illiterate or semi-literate Jews "enemies." He is clearly gesturing toward them as a population within the rubric of Jewish peoplehood. It does, however, resonate as a subtle expression of division and difference within the Jewish community itself, even as the largest division signified in the elegy is the one between the Jews as a nation within England and the mainstream of the English nation whose head of state is being mourned.

Hurwitz's representation of the tears of the people he insists are "grateful" is not mere irony, however. He is ever mindful that the Jews of England in 1820 indeed benefit from various protections under the laws of England, notwithstanding the various disabilities under which they still labor. They are much safer in England in the early nineteenth century than they are in most locations on the continent, and this is a fact that further inflects Anglo-Jewish identity. Hurwitz is sincere in his belief that gratitude is due. He is also sincere in his belief, largely shared by the Jewish leadership of the time, that the Jews have a special responsibility to showcase publicly their pleasure in such freedoms and largesse as England has granted them. Hurwitz is an interesting case because he was fervently committed both to the English acculturation of Jews and to specialized Jewish religious and Hebrew learning. He also recognized the immense importance of "correcting" the Christian mainstream's understanding of the Jewish religion itself. He was further adamant that however well integrated the Jews become, they still ought to master the Hebrew language and Jewish learning. Like many Jewish scholars of the time, David Levi among them, he understood that by the early nineteenth century, English translation of Hebrew prayers, and even English translation of the Hebrew Bible, are unavoidable necessities. In 1826 Hurwitz himself published in English *Hebrew Tales Selected and Translated from the Writing of the Ancient Hebrew Sages to which is prefixed an Essay on the Uninspired Literature of the Hebrews*. Ruderman describes it as "the first rabbinic anthology in English."[42] Hurwitz was in line with the Jewish scholars and leaders of his time in trying to fashion an understanding of Judaism that would be compatible with English culture. In an extended examination of the work, Judith Page has convincingly argued that in *Hebrew Tales*, Hurwitz "wanted to show the compatibility of traditional Jewish wisdom and contemporary British culture . . . and to cultivate a new tradition that would make Jews more at home in Britain and Britain more hospitable to Jews and Jewish culture."[43] Since Jewish culture in England tended to focus on the Bible and not on rabbinical writings,[44] the project of *Hebrew Tales*, for which Coleridge himself contributed three translations, signals a crucial effort to educate not only the Christian mainstream, but the Jews themselves. As Ruderman points out, "By translating the most familiar compendium of rabbinic moral maxims, he hoped to show that Judaism was consonant with a universal moral and rational faith common to all humanity. In the context of England, he was the first Jew to attempt to rehabilitate the image of rabbinic Judaism through English translation."[45] Rehabilitating rabbinic Judaism by showing its consonance with universal morality is not tantamount to erasing differences: this is no simple erasure of difference. The distinctiveness of Judaism stands as a marker of difference for the Jews in this English world, and it is a distinctiveness that Hurwitz seeks to make *compatible* with, as opposed to identical to, English culture. For Hurwitz, the emphasis on compatibility is not merely in service of relieving anti-Jewish sentiment: it serves the purpose of educating the Jews themselves about the worth of historical rabbinic wisdom. If Hurwitz is rehabilitating the image of rabbinic Judaism, he is also drawing attention to it.[46]

Universal Values and Jewish Particularity

Hurwitz became the first professor of Hebrew at University College London, and he took the opportunity of his introductory lecture, delivered on November 11, 1828, to hope for both a dawning equality and a more rigorous education for the Jews. In terms of the former, he speaks unquestionably as a Jew conscious of the monumental significance of his election to the position: "Could I feel it other than as an almost overwhelming felicity, that I could regard my own election as a sign and pledge of the fulfilment of the auspicious promise, that the differences in the degree of those qualities, which in kind distinguish man from the brute, *Reason*, I mean, and the *will* in harmony with *Reason*, should alone and exclusively be allowed to distinguish man from man."[47] If Hurwitz as Jew is here speaking somewhat as a Deist, then he is doing so in his aspect as Hebrew teacher to both Jews and Christians, but with a lesson to the Christians about Jewish universalism, and a lesson to the Jews about Jewish particularism. The Jews, with a peoplehood and a religion that can be universalized in its main import, are not *essentially* to be distinguished by others. Reason alone should distinguish man from man. But when he turns to the Jews, he makes it clear that their Jewish learning serves not only a spiritual purpose, but also a political one:

> O! do not, I beseech you, neglect an opportunity which you cannot prize too highly.—And O! Let me conjure you, let it no longer be in the power of your Detractors to say, that we aid the ignorance of our oppressors, by our own aversion from knowledge; and that we are accomplices in the superstitions, which have been the cause and pretext for our persecutions, by fostering superstitions of our own, scarcely less gross, and alas! Not always free from the same persecuting character.[48]

Later in the lecture, he exhorts the Jews to educate their children, again in terms that recall their political and social privations, even as it recognizes the specificity of Jewish religious particularity:

> If, then, you prize your Religion—and I know ye do —since for what else but for your Religion do you suffer Privations, and Exclusions, and the bitter taunts of your Detractors!—If you value the inspired writings of your Divine Legislator, Pious Kings, and Eloquent Prophets—and I know ye do, for even now I behold amongst you many, many, who are as distinguished by general knowledge, as by the particular knowledge of the Holy Law, and its sacred accompaniments—Then, by these Holy Writings, and by that Religion I conjure you, and solemnly intreat you, not to neglect the golden opportunity which this Institution offers you. Bestow upon your sons those manifold blessings which flow from a Superior Education, and

prove that you know how to value the Sympathy with which the Founders of this University have contemplated your privation.[49]

Hurwitz is conscious of addressing the Jews as those who reflectively recognize that they "suffer Privations, and Exclusions, and the bitter taunts of your Detractors." His poetic citation, in his elegy for George III, of the enemy within, but only as such citation is accessible to those readers in possession of Jewish and Hebrew literacy, now takes on greater resonance and significance. To be united as a Jewish people with a common language and a common learning becomes, for Hurwitz, one route to greater acculturation within Protestant England. Gratitude and frustration are the two poles in which he here moves, and they are inextricably linked: gratitude to the host country that, frustratingly, rejects full hospitality; and gratitude and frustration within his own Jewish community that all the same must be presented publicly as unified in gratitude.

It is for this reason that the histrionics of the poem recall even the elegy to Princess Charlotte. The first line of the Hebrew's second stanza refers to Jeremiah 4:31, but only in allusion. Mays translates the first line as "For the cry of a woman in labour, the cry of anger and disturbance." I would quarrel with this translation because the Hebrew original in fact does not include the words "of a woman in labour." The latter is an interpolation based, I would presume, on the context from Jeremiah, in which the line קול כחולה שמעתי (*kol k-holah shamati*), meaning "I hear a voice as of one in travail,"[50] is followed in the Hebrew Bible by the reference to the anguish of a woman in childbirth. The rest of Mays's translation is accurate, and I quote the full stanza in his rendering:

> For the cry of a woman in labour, the cry of anger and disturbance,
> the cry of the rending and breaking of hearts,
> the cry of wailing from sons and fathers,
> I have heard, I am afraid, and my soul is disturbed.

The Coleridge rendering strips the language not only of its biblical reference, but also of its excessive histrionics:

> A fear in every face I find,
> Each voice is that of one who grieves;
> And all my Soul, to grief resigned,
> Reflects the sorrow, it receives.

Coleridge makes Hurwitz sound somewhat paranoid, or as if the Jews in the synagogue now meet each other's fear of the political future with uncertainty and anxiety. It also, of course, sustains the allusion to the "Dejection Ode" established in Coleridge's translation of the first stanza. The Soul reflecting the sorrow it receives echoes that ode's wistful recognition that "we receive but what we give." We do not, in fact, necessarily receive what we give to the nation. Certainly the disenfranchised do not. The overstatement in Hurwitz's stanza, especially in context of the Regency having ruled the throne during George III's illness, is one that could have been observed by an exclusive coterie. It is unclear if Coleridge took his cue from Hurwitz's own desire to cool the emotional temperature of the Hebrew dirge, or if he was merely bringing the poem under the compass of his own poetic predilections. It is important to remember that this pamphlet was printed as a face-en-face, and that Coleridge was not translating for a wide general public. This would suggest that to the extent Hurwitz was guiding or at least sanctioning the translation, his eye on the differences between his Hebrew and Coleridge's English was intended to take account of the division within the congregational community of Jews themselves. And why would the greater cry, the excessive zeal of mourning, be reserved exclusively for the Hebrew? The Hebrew-literate Jews are the ones who are able to recognize the echoes and allusions to biblical texts, and to understand the denuding of such references in the English translation. They are the ones, that is, who in this elegy recognize their own distinctiveness, their own difference, both from the other Jews in the sanctuary and the wider community. They are also the ones who would fully apprehend the significance to Hurwitz of Hebrew, as a potential unifier of the Jewish people (which is, lamentably for Hurwitz, deteriorating) and as a guarantee of Jewish continuity throughout history in the diaspora. Hurwitz was no supporter of Yiddish as a unifying language, for example. For Hurwitz, Hebrew is the privileged legacy of the Jews, and the Hebrew Bible is the privileged inheritance of the Jews, and as such Hurwitz is dedicated to ensuring that even in the land where the Jews are enjoined to show their gratitude to the government and to the governor of the Church of England, they are also enjoined to learn their Hebrew and know it well.

But Hurwitz surely knows too that what he is asking of his fellow coreligionists is the fashioning of a complicated identity: an Englishman fully acculturated, fully committed to the expression, indeed even the conviction, of loyalty to England, held by a Jewish people always conscious also of their distinct peoplehood, and who acquire distinctive markers of their difference:

fluency in Hebrew, fluency in Jewish religious knowledge, observance in Jewish ritual. The English Jew who loves England and further understands himself in terms of his Jewish inheritance is a creature whose subjectivity is marked by tensions that define him at the deepest level of self-understanding. When Hurwitz writes elegies for the English royal family, he is implicitly pledging allegiance both to English literary history and the English Crown. The people shed tears, and they are the tears of a grateful people. The allegiance to literary inheritance is further underlined by the spectacle of Coleridge as translator, and it is reinforced by the public gestures to English literary norms. But the pledge of allegiance now clearly emerges as an allegiance also to specifically Jewish continuity: the elegy of allegiance to the English monarch is written in Hebrew and laden with a Hebrew-biblical intertext that functions also as an implicit plea for deep Jewish learning among the English Jews. It further functions as a qualification to the tears of gratitude. Some of the tears shed must also be tears of frustration. Others are tears of shame and regret. The assertion that the speaker's soul "is disturbed" is an elegiac cliché even as it is the English Jew's recognition of necessary self-reflexivity within the poem: Hurwitz is writing a poem, in part, about how the poem is understood, and how it ought to be understood.

It is difficult to read Hurwitz's dirge in Hebrew without being overwhelmed by the biblical intertext. At every opportunity, at every expression of grief for the loss of King George III of England, Hebrew-speaking Jews are reminded of their specifically Hebrew inheritance, their specific cultural and spiritual privileges *as* Jews, even as their concomitant frustrations and privations are brought to the fore in the process. To be so reminded while reading an overblown elegy for a British monarch who opposed the abrogation of disabilities for those outside of the Church of England is tinged with irony, however qualified by the other real grounds for gratitude. This back-and-forth between the Hebrew original and the facing-page translation is a real insider's strategy, one that comes packaged with a clear and one-sided indication of who is center and who is margin. It is flattering, too: the Jews of the congregation reading through Hurwitz's Hebrew dirge must of necessity become conscious of their own incessant noting of allusions and references, even as they would have been acutely aware of what their non-Hebrew-speaking congregants would be missing. They are the insiders, even within the synagogue attended exclusively by Jews—another ironic reversal given that more traditional, religiously educated and Hebrew-literate Jews are the very ones who are least assimilated into mainstream English culture. There are very few contexts in which such Jews in nineteenth-century England are portrayed as privileged insiders, especially where a subject involving the royal family is concerned. Singing the Lord's song in a foreign land is not the same as singing the songs for the British monarchy in England. As such, the translation functions as a more conventionally public dirge for the king—the Jews *ought* to show their gratitude, they ought to demonstrate mourning, and one of their literate, cultured leaders (Hurwitz) ought daringly to foreground his right to participate in the public, communal mourning for the monarch. The translation fulfills this function. The Hebrew original, however, is closer to a singing of the Lord's song in this foreign land. It is a song that only the Jews could sing, and that only the most Hebrew-learned of the Jews could fully comprehend, both in its allusiveness and in its subtle ironies about the practice of Jewish allegiance in England.

Such Jews apprehend the imagery of a woman in labor in the second stanza; perhaps some of them will recall this dominant image from the dirge for Princess Charlotte. It is not entirely consonant with the imagery of the rest of the poem. The Jews are not laboring to birth a new dawn in the wake of the king's death, but they are aware of the self-divisions, as described above in the discussion of the allusion to Psalm 55. May they be described as wailing, in the terms of rending and breaking of hearts? Not entirely, or at least not in reference to this particular moment of loss. In stanza 14, the imagery shifts from a woman crying in labor to a woman sitting like a widow; however, in the former, the cry seems to be the cry of the "Grateful People." In stanza 14, the specificity is absorbed into the image of Britannia. Here is Mays's translation:

> And Britannia, sitting like a widow,
> Desolate, widowed, like those going down to the grave:
> for great is the pain, strong the wound;
> and grief is closed up in her like a smelting fire.

For this stanza, Coleridge's translation generalizes a grief that is noted specifically by the Jews:

> Beyond the mighty Isle's extent
> The mightier Nation mourns her Chief:
> Him *Judah's Daughter* shall lament,
> In tears of fervour, love and grief. (italics mine)

Hurwitz's lines echo Lamentations but do not quote it exactly. The first line of stanza 14 in the Hebrew takes up the word for "like a widow" (*k'almanah*, כאלמנה) as used in Lamentations, which figures Jerusalem as widowed among the nations after the city and the Temple were destroyed by the Babylonians. Historically, this occasioned the Babylonian exile of the Jews, for which Psalm 137 is the other most familiar lament: "By the rivers of Babylon, there we sat, sat and wept, as we thought of Zion." This is followed in the psalm by the equally familiar declaration:

> How can we sing a song of the Lord on alien soil? If I forget you, O Jerusalem, let my right hand wither. If I forget you, O Jerusalem, let my tongue stick to my palate if I cease to think of you, if I do not keep Jerusalem in memory even at my happiest hour. (Ps. 137:4–6)

Psalm 137 is one of the key texts of Jewish culture and Jewish collective cultural experience. For a people tasked with publicly declaring their primary allegiance to England, Psalm 137 presents potentially vexing implications. If Jerusalem must be the chief joy of the Jews, where does that situate Jewish loyalty to the land of England? English Jews found they had need on a fairly regular basis to defend their allegiance to England, lest they be dismissed for their allegiance to Judaism as a nation unto itself, or especially lest their English allegiance be questioned relative to their allegiance to the present concrete actuality of the Holy Land, Palestine having recently gained a more concrete reality in the eyes of readers of English travel books.[51]

Establishing the Standing to Mourn a King

Indeed, in 1833 William Cobbett (whom I discuss briefly above in relation to the English blasphemy laws), the radical populist, journalist, and parliamentary member for Oldham, had pronounced in the House various slanders about Jewish ritual, alleging that the Jews regularly blaspheme Christ in their synagogues and crucify Christ in effigy once a year. Cobbett, the author of *Rural Rides* (1830), was a champion of agricultural England, and known widely as the friend of the poor, the disenfranchised (he was a vocal supporter of the 1832 Reform Bill and a strong proponent in favor of Catholic emancipation), and agricultural laborers. He was also virulent in his hatred of Jews and his opposition to Jewish emancipation.⁵² Hurwitz himself countered with a published pamphlet, "A Letter to Isaac L. Goldsmid, Esq. F.R.S., Chairman of the Association for Obtaining for British Jews Civil Rights and Privileges, on Certain Recent Misstatements Respecting the Jewish Religion."⁵³ The letter begins by apologizing for the need to refute such preposterous charges in the first place. This is not because such aspersions are without precedent. Hurwitz recognizes that the charges are consonant with the standard libels promulgated in various countries throughout history. His insistence that, at first thought, he considered it unnecessary to address the aspersions, all the same recalls the long history of persecution with which the Jews have had to contend: "That in our enlightened days, when so many sources of information are open to the diligent enquirer, there should be found any well educated man so ignorant of our laws, customs, and manners, as to renew against us charges, first invented in the darkest ages by our enemies for the basest purposes, may well excite our astonishment."⁵⁴ Hurwitz decides "on mature consideration" that they ought to be refuted anyway. He cites the authority and precedent of Flavius Josephus in the latter's refutation of the slanders against the Jews by Apion the Grammarian. The speaker from Oldham, contends Hurwitz, has more influence than Apion did in Josephus's time, all the more reason for Hurwitz finally to speak out. Before he proceeds to simply refute the charges in straightforward fashion, he quotes at length from Josephus's "Flavius Josephus against Apion." What he chooses to quote is telling, and I cite only a selected passage:

> Yet, because there are a great many men so very foolish, that they are rather caught by such orations, than by what is written with care, and take pleasure in reproaching other men, and cannot abide to hear them commended, I thought it to be necessary not to let this man go off without examination, who had written such accusations against us, as if he would bring us to make an answer "in open court."⁵⁵

Perhaps these are not such "enlightened days," as Hurwitz refers to the present in his opening discussion in the pamphlet. The displacement onto Josephus of the disgust for those who would believe such ancient slander against the Jews is hardly a real deflection of his indignation. Hurwitz would prefer to think of these contemporary days as ones in which no educated human being could give serious ear to preposterous charges "invented in the darkest ages by our enemies for the basest purposes" but, as Josephus indicates many hundreds of years before him, there are enough among us who really are "so very foolish" to warrant a public refutation, as if it were "in open court."

Hurwitz proceeds to refute the charges easily enough. What is most interesting about his defense, however, are the appendices to the pamphlet. These are all concerned not with refuting ancient slanders about the Jews as Christ killers or Christ blasphemers, but about the Jewish allegiance to the Crown, or indeed to any society in which the Jews live. The point is that the pressing concern represented by the slander is not its real content, but the way in which it stands as synecdoche for the outsider status of the Jew. Jewish integration into English society must be publicly emphasized in terms of Jewish loyalty to English society and its rulers. It is therefore only somewhat surprising that immediately following Hurwitz's refutation of the charges, there follows a copy of translated extracts from the conference of the "Sanhedrin" convened by Napoleon Bonaparte in France in 1807, "for the purpose of declaring what are the Principles of the RELIGION OF THE HEBREWS, respecting their Social and Political Relations, and which was composed of about 80 of the MOST LEARNED JEWS OF FRANCE AND ITALY."[56] The extract emphasizes the commitment of the Jews to their land of residence, whatever that residence may be:

> It having appeared to the great Sanhedrim, that the nations among which the Jews have for many generations dwelled, are not sufficiently informed of the feelings of sociality and brotherhood entertained towards them by the body of men, so that both in France and the kingdom of Italy, a degree of uncertainty exists as to the question, whether the Israelites of those two states consider their Christian fellow citizens as their brethren, or as strangers.[57]

It is clearly not simply the French and Italians who are "not sufficiently informed" of the regard in which Jews hold their fellow non-Jewish countrymen. The Sanhedrin go on to clarify that Jewish law requires that Jews love their neighbors as they love themselves, and that this dictum must be generalized to admit love of those who dwell in the same country, indeed who extend to them national hospitality. It is emphasized that this is a truth "universally recognized both by those teachers, who have most authority among the Israelites, and by every Israelite who is not ignorant of the principles of his Religion."[58] They conclude by advising that this message be recognized by all dwellers in all lands: "For these different reasons the Great *Sanhedrin* commands all Israelites in the

French Empire, the Kingdom of Italy, and elsewhere, to live with the subjects of every state in which they dwell, (since all these acknowledge God, the Creator of Heaven and Earth), as with their fellow citizens and brethren; for so the Letter and Spirit of our Holy Law require."[59] In England, in France, in Italy, indeed everywhere: the Jews are required, by their own law, as proclaimed universally by the greatest rabbis and understood by all Jews who know anything at all of their religion, to love the neighbors among whom they dwell. Hurwitz could have included any number of pamphlets or opinions from English sources, but he begins with a pronouncement that would be recognized as authoritative from a universal perspective. The "Great Sanhedrin" convened by Napoleon did not, of course, actually possess the legislative authority of antiquity. The name is suggestive of the tremendous authority exercised by the ancient Jewish court of the Sanhedrin, and in this pamphlet, the appearance of authority is precisely what is needed to emphasize to the majority population that the loyalty of the Jews to Crown and country is a matter not only of personal pride but of Jewish religious statutory requirement. We might recall the exclamation in the elegy for Charlotte that the Jews will observe an anniversary of mourning on the date of Charlotte's death. As a specifically Jewish ritual of obligation to remember and commemorate, the anniversary ritual does not normally extend to those without blood relationship to the mourner. But the need to establish the depth of Jewish sentiment for the royal family is enough to warrant a tentative revision, at least in poetic fancy, of the ritual obligation.

It is for this very reason that the pamphlet continues with an extract from the catechistic "Elements of Faith: for the use of Jewish Youth of Both Sexes." Published in London in 1815, the pamphlet emphasizes that even from their youth, Jewish students are taught to love their neighbors as themselves, and that this extends to the mainstream population in the country of which they are a minority. One of the questions reads as follows: "As we are the children of Israel, who live in the hope and expectation of the coming of the Messiah, and the return to our country Judea, is it equally incumbent upon us to love the king and country in which we at present reside, and to obey all its laws equally with the rest of its inhabitants?"[60] The answer, which begins with the emphatic word "certainly," is that until the Messiah actually arrives, the Jews must obey the laws of the country, and regard the king of the country in which they reside as "a king of Israel." The answer is indeed somewhat drastic, but strong semantic measures, perhaps, are the key to making the point in this regard. There must not be seen any incompatibility between the longing to return to Zion and the Jewish loyalty to the Crown of England: "and we are in duty bound, equally with all its inhabitants, to respect and obey the king and ministers who form the government, as it is directed by Jeremiah—seek the peace of the city whither I have caused you to be carried away captives, and pray unto the Lord for it, for in the peace thereof shall ye have peace (Jer. 19:7)." Such is the apparatus surrounding Hurwitz's very straightforward defense of the Jews against the slander from Cobbett. This is an apparatus that leaves those particular slanders well behind, and goes right to the heart of the matter that is of far more pressing concern: *how* the Jews convey their commitment and loyalty to England, especially in a historical moment when, general liberal toleration notwithstanding, so much is potentially at stake in the meaning attributed to Jewish utterance. If Hurwitz encodes elaborate refractions within his Hebrew poetry that commemorate members of the royal family, that is because the subjectivity of the acculturated English Jew is a subtle negotiation.

The culturally sophisticated English Jew is on remarkable display in the most unlikely of places: in the appendix to Hurwitz's *A Grammar of the Hebrew Language*, published in two parts in 1835 (expanded from a version of 1829). This text is meant as a primer for learning Hebrew, one directed to both Jews and Christians. The appendix is subtitled "Extracts from Scarce Hebrew Books," and the author claims to offer such extracts for practice in reading. In fact, many of the texts are not extracts from scarce Hebrew books at all. Indeed, it is a veritable anthology of cultural as well as biblical and talmudic documents that are of interest to Hurwitz. The translations into Hebrew are from Latin, German, French, Italian, and English. They may well provide the student with practice in reading Hebrew, but Hurwitz is clearly also interested in advertising the more worldly and liberal cultural tastes of the professor of Hebrew Language and Literature and the author of Hebrew grammars. Examples include a Hebrew translation of part of Boethius's *Consolation of Philosophy* with the corresponding Latin; translations of Italian poetry by such authors as the eighteenth-century Pietro Metastasio; and Hurwitz's own Hebrew translation of "God Save the King." A poem by the Italian Jewish poet Moses Chaim Luzzatto, "The Contented Shepherd," is offered, as is poetry by Hartwig Wessely, the German Jewish Hebraist. One interesting addition includes a paraphrase of the eighth psalm, for which Hurwitz supplies the following footnote: "From כהונת אברהם (*kehunat Avraham*), a poetical paraphrase of the whole of the Psalms, by R. Abraham Ben Shabthi HaCohen. This work, written in almost every kind of metre, evinces uncommon skill and a wonderful command of language, and is therefore deservedly esteemed."⁶¹ The eclectic, cosmopolitan Hurwitz spans the ages and centuries and cultures, pronouncing with authority on the worth of poetry, philosophy, and sacred texts. Indeed, the cosmopolitan Hurwitz is including such specimens in an anthology dedicated to the advancement of specifically Hebrew learning. This is the same author who, in his introductory lecture at the University of London, turns at one point to the Jews in particular and urges them that "a scientific acquaintance with the language of their Forefathers must be the basis of all *liberal* education" (italics mine).⁶² This is the Hurwitz who writes the elegy for King George III of England, a poem of a "grateful people" whose place within culture is also the place where they can sing the Lord's song in a foreign land.

Jerusalem, or the New Jerusalem, is envisioned by Blake as taking root in "England's green and pleasant land."⁶³ Britannia may well be the New Jerusalem, and the tradition of British Israelitism may well enable a reader to associate Hurwitz's "Britannia" in stanza 14 with both Britain and the Jews,⁶⁴ but the primary reference must be grounded in a complex irony: Britannia bereft of George III is poetically figured in terms that recall the fall of Jerusalem and the first great exile of the Jews into diaspora, the very exile that occasioned the singing of primary allegiance to Jerusalem above all else. Both Psalm 137 and Lamentations, which is one of the texts read on Tisha B'Av to commemorate the fall of Jerusalem and the destruction of the first and second Temples, are central canonical texts of Jewish exile and longing for return to Zion. Hurwitz's Hebrew provides the reader with a conflation of the Jew mourning for Jerusalem in exile with the Jew mourning for George III, also in exile from Jerusalem, *and* with an image of England *as* the fallen Jerusalem in the wake of the king's death. The result is a description that foregrounds the exilic suffering of the Jews even in the midst of the Jews' appreciative elegy for a king of England. The irony, again, is necessarily qualified by Hurwitz's desire to represent a Judaism compatible with English tastes and sensibilities and a Jewish people loyal to the Crown.

The first part of Lamentations makes reference to allies become foes, another intertext that recalls the previous one about internal enemies. Jerusalem as widow is not comforted by her allies:

Bitterly she weeps in the night,
Her cheek wet with tears.
There is none to comfort her
Of all her friends.

> All her allies have betrayed her;
> They have become her foes.
> Judah has gone into exile
> Because of misery and harsh oppression;
> When she settled among the nations,
> She found no rest. (Lam. 1:2–3)

We will recall the references to Tisha B'Av from the elegy to Charlotte. To cite Lamentations in an elegy to King George is to figure, at one level of reading, the mourning in terms of the expression of the most extreme grieving historically performed by Jews in response to their most catastrophic collective loss: Jerusalem and the Temple. This allusive reference is consistent with the "tears of a *Grateful* people." Alternatively, it serves the purpose of reminding the Jews of the corrective perspective: we mourn George, but after all this is not the loss of Jerusalem and the Temple; Jerusalem and the Temple have already been lost. The Jews already situate themselves in the exilic dispersion. In the peculiar subjectivity of Jewish English existence, both of the above scenarios are held at once: the death of the king is represented as a grievous loss because, in some respects, that is what the post-exilic Jew is enjoined to do; further, the death of the king signals England as but one corner of that dispersal, and the Jews are the widows not again, but still. We would do well to recall the dictate of Jeremiah commanding the Jews to seek the peace of the city; God tells them to "seek the peace of the city whither I have caused ye *to be carried away captives*" (italics mine).

Earlier I cited Coleridge's reference to his own "Dejection Ode," and the counter-reference supplied by Coleridge's familiar utterance, "We receive but what we give." Indeed, the famous lines following, "And in our life alone doth Nature live," obtrusively recall us to a dynamic figured in the Charlotte elegy as well: the natural world is not brought to bear in this elegy to George III. There are fewer such natural references in the biblical intertext cited by Hurwitz in the Hebrew; however, Coleridge "translates out" any natural or pastoral context. Ostensibly, this elegy is decidedly not pastoral elegy. The fifth stanza contains a significant allusion to Joel, one which only initially would reinforce an anti-pastoral ethos (from the discursive translation of Mays):

> The sun has set! The light of eyes is darkened.
> A cloak of darkness clothes the moon.
> The stars have withdrawn their brightness from shining.
> And every heart is sick, and every eye has water.

The relevant words from the third line of the stanza—כוכבים אספו נגהם—quote directly from the Hebrew Bible. Joel is one of the minor prophetic books, which begins with a description of the effects of a terrible locust plague that has laid waste the land. As I have noted above, Joel 1:8 is the source for the Tisha B'Av poem that Hurwitz quotes in the Charlotte elegy, and which urges its hearers, "Lament—like a maiden [girded] with sackcloth for the husband of her youth." The prophecy in Joel then turns to the restoration promised by God, who is roused on behalf of the *land*:

> Then the Lord was roused
> On behalf of His land
> And had compassion Upon His people.
> In response to His people
> The LORD declared:
> "I will grant you the new grain,
> The new wine, and the new oil,
> And you shall have them in abundance.
> Nevermore will I let you be
> A mockery among the nations." (Joel 2:18–19)

Pastoral rejuvenation enters explicitly with an address to the land itself:

> Fear not, O soil, rejoice and be glad;
> For the Lord has wrought great deeds.
> Fear not, O beasts of the field,
> For the pastures in the wilderness
> Are clothed with grass.
> The trees have borne their fruit;
> Fig tree and vine
> Have yielded their strength. (Joel 2:21–22)

Coleridge's translation of stanza 5 hints at the tradition to which Hurwitz alludes, only to deflect it:

> Lo! of his beams the Day-Star shorn,
> Sad gleams the Moon through cloudy veil!
> The Stars dim! Our Nobles mourn,
> The Matrons weep, their Children wail.

The first line of the stanza contains an asterisk that leads to a footnote provided by Coleridge: "The Author, in the spirit of Hebrew Poetry here represents, the Crown, the Peerage, and the Commonalty, in the figurative expression of the Sun, Moon, and Stars." The footnote provided by Coleridge establishes the conceit that in this stanza at least, the biblical allusion is being drawn out for the benefit of non-Hebrew readers. The claim here that the Crown is the Sun, whose eclipse is being mourned, diverges significantly from the actual source. In Joel 2:10 and in Joel 4:15, we have the Hebrew words for "And stars withdraw their brightness," as well as "sun and moon are darkened." Hurwitz directly quotes the Hebrew for "stars withdraw their brightness," but "sun and moon are darkened" from Joel are words rendered somewhat differently in Hurwitz's poem and in the translation. What is most significant here is that Coleridge in his footnote may well be referring to conventions of Hebrew poetry, but they do not necessarily apply to Hurwitz's use of them in the original Hebrew, which he is putatively translating. The context for the dimming of the stars and sun in Joel 2 is the locusts, figured as God's army avenging the sins for his people Israel. The context for the dimming of sun and moon in Joel 4 is the prophecy of the judgment day of the Lord in "the Valley of Decision" (4:14), where "the Lord will roar from Zion" (4:16) and finally ensure "A refuge to the children of Israel" (4:16):

> And you shall know that I the Lord your God
> Dwell in Zion, My holy mount.
> And Jerusalem shall be holy;
> Nevermore shall strangers pass through it.
> And in that day,
> The mountains shall drip with wine,
> The hills shall flow with milk,
> And all the watercourses of Judah shall flow with water.
>   (Joel 4:17–18)

For Hurwitz, the tangle of Hebrew allusions brings to the fore the pastoral as a feature of prophecy, which Hurwitz suggests in ways that recall his appropriation of pastoral conventions in the Charlotte elegy; in that poem, as in the elegy for George, the pastoral exists in Hebrew allusion only, and therefore is accessible to a select audience only. The pastoral to which Hurwitz alludes is anchored not in English history, but in the biblical Hebrew text. Coleridge's "we receive but what we give / and in our life alone doth nature live" ("Dejection: an Ode") is the counterpoint to Hurwitz's invocation of a biblical prophetic pastoral, one that figures access to arcadia not as a Coleridgean reaching out of the spirit, but as divine recompense for the broken-hearted children of Israel. Dejection meets nature, but where Coleridge's ode ends with the nightmare of nature gone awry, Hurwitz's mourning consigns nature not only to the footnotes, but to the notes that may be read and interpreted only by the select few. The other readers, those without Hebrew, are not consigned to the nightmare of a nature that will not meet us halfway, as is Coleridge's dejected speaker; rather, they are jostled forward in the poem's elegiac consolation of remembrance and communal affiliation with the great company of the English nation who mourns in parallel consort. Even the Hebrew in mimetic translation does not itself access the pastoral restoration of the Jews in Judah without the Hebrew *biblical* context alluded to in the Hebrew poem. This is a subtle engagement indeed with the complexities of Anglo-Jewish identity. In the English translation, the death of King George III of England is the very diminution of the sun, stars, and moon. Such natural forces as are suggested by this triplet pertain to the figuring of the death of George as the eclipse of spiritual and political light, guidance. Only the restoration of the throne to right rule—the succession of the next King George—will restore the natural order of light in the world. In the Hebrew context for the biblical allusions, it is the locusts that must be cleared from the land. When God passes judgment and restores a pastoral peacefulness to the land, "strangers shall not pass through" Zion. England is not the site of a Jewish pastoral prophecy. Hurwitz's Hebrew underlines and emphasizes this point. In asserting the cultural authority and English nationalist inheritance advertised by the elegy to George, Hurwitz still registers his separation from English pastoral. That affiliation, as described earlier in this chapter, is not available to him. The consolation and cultural authority of a pastoral inherited from the Hebrew biblical text is the greater affiliation and greater solace in this elegy. Pastoral consolation is still among the desiderata of the English Jew; *English* pastoral can be at best only a diluted consolation, however.

In the April 1833 volume of the *New Monthly Magazine and Literary Journal*, the editor Edward Bulwer-Lytton, the popular English author, offers an opinion on "Cobbett and the Jews" as part of the "Monthly Commentary." Its defense of the Jews against Cobbett's complaints underlines the general recognition of Jewish alienation from English pastoral, and it sheds light on the clarity of understanding among those who would defend the Jewish presence in England:

> Cobbett's objection to the Jews is that they don't plough: he would ask who could produce a Jew who ever dug, who ever went to plough? It is only very lately that Jews have been permitted to hold land: how were they to learn to plough? The only piece of earth that Jews of former years were permitted to possess was a burying-ground: and this little farm the Jews dug and trenched, after all the approved principles of the drill-husbandry. . . . The two *foibles* of the English (as also, in another sense, their source of strength) are their love of the country and their adoration of the sea. Cobbett appears fresh from a chapter of Cottage Economy or Indian Corn; and the "stinking Jew" is put under his nose. Pah! He has no toleration for a suppliant with a beard. . . . His nostrils are full of the perfume of new-mown hay, and shall he suffer a skunker between the wind and his nobility?[65]

This lively quotation is exactly to the point (which is why I quote the first part as an epigraph to this chapter). The Jew in England, as understood by Cobbett and his ilk, is the skunker between the perfume of new-mown hay and the English nobility. The writers' masterly defense of the Jews peels the patina of self-righteousness from the skin of pastoral privilege. In so doing, they remind us of an attitude about Jewish propensities and Jewish belonging pervasive still in 1833, one that helps to clarify the subtler aspects of alienation to which writers like William Hazlitt, whom I discuss in the introduction, respond. They also remind us of one of the grounds for the genuine gratitude of the English Jews. After all, a public magazine could expose such anti-Jewish slander; it could also understand the import of the self-contradictions exemplified by Cobbett. When English Jews like Hurwitz speak of their longing for integration within the fabric of the English nation, it is with the consciousness of a cultural landscape that includes such diametrically opposed positions on the affiliation of the Jews.

Returning to Hurwitz's elegy, we will recall Emma Lyon's adaptation of Psalm 72, discussed in the previous chapter, which asks for God's endowment of the king with good judgment and righteousness. Hurwitz's stanza 7 begins in the Hebrew with a direct quotation of Psalm 72:8, "Let him rule from sea to sea." Psalm 72, "Of Solomon," situates the prayer to God for the strength and goodness of the king within a plea for the succor of the people. That succor is framed, in the psalm, as the bounty of divinely blessed nature: "Let the mountains produce well-being for the people, the hills, the reward of justice (72:3). The first line of Hurwitz's stanza, translated by Mays as "He ruled from sea to sea," is a fine counterpoint to the Israelites' mastery of natural forces as suggested in the psalm immediately cited in the stanza. The stanza proceeds to offer an encomium that offers particular complications, as its enthusiasm for George's religious liberalism could be read either as ironic, as criticism of the king by indirection or, alternatively, as simply stretching the limits of Jewish praise for an English king in 1820. Mays's translation of the stanza is a fine rendition:

> He ruled from sea to sea, in the mountains of the East.
> Over many peoples, differing in their laws.
> Their well-being he sought, he ruled over them like a father.
> He said, God tests the heart—not man.–

The Jews at this point had not yet obtained political emancipation, which was not to arrive until 1858. The liberal toleration and protection that George extended to the Jews did not include recognition of full civil or political rights. The legacy of the king under whom the American colonies were lost and far-flung wars were waged has indeed undergone, as noted, many reversals of historical judgment. There were periods during George's reign when his popularity among his subjects was high; there were other periods during which he was mocked widely as ineffectual. Still, Hurwitz would not have been unaware of the hyperbolic nature of praise for the king whose rule from sea to sea, whose rule over many peoples, differing in their laws, makes a weak comparison with Solomonic wisdom, as implied in the first line of the stanza. More to the point, the wording for "differing in their laws" is, as Mays points out, an allusion to the Book of Esther 3:8. The allusion in the Hebrew is not an exact quotation. The Hebrew of the Book of Esther—ודתיהם שנות—"whose laws are different," comes from the words of Haman, historically understood as among the worst enemies of the Jewish people. A vizier in the court of King Ahasuerus (Xerxes I), he resolved to kill all the Jews in the kingdom, in part as a response to a Jew—Mordechai—refusing to bow down to him. The biblical verse to which Hurwitz alludes follows Haman in his efforts first to make the king understand the fundamental differences of the Jews from the mainstream population, and then of his need to exterminate them:

> Haman then said to King Ahasuerus, "There is a certain people, scattered and dispersed among the other peoples in all the provinces of your realm, whose laws are different from those of any

other people and who do not obey the king's laws; and it is not in Your Majesty's interest to tolerate them. If it please Your Majesty, let an edict be drawn for their destruction, and I will pay ten thousand talents of silver to the stewards for deposit in the royal treasury." Thereupon the king removed his signet ring from his hand and gave it to Haman son of Hammedatha the Agagite, the foe of the Jews. And the king said, "The money and the people are yours to do with as you see fit." (Esther 3:8–11)

The story of Purim and its allusive significance for nineteenth-century Anglo-Jewish poets become clear again in the chapter on Grace Aguilar. In this particular instance, we have Hurwitz himself taking up the words of Haman, "the foe of the Jews." He does so, however, in the midst of putative praise for King George III's protection of them, which is already somewhat qualified by the situation of the Jews through his reign. The historical significance becomes tortuous, however, when we remember that King Ahasuerus's wife, Esther, is Jewish, a fact unbeknownst to the king at the time of Haman's persuasion. It is only when Esther pleads on behalf of her people that Ahasuerus, swayed by his beloved Esther, reverses the decree and has Haman hanged on the very gallows prepared for Mordechai. In Esther 3:8, Haman insists that the Jews do not follow the king's laws. In fact, so bound to following the king's laws are the Jews that when Esther is summoned to the court to become the queen of Ahasuerus, she obeys, disregarding the Jewish proscription against intermarriage. The king's laws are to be obeyed, short of apostasy. In the Book of Esther, one subtext is Jewish subservience to the whims of the king. The Jews who have other laws, who understand themselves as another people, are the Jews who all the same acknowledge the temporal supremacy of the king in the country of their domicile, whatever it may be. This is not merely good manners; it is political expediency. Queen Esther's relationship to the king enables her to plead for mercy. She first saves Mordechai. Then, after Haman is killed, she falls at the feet of Ahasuerus and weeps, begging him to avert the evil plot by Haman:

"If it please Your Majesty," she said, "and if I have won your favor and the proposal seems right to Your Majesty, and if I am pleasing to you—let dispatches be written countermanding these which were written by Haman son of Hammedatha the Agagite, embodying his plot to annihilate the Jews throughout the king's provinces.

For how can I bear to see the disaster which will befall my people!
And how can I bear to see the destruction of my kindred!" (Esther 8:5–6)

Jewish difference is herein underlined, and it is this description of difference that Hurwitz arrogates for his poem even in his expression of gratitude, on behalf of the Jews of England, for such protections as George afforded them. Esther is the king's wife, and to him she is subservient. Her "People" fated for destruction, however, are the Jews. Jeremiah, too, in exhorting the people to seek the peace of the city, reminds them, "For in the peace thereof shall ye have peace" (KJV). The Book of Esther has historically provoked commentary and discussion about the trials of Esther and her willingness to marry outside the faith. The story finds its way into various talmudic tales as well. It is a book with a complicated history of exegesis, for it situates the Jew very clearly as a foreigner within a land in which the Jews must not take their rights for granted. Hurwitz is not drawing parallels between George and King Ahasuerus, or between George and Haman. He is appropriating one of the central biblical narratives of survival in a hostile country through the good intercessions of the Jews with the king. This is emphatically not a claim against England as hostile so much as it is an echo of a foundational narrative about Jewish history and Jewish survival and continuity throughout history. When Hurwitz inherits the form of the gracious English elegy for a potentate, he also inherits the Jewish legacy of recognizing the Jew's stake in understanding his relationship to the potentate. No such nuance is conveyed in the translation of Coleridge:

> His Love was bounded by no Clime:
> Each diverse Race, each distant Clan
> He govern'd by this truth sublime,
> "God only knows the heart—not man."

In this context, we do well to remember Lord Byron's mockery of George in *The Vision of Judgment*. The narrator, satirizing Southey's sycophancy toward the memory of George, reminds us both of the pomp that of necessity accompanies commemoration, and that non-members of the Church of England have "shammed." Given George's opposition to emancipation for Catholics, Nonconforming Protestants, and Jews, and given his opposition to American independence, Coleridge's translation reads as simply hyperbolic nonsense, especially if read as the putative meaning of an orthodox Jew. But Hurwitz is navigating the tension of his diverse inheritances through a masterful manipulation of allusion and citation. In this, Coleridge's translation is perhaps aggressively clever in the last line of the above stanza; citing 1 Kings, God indeed only knows the heart, not man. In this instance, God alone—and those who read and understand the Hebrew allusions—know at least one aspect of the heart of Hyman Hurwitz in his encomium to George III.

The elegy concludes with a prayer to God, rendered by Coleridge as "hymn." In the Hebrew, the concluding section is called תפלה (*tefillah*), "prayer." It functions, in a manner reminiscent of Jewish liturgical custom, as a request for God to hear the prayer of the petitioners. The difference is telling, as *tefillah* was the name used for the *Amidah* during talmudic times, the *Amidah* being the central liturgy in organized Judaism. The refrain is repeated five times, and in the Hebrew it in fact directly quotes from the *Amidah*'s well-known petition for God to "hear our voices." Here is the Hebrew of the refrain:

רחמיך אל! נעמו.
חסדך וטובך עצמו.
אנא אל! שמע קולנו
ורצה את תפלתנו

I offer now Mays's translation:

Your mercy O God! Is pleasing.
Your faithful love and your goodness are strong.
Wherefore O God! Hear our cry
and grant our prayer.

I would suggest that the last line would be better understood as expressing a wish that God "desire" (rather than "grant") our prayer, in the sense of "accepting" the prayer. Furthermore, for Mays's "cry" ("Hear our cry") I would suggest "voice," the standard rendition in most translations of the original source in the *Amidah*. I offer now the relevant lines from the *Amidah*:

שמע קולנו יהוה אלהנו חוס ורחם עלינו, וקבל ברחמים וברצון את תפילתינו.

As in Abendanon's poem discussed above, the allusion to the Hebrew *Amidah* could not be missed by any synagogue-attending Jew with the least smattering of Hebrew. It may be translated as follows:

Hear our voice, O Lord our God; spare us and have mercy upon us,
and accept our prayer in mercy and favor.

Coleridge makes of the refrain a jingoistic and more familiarly Christian-sounding stanza:

Thy mercies, Lord, are sweet;
And Peace and Mercy meet,
Before thy Judgment seat:
Lord, hear us! We entreat!

Coleridge has "Peace and Mercy meet" where Hurwitz has lovingkindness and goodness joined in "strength." Coleridge does pick up the emphatic nature of what he translates as "Lord, hear us!" The reference from the *Amidah* of this verse is to the sixteenth benediction, in the middle section of the *Amidah*. There is a tradition that these prayers were spoken by the Israelites in their slavery in Egypt; it has an impressive provenance, that is, one that even predates the desert, when the very foundational narrative of Judaism begins: we were slaves in Egypt. During the *Amidah*, the community makes petitions that are statutory. When this sixteenth benediction is offered, the point of the "Hear our voice" segment, personal supplications and meditations may be inserted as well. The request to be heard by God, however, does not refer only to such private additions. The plea to be heard refers to the full liturgical experience. The very next line in this part of the *Amidah* continues, "for you are a God who hears prayers and supplications." It concludes by announcing, "Blessed are you God, who hears prayer." This is not the only time in the Jewish liturgy in which we witness the plea for a voice to be heard by a God who is defined by His ability and willingness to hear. In fact, it is a dominant motif, one encapsulated by its position in the *Amidah*.

If Hurwitz has situated his elegy within the norms of English patriotic expectations, he absorbs such patriotism into the Jewish liturgical inheritance of the "extra" petitions permitted during the sixteenth benediction of the *Amidah*; that is, the conclusion of the poem reminds us of the structure of formal possibilities for shaping our utterances and prayers. At this point in the *Amidah*, extra supplications are permitted. So, too, does Hurwitz remind us and insist upon the propriety of his praise for George III and his supplications on behalf of the health of the royal family.

We are herein returned to the motif that pervades my reading of Anglo-Jewish poetry: the emphasis on trying to understand the *meaning* of establishing a voice, especially where the intimacy of one's own subjectivity is challenged precisely by the conflicting demands of hearing and being heard. To project a voice into the public sphere is no guarantee of being heard in the fullness of the speaker's complexity. More pressingly, neither is it any guarantee that one has constituted a voice that is fully answerable to the demands of one's own private self-divisions. This prayer with which Hurwitz concludes his elegiac encomium to George III is one that finally throws into definitive relief the tensions inherent in defining a voice that is heard over the din of gratitude, frustration, and alienation.

CHAPTER 3

The Early Efforts of Celia and Marion Moss

> A Jew may be born in England—he may be bred there—he may speak the language, obey the laws, conform to the customs of an Englishman; he may cigar it, drink it, game it, race it, box it, as naturally as the most genuine bit of John Bull extant—and be an alien to all intents and purposes notwithstanding.
> —*The Spectator*, May 8, 1830

In 1839, Marion and Celia Moss published their first volume of poetry, *Early Efforts: A Volume of Poems, by the Misses Moss, of the Hebrew Nation, Aged 18 and 16*. It is a volume laden with multiple—and often mutually contradictory—presentations of subjectivity, many of them relating to their Jewish authors' consideration of England as a nation, an idea, and as an anchor for identity. The year 1839 also marks the publication date of Thomas Carlyle's pamphlet *Chartism*, in which he invoked "the condition of England question," a phrase he coined to elucidate his dismay at the plight of the working classes and the consequent upheavals then roiling the nation. The condition of England, in fact, was to be taken up as a touchstone phrase for the effects of industrialization on the working poor; the "condition of England" novel, a subgenre of early Victorian fiction, soon came to prominence, Dickens's *Hard Times* being the most accessible example. In citing Carlyle in relation to my introduction to the Moss sisters in this book, I hope to shed further light on some of the contexts for Anglo-Jewish late Romanticism, especially as they affect the self-understanding of its authors. I do not suggest that Carlyle or the Mosses were reading one another at this point, and I am not positing direct influence. Rather, my consideration of the condition of England provides another forum in which to understand not only the grounds for agitation on the part of the disenfranchised, but also the self-contradictory positions about the idea of England as taken up with remarkable poignancy by the Mosses in their poetry. Beginning this chapter with Carlyle enables me to gauge one reading of the climate of ideas in which the Mosses are immersed, one that adds further texture to the larger study. In so far as the stability of English identity depends, in part, on the cultural reification of hearth and home within the wider confines of the landscape, the basic questions about the quotidian reality of English subjects are increasingly being asked throughout England, not just by the Jews. This is a dynamic we have seen before in this study: whose hearth, whose home, whose valorized landscape? These are questions for the champions of disenfranchised industrial workers no less than for Jewish authors, and although the defining concerns of the workers are by no means identical to those of Jewish authors, the comparison is illuminating. For both quasi-groups, England has been, at turns (and sometimes simultaneously), alienating, sheltering, dismissive, grudgingly tolerant. I would appropriate Carlyle's questions of 1839 as a springboard into a discussion of the Moss poets' volume of 1839, and its vexed reflections on their experience of England's condition, as a forum for further taking the measure of the paradoxes and contradictions of one frame of reference within the majority culture.

The Condition of England (and of Its Jews)

The immediate occasion of Carlyle's pamphlet was the radical campaign being undertaken by the Chartists demanding reform of parliamentary rules.[1] Having collected more than 1.25 million signatures for "the People's Charter," which had been composed for the London Working Men's Association, the Chartists nonetheless failed to realize any of their goals when they presented the Charter to the House of Commons in June 1839. These included goals intended to address deficits in the Reform Bill of 1832, which enlarged the franchise, but only for property-owning middle-class men. Now the Chartists were demanding universal male suffrage; constituencies of equal size; secret balloting; payment for members of Parliament; parliamentary elections to take place every year; and abolition of the property qualification for becoming a member of Parliament. The unrest that followed the rejection of the

People's Charter was widely seen as confirmation of the putatively radical nature of the demands. Indeed, for many, the fear of Chartism and the Chartists became linked with the memory of the French Revolution.[2] Carlyle took up the subject of Chartism in large part because he wished to champion the rights of the working classes, but not always on terms that would frankly make common cause with most Chartists themselves. For Carlyle, the neglect of and ingratitude toward the working classes were scandalous, and the official suppression by force of those who continued to agitate for reform was a spectacle that diminished the integrity of Parliament:

> A Reformed Parliament, one would think, should inquire into popular discontents before they get the length of pikes and torches! For what end at all are men, Honourable Members and Reform Mem bers, sent to St. Stephen's, with clamour and effort; kept talking, struggling, motioning and counter-motioning? The condition of the great body of people in a country is the condition of the country itself.[3]

Are Jews properly a part of the "great body of people in [the country]"? May they be counted within the great body, inextricably within it? These are questions that do not occupy Carlyle specifically, of course, but in the wake of the political and cultural changes of the times, changes that occasion deep questions about the condition of the historically disenfranchised and ignored, they are questions that do naturally arise among the Jews and among those who contemplate the condition of the Jews in England. Remember that the historical struggle to abolish the Jewish civil and political disabilities ended, depending on how one counts, either in 1858, when Lionel de Rothschild took his seat in the House of Commons, or 1871, with the abolition of the University Tests Act, which suspended the requirement to subscribe to the articles of the Church of England as a condition of holding fellowships in England's ancient universities.[4] The immediate catalyst for the agitation that led up to this political change was, in fact, occasioned by Numa Hartog, son of Marion Moss. He had been named "Chief Wrangler" at Cambridge University, but was unable to take up the fellowship that came with it because he was a professing Jew.[5] I will return to such implications later, but it is important to note now that the condition of England question involved a limited engagement with only a circumscribed number of the disenfranchised. The great glorious nation could not function with most of its working poor living in deplorable conditions, but "nation" was still defined on "the true faith of a Christian," and national Christianity, which meant Church of England Anglicanism, could not, for most people, be separated from the central meaning of Englishness, especially as the forging of the meaning of the nation was still very much an ongoing concern. What is the condition of Jews in England when it is unclear if Jews can be understood as *of* England? Indeed, what is the condition of Jews in England when "England" is increasingly recognized as a concept still in the process of being constituted?

Among the remedies proposed by Carlyle for the deplorable nature of the condition of England was a stronger proprietary role to be played by the landed aristocracy. Not content to see the Chartists' demand for autonomy on its own terms, he asked that the aristocracy match its privileges to its tacit obligations, which included proper guidance, or shepherding, of the working poor. As Michael Levin argues, "For Carlyle, then, the truth of power was that it carries the obligation of proper leadership."[6] The neglect by the governing classes—and "governing" is how he perceived their proper role—is the immediate cause of the unrest, and Carlyle warns that further unrest will follow in the absence of firmer guidance. Such direction can only be forthcoming when understanding of and sympathy for the working classes are present:

> The struggle that divides the upper and lower in society over Europe, and more painfully and notably in England than elsewhere, this too is a struggle which will end and adjust itself as all other struggles do and have done, by making the right clear and the might clear; not otherwise, than by that. Meantime, the questions, why are the Working Classes discontented; what is their condition, economical, moral, in their houses and their hearts, as it is in reality and as they figure it to themselves to be; what do they complain of; what ought they, and ought they not to complain of?—these are measurable questions; on some of these any common mortal, did he but turn his eyes to them, might throw some light.[7]

This effort to understand the heart and soul, as it were, of the working classes is joined both to a remarkable effort to understand further their own self-understanding ("and as they figure it to themselves to be") and to a paternalistic effort to understand what they ought not to be complaining of. Carlyle here treats class as if it were a category for identity; that is, he harnesses rhetoric better suited to discussion about belief. The conceptions of Englishness as well as class to which Carlyle subscribes are generalizations in which some segments of the population would never have been able to locate themselves. This provides me with a particularly apt segue into a discussion of the publication of *Early Efforts* in 1839. For in 1839 we are in the midst not only of the political agitation known as Chartism but of the period during which Jews are gaining greater integration into the mainstream of English life.[8]

Familiarization, however, is not tantamount to cultural integration. For the Jews of England still, self-understanding is related to a complicated rapport with the English political nation as well as the English cultural inheritance. Furthermore, the literary expression of that relationship throws into sharp relief Jewish authors' conflicted apprehension of the subtler forms of alienation. Where Carlyle asks what it means to be a working-class Englishman in 1839, and what that very question means to working-class Englishmen, the Moss sisters in their poetry interrogate the meaning of subjectivity within the paternalistic structure that Carlyle identifies also as the remedy for Chartism.

Finding a Voice

The Moss sisters experiment with the posture that they may take their cultural authority for granted, as if no impediments, political or existential, could obstruct their lyric power. The question of cultural entitlement surfaces explicitly only when their youth and status as women are foregrounded. Otherwise, to sing the Lord's song in a foreign land itself is offered as their just inheritance, even as the English Jew in their poetry is presented often in the exile's habit, longing for Zion. Such forthrightness is perpetually subjected to ironic reflection; their poetry, which often stages a confidence in the simplicity of their hybrid identities, also pulls the rug out from under their own self-definitions. Entitled, yet self-consciously in exile; mature in insight, yet with a still nascent identity; grateful for safe haven, yet angry at England's history of inhospitality and violence toward the Jews: what we have, finally, is the presentation of a self-hood hovering between various anchors. If this does not quite leave them lost at sea, then it does make for a perpetually shifting landscape.

Celia and Marion Moss jointly published their first and only book of poetry in 1839, when they were eighteen and sixteen, respectively. The poems are presented as if by a single voice; authorship is not differentiated until the back of the volume. Though the book did go into a second edition, and though they continued to publish poetry in periodicals occasionally throughout their lives, this was their only book of verse. Both women went on to write prose fiction, both together and individually, and Marion, now Marion Hartog (having married Alphonse Hartog in 1845), established the *Jewish Sabbath Journal* in 1855, the first Jewish women's periodical in history.[9] The title of the poetry collection, *Early Efforts,* is obtrusively apologetic not on account of the Jewish preoccupations of much of the verse, but because the authors are merely teenagers. Likewise the preface, which pleads, "If we have been too presumptuous in deeming them fit for publication, we are sure that sufficient allowances will be made for all the disadvantages under which we have laboured, and which are at all times inseparable from first attempts." In this, the Moss sisters are merely conforming to the convention by which women present their poetry. A prefatory apology for the presumption, like the one written by Emma Lyon discussed in Chapter 1, both establishes necessary deference and disclaims it. I suggest that the signaling of juvenilia, however, is not the only sense in which the collection is an "early effort." It is early in its nascent effort at self-definition; more broadly, it is early in its positioning of the Jew, and especially of the Jewish woman, within English society: the effort to define the English Jew within, and relative to, mainstream English culture is still immature in this part of the nineteenth century.

The Moss children grew up with many of the benefits of a secularizing household. Their father read secular literary books aloud to the family, including the poetry of Byron. When the girls were discovered writing their own poetry, however, their father objected: girls should not be participating in activities that could distract them from the duties of femininity or make them less marriageable. The first challenge to their cultural adeptness, then, was their father, who threatened to burn their books if they persisted in their writing efforts. Having been threatened with destruction of their books, the girls coped with the crisis by committing their favorite works of literature to memory.[10] As such, the English canon, or at least parts thereof, were fully internalized, digested sufficiently to guard against any external opposition. If Jewish identity is at odds with English culture, at least in part, then here we have an instance of Jewish social norms inverting the budding process of Jewish cultural emancipation. No Emma Lyon, with her brilliant inheritance of learning at her father's knee, the Moss sisters learned from their father both the love of English literature and the lesson that producing it would be a negation of their proper identity as perceived by the Jewish father. For all these histrionics, they took up the pen again and published *Early Efforts* when their father fell ill. This was undertaken to supplement the family income, and there is no suggestion that they met with resistance from any family members.

It is no wonder, then, that many of their early efforts to write poetry are early efforts to define themselves as Jewish women within the English nation. What iteration of the writerly self could they possibly produce under the shadows cast by their earliest childhood efforts, ones that yielded only a father's volatile scorn? One immediate need would be to present themselves as feminine still, authentic women still, and entirely in compliance with traditional expectations. Still marriageable and still infused with the spirit of sensibility, then, they offer pious versions of themselves that would put their conservatism beyond doubt. They include lyrics of sentimental reflection such as "To a Young Mother," "To a Robin," or "The Tear of Sympathy." Not to be perceived as distracted from the duties of femininity, there are sufficient lyrics in this collection to reassure any interested suitor or ambivalent father. "To a Young Mother" is paradigmatic in this regard:

> Thou hast heard thy child speak, and Oh! What is more dear
> Than the first prattling accents of childhood to hear;
> To the heart of a parent a bliss worth all blisses,
> And the mouth of the speaker is cover'd with kisses.[11] (p. 2)

The unremarkable sentimentalism here appears superficially to lack nuance. The lyric's authors are surely qualified for marriage and child-bearing. They are young, conventional women writing these lines, and nothing more. Or are they?

These are young women who know something also about the relationship between a child's speech and the parent's response. They are vividly attuned, then, to a corresponding dynamic: the relationship between the presumption of lyric authority and the audience that processes lyric. The simplicity of the above-quoted lines is suggestive of the complications of their own efforts to be heard. Focusing as it does on the parent's pleasure in hearing the child's first words, one may perhaps detect some resonance of the girls' first efforts at writing poetry. In their case, however, the pleasingly simple paradigm is inverted: their father became enraged, after all, when they were discovered writing poetry, and he threatened to burn their books if they did not leave off writing. The speaker of this poem celebrates first and foremost the child's first words, the "first prattling accents of childhood." The qualities of listening, and of knowing when to listen, and of knowing when and when not to speak, in fact function as clear leitmotifs throughout the collection. The Jews are represented in "The Feast of Trumpets" (referring to the Jewish New Year, Rosh Ha-Shana) as "the listening people" (43). Lovers in this volume not only speak but also listen with particular acuity, as do the pious. What does it mean to be heard, then? This is a question that has been persistently asked not only of Jewish poets, not only by women poets more generally, but by all those who toil in lyric.

It is a question that is also asked in interrogations of the condition of England that seek to access the self-understanding of the conventionally disenfranchised. If the effort is made more difficult by being a woman, and yet more difficult by being a Jewish woman in a Christian land, and still more complicated by being young and inexperienced, it surely becomes even more vexed if the authors are young Jewish women whose father threatens violence to their books if they continue to write. This is no mere biographical reduction of the poetry. For if *Early Efforts* is anything, it is an uneasy effort to establish credentials in so many different venues that the collection finally reads as a disconnected series of experiments in the fashioning and presentation of selfhood. I would suggest that the very political as well as cultural conditions in which they are situated in England undergird such volatile self-fashioning. The voice that performs the fashioning will now be my concern.

The Moss sisters are themselves canny listeners, and they persistently represent the speaking voice as deeply invested in interpreting sounds and in gauging their effect on others. In 1833, John Stuart Mill famously tried to define lyric poetry, and his very Romanticism-inflected response was to distinguish it from eloquence, which is merely heard: lyric is "overheard."[12] But this notion of an overheard lyric voice communing with its own subjectivity depends for its efficacy on a confidence in the consensual understanding of the audience that overhears, a recognition encountered by each of the authors studied in this book.

Canonical Romantic poets, to be sure, sometimes ironize and inflect such assumptions, but received notions about the relationship between lyric and reading audience retain a privileged position throughout the period. Romantic subjectivity is still the ground of a common understanding that presupposes that we all know—if only we could truly hear—that which is most permanent and enduring in human nature. It depends, in other words, on a subjectivity that takes its place within a fiction about an identifiable common humanity. The generalization of the human and the confidence in the subjectivity of the overhearing listeners are diluted in this volume by the Moss sisters. The definition of subjectivity to which they sometimes gesture does not quite take root in them, at least not with categorical or unquestioned stability. Carlyle chastises Parliament for its inability to establish insight about the dissatisfaction of the nation and for its refusal to give voice to those who are incommunicado, by which he understands the vast body of the people. The Mosses are preoccupied with the various meanings of voice, but neither the voice of Parliament nor the voice of Carlyle's outrage could properly appropriate their unique position. It is not that the Moss sisters are industrial workers, of course; I draw the analogy because neither are they members of the landed aristocracy nor, for that matter, of the English nation as conventionally defined. Of Parliament—and remember, professing Jews were excluded from becoming members—Carlyle complains: "Whatsoever great British interest can the least speak for itself, for that beyond all they are called to speak. They are either speakers for that great dumb toiling class which cannot speak, or they are nothing that one can well specify" (154). Since "the Collective Wisdom of the Nation has availed us as good as nothing whatever" (154), Carlyle is left to wish for "a genuine understanding by the upper classes of society what it is that the under classes intrinsically mean; a clear interpretation of the thought which at heart torments these wild inarticulate souls, struggling there, with inarticulate uproar, like dumb creatures in pain, unable to speak what is in them!" (155). The Mosses address themselves to the nuances of voice, to the inchoate longings of their souls as much as to the incapacity of their interlocutors fully to comprehend their utterances. They constitute their voice, however, in the full knowledge that they do not fully qualify for membership within the generalization of English community by which they could be spoken for.

It is with such a dynamic in mind that I return to one of the questions that I raised earlier—how naïve, or how unsophisticated, is the voice in the lyric "To a Young Mother"? It is important to recognize that this voice is staged in a volume that contains other iterations of agency, which in fact makes it more difficult to construe its significance. In this poem, other sounds are contrasted with those of the child, and all of those other sounds pale in comparison. But the parent's role as listener also plays a crucial part in the literary inheritance of this particular poem and more generally claimed by the Moss sisters. Coleridge's famous "Frost at Midnight" tells of the absolute silence which forms the background to the sound of his son's breathing. It is this sound, which he fondly hears while thinking about the disappointments in his own life and early childhood, which connects with nothing less than the eternal language of God:

> Dear Babe, that sleepest cradled by my side,
> Whose gentle breathings, heard in this deep calm,
> Fill up the interspersed vacancies
> And momentary pauses of thought!

> . . . .
> . . . so shalt thou see and hear
> The lovely shapes and sounds intelligible
> Of that eternal language, which thy God
> Utters, who from eternity doth teach
> Himself in all, and all things in himself. (ll. 44–62)

Coleridge's fond listening perhaps provides an interesting contrastive point with the Moss poets' father. A father who listens, in fact, is precisely the chief fantasy conveyed toward the end of the *Early Efforts* volume, in a lyric entitled "Father's Lament." Here the poetess has been killed off, for reasons we are not told, and the father laments the loss of his daughter by way of lamenting the loss of her poetry. In this poem, the father, like the father of "Frost at Midnight," has heard "the stillness of the evening hour" broken only by the sounds of his child. The silence now comes from the silencing of her voice forever. The lament of this father, then, focuses the daughter in the terms of her voice, and he processes his grief through the prism of his praise for, and regret at the loss of, her song.

> The cloud of death thy brow hath shaded,
> Thy cheek hath lost its healthful glow,
> The luster of thine eye hath faded.
> Thy joyous laugh is silenced now;
> And never more shall song or smile
> Of thine, this aching heart beguile.
> . . . .
> Oft have I heard thy sweet voice break,
> The stillness of the evening hour;
> Oft have I heard thy lute awake
> Soft echos with its thrilling power,
> That voice of melody is mute,
> And hush'd for ever is thy lute.
> No voice shall e'er attempt to sing
> The heavenly strains that thou hast sung;
> No hand shall dare to touch a string
>
> O'er which thine own hath once been flung
> I'd rather rend thy lute in twain,

Than it should breathe of joy again.
The very breeze that murmurs by
Thy bow'r at eve, and wakes its strings,
This riven heart with agony,
That's almost wrought to madness wrings,
I cannot, cannot bear to hear
Sounds that were once to me so dear.
(pp. 119–120)[13]

The voice of this overheard poet is mute. The father is bereft of a voice. And it is voice that defines the highest authority for the Mosses ultimately, even through their highlighting of versions of themselves that conform to feminine norms. In this, we might be reminded of Psalm 29, which is central to the synagogue Torah service:

The voice of the Lord is powerful; the voice of the Lord is full of majesty. The voice of the Lord breaketh the cedars . . . (29.4–5)

Early Efforts shifts dramatically in its mode of presenting its authors, but it is unwavering in its recognition of the importance of establishing a voice and of construing the audience that processes voice. However we read this instability, it is clear that they are performing various allegiances, some of them mutually contradictory, and performing various identities. In some ways, they are gesturing toward the cultural conditions by which their voice could only ever be unstable, could only ever be fraught with tensions that undermine its efforts at definitive self-definition. Such poems as "To a Young Mother" establish their authority as women possessing the gift of sympathy, and as young women who know their place. Other poems present encomiums to England, queen of the waves and example to the nations. Here they reveal themselves to be fierce patriots, sharing in all the nationalist fervor of any true Englishman born and bred to pride in the land. Still others are dramatic monologues whose speakers are Jewish exiles mourning for Jerusalem. The boldest of the poems in this collection presents a narrative documentary of the infamous York Massacre, the terrible massacre by an angry Christian mob of the Jews of York in 1190. This is the only poem that contains explanatory, historical footnotes, lest any English countryman not realize fully the reality of the historical relation between Christians and Jews in England. The authority of the oppressed, of those who remain tenaciously strong through adversity, is herein thrown into relief; I return to this poem below. The collection is peppered also with instances of quiet protest, subtle self-assertion, and sometimes even strident affirmations of feminine identity that defy conventional stereotypes.

The Moss poets wage war on the traditional notions of feminine beauty, insisting that strength of mind is paramount. In "The Fadeless Flower," a lyric of quatrains that is suggestive of an English sonnet without the concluding couplet, they recall Shakespeare's musings on beauty and mutability; however, what truly endures is not writing, but intellectual power:

> The finest form will moulder in the dust;
> The brightest eye will sink into decay;
> The fairest brow will wither 'neath death's touch;
> The sweetest flowers soonest fade away.
> Why then, by man, should loveliness be deem'd
> As the best gift bestow'd on woman-kind;
> The brightest germ from whence her actions spring,
> The noblest gem of woman, is her mind.
> That mind that never yields beneath despair
> That still shines forth in sorrow's wasting hour;
> That will resist the keenest sting of care,
> This, this, in woman is a fadeless flower. (p. 78)

Spirit over flesh; mind over matter: the triumph of mind is the triumph of endurance and defiance. Shakespeare's sonnets, of course, would resist mutability through the immortalizing capacities of verse. The beauty of the beloved is sustained through the mind's creation of artifice: "Yet, do thy worst old Time, despite thy wrong, / My love shall in my verse ever live young" ("Sonnet 19" 13–14).[14] Art, he insists, immortalizes beauty. The "gem" of the "mind," the true "fadeless flower," for the Mosses is neither Shakespeare's enduring art nor Wordsworth's sustenance in nature. The poem not only redefines the value of beauty and of women, it redefines the metaphoric significance of "flower." The Moss sisters are herein not rejecting the pastoral so much as they would appropriate it to signify that which is entirely detached from pastoral. In this, they are decidedly Jewish in sensibility and defining their Romantic inheritance in terms consonant with that Jewish identity; that is, they recognize the subtleties of their alienation from the pastoral inheritance of English Romanticism even while mobilizing alternative strategies to access it. Wordsworth sings that the "mind of man becomes / A thousand times more beautiful than the earth / on which he dwells" (*The Prelude* 13.446–448). For Wordsworth in "Tintern Abbey," the mature mind has gained sufficient critical distance from the all-consuming love of nature to be able to feel, finally, "A presence that disturbs me with the joy / Of elevated thoughts" (94–95): nature converts itself into a giver of that which is beyond the tactile. For the Mosses, the permanence of intellectual and spiritual beauty, the "fadeless flower," dissolves the image of visual spectacle altogether. The iconic Romantic sign (after grazing sheep) by which beauty in nature is conventionally valorized—the flower—is converted to an assertion that pastoral commonplaces can be transcended. What is a human being? Dust. What is a woman? She who can determine her will. The abstraction of mind endures, and it need not be converted into artifice. It does not bow to despair or sorrow or the sting of care. It "never yields," it "resists." In woman the fadeless flower is the stuff of revolution.

It should therefore come as no surprise that they position a song of Jewish protest as belonging to a girl. "The Jewish Girl's Song" is an apostrophe to Judea, lamenting the destruction of the Holy Temple. As Nadia Valman has shown, such poems represent the Moss poets appropriating "the rhetoric of early Victorian femininity as a literary strategy in the cause of Jewish rights.[15]" A twenty-line poem, its concluding eight lines reveal all of the glories of the "fadeless flower" as the speaker muses on the reversal of the enemy's fortunes:

> But weep not, thy day-star again shall arise!
> Again shall thy children be rank'd with the free,
> While Rome is a thing which all nations despise,
> The proud city itself is a ruin like thee!
> She laugh'd at thy fall, thy destruction enjoyed,
> But she who destroyed thee herself is destroyed,
> Her shrines too are fallen, and trampled her fanes,
> And nought but the shade of her glory remains. (p. 83)

There are many laments for Jerusalem and for exile throughout the volume. Some poems assume the voice of an unidentified woman lamenting the loss of a love in battle, while others narrate a tale of war and captivity in unspecified lands by indeterminate people. Exile and loss, then, are motifs throughout the poetry, and they are intermittently narrowed to describe exile and loss suffered by the Jews. "The Jewish Girl's Song" is remarkable for its title, as nothing else in the poem itself would suggest that the lyric is uttered by a girl. And since the collection in which the poem appears is written by Jewish girls, the significance is self-referential in ways that acknowledge both the strengths and limitations of the authors' self-fashioning. This is a poetry of exile that resists the elegiac. It is a poetry that resonates with the multifaceted self-positioning of the Moss sisters: Rome is not to be equated with England, but neither are the Moss sisters free to ignore their complicated inheritance, one which recognizes their affiliation with a history of exile as much as their intricate negotiations of the subtler forms of alienation within their contemporary England. The poem's speaker does not call down vengeance upon Rome; she merely observes the justice of its ironic reversal, that "she who destroyed thee herself is destroyed." Who is this Jewish girl voicing the song of tenacity and vengeance? Strong of mind, unyielding to the despair of exile, this is a girl whose triumph over pain is the indulgence in schadenfreude. Is this really the fadeless flower? Strong and defiant, she describes her people as unbroken:

> The wild deer in freedom bounds over thy plain,
> But thy once happy people in exile remain;
> Yet their hearts still yearn to thee, their spirits unbroke,
> Tho' forced to submit to the Edomite's yoke.

Still in exile, still yearning to be free, and finally triumphant in angry vengeful pride, this is truly the song of a Jewish girl whose strength of mind has found no other outlet. If she recognizes herself in the mirror of her enemy's face, then she does not assume the blame. "Her shrines too are fallen, and trampled her fanes," she exults, but her people, though unbroken in their devotion to Judea, are still in exile.

The voice of exile is a voice all the same. It is the voice of the fadeless flower no less than the voice of the father finally recognizing the value and the authority of the daughter's voice. It is the voice that joins itself to several proud histories in which voice is the ground that defines one's cultural authority as well as one's cultural belonging. And it is this question of specifically cultural belonging that defines the Moss sisters' apprehension of the conditions of England in which they labor in lyric. Their poetry cannot rest on confidence in the consensual understanding of the meaning of landscape, or of literary inheritance, or of quotidian ease of being. As such, their voice is not registered within the public recognition of what constitutes the condition of England. Still, it is a voice tenacious in its insistence that the effort is early, that it may yet project itself into a horizon that recognizes its being.

The York Massacre

"The Massacre of the Jews at York: A Historical Poem" takes up the subject of England's self-definition, or at least one aspect of it, astonishingly, from the perspective of the Jews who would interrogate its congruence with the received orthodoxy of England's historical meaning. York Castle, as I described briefly in the previous chapter, is the site of the infamous York Massacre of 1190, where 150 Jews had taken refuge from an angry mob, and where they chose to commit mass suicide rather than submit to conversion. The Mosses' poem about it is the only one in the volume with footnotes. Like Charlotte Smith's footnotes for "Beachy Head," which establish her scholarly, scientific and cultural authority on the subject matter of the poem in defiance of conventional expectations for women,[16] the footnotes of "The Massacre of the Jews at York" throw into sharp relief the historical reality which they have mastered, and which they read against their inheritance of English values even as they define their self-positioning as Jews. In the footnotes they quote from Henry Milman's 1830 *History of the Jews* to emphasize that their historical tale has the sanction of scholarly history, and not only Jewish history. If they apologize in their preface to the volume as a whole that the poetry is merely an *early* effort on account of which they have presumed upon the public—again, the conventional disclaimer for women poets at the time—the citation of Milman requires no such special pleading, and by extension, neither should their presumption to narrativize English history as it relates to the Jews. Milman was an Anglican priest, a highly regarded poet, dramatist, essayist and historian, whose idiosyncratic treatment of the Jews in his *History of the Jews* was heavily criticized by his peers. Still, he had a brilliant university career as Professor of Poetry at Oxford; and though by the time he was made Dean of St. Paul's in 1849 it was already ten years after the publication of the Mosses' *Early Efforts*, by 1835 he was already Canon of Westminster. Milman went on to write a history of Christianity as well in 1840. His family also enjoyed notable connections, as his father was physician to King George III.[17] I cite these instances of his public authority to emphasize the role his imprint plays in the Moss sisters' poem on the York massacre. They appropriate Milman as an authority with public standing not only as a scholar but as a highly respected Church of England luminary. And they fully presume upon this arrogation of the status of the Very Reverend Canon of Westminster precisely to qualify the import of Christian violence against the Jews in the context of the meaning of English nationhood. It is a "historical poem," a tale of truth, and as such, resonates with the national tales common in the Romantic period. Indeed, as Katie Trumpener reminds us (discussing primarily fictional prose), "The national tale is a genre developed initially by female authors, who from the outset address questions of cultural distinctiveness, national policy and political separatism."[18] Only here, the nationalist sentiment is qualified by a volume that intersperses encomiums to England with laments for the dispersal of the Jews, and lyrics of exilic longing for Zion. Nationhood in this poem, "The Massacre of the Jews at York," is defiantly a reference to specifically Jewish nationhood as conceived by two young English women who are also insistently English, but its implicit assertions of cultural distinctiveness are refracted through a prism of longing for the majority culture to affiliate with *their* insistence on the true valor of England.[19] The enmity of medieval Christendom toward the Jews, and the more recent memory of the qualifications to hospitality with which it resonates, become the signature not of dislocation for the Jewish poets, but rather of a defiant belonging within England and within its cultural heritage. This is a rather remarkable turning of the tables. It also reminds its readers of another meaning of nationalist pride as expressed in more conventional forms of Christian English nationalism. This *is* a historical poem, and its historicity is implicitly sanctioned by no less an authority than the Very Reverend Henry Milman. In the logic of the poem's structure: It really happened like the poets are telling it; see the footnotes. But it is not *merely* history, and that is what makes all the difference. It is a historical *poem*, and its length and narrative style suggest near epic ambitions. As such, it presumes upon the authority of literary inheritance and lyrical rendering even while staking its claim to historical accuracy. This epical poem about the Jews as outcasts implicitly becomes a poem about their cultural belonging, even as it presumes to define the essence of Englishness for the majority English culture.

The poem is prefaced by a quotation from Byron, one of the *Hebrew Melodies*, "From the Day of the Destruction of Jerusalem by Titus": "And scattered and scorn'd as thy people may be, / Our worship, O Father, is only for thee." If Byron presumes upon the authority of Jewish voice in grieving for the ruins of Jerusalem and the Temple, then the Moss sisters presume as Englishmen and as Jews beholding the site of York Castle, an English monument. The epigraph from Byron may well elevate their participation in Jewish nationalist longing to the status of high Romantic lyric, but the voice of their poetry is obtrusively not an appropriated language. Unlike Byron, they speak not in the voice of exile, but in the recognizable idioms of English historical poetry, and they localize themselves in time and place, at the castle, in 1190.

> There is an old and stately hall,
> Hung round with many a spear and shield,
> And sword and buckler on the wall
> Won from the foe in tented field. (p. 11)

The "scattered and scorn'd" people of Byron's lyric that prefaces the poem are here the Jews of glorious England, and if they are scattered in the sense of dispersed from Jerusalem, and scorned in this English pogrom of 1190, the position of their poetic speaker is very much *of* England. In fact, they are the English who recognize that the English monument itself is displaced from its "natural" duty: "Yet there no warrior bands are seen, / With martial step and lofty mien." There are no warriors, only Jews prepared to die "the death of the brave, for the laws that he gave," who have taken shelter from the murderous mob, themselves not warriors but "savage beasts" who "hunt us down" (13). And let it be known that these Jews sheltering in the *English* monument are represented as the *real* Englishmen; as the footnote to Milman confirms, the Jews came in homage to the newly crowned Richard I, but were excluded from their offering by the courtiers and others, worried that the Jews "were likely to blast all the prosperity of the reign by their ill omened presence" (19). The eternal exile is still the stalwart Englishman. And the Jewish poets are telling an *English* tale.[20] In telling this English tale, then, the valor and the promise of English nationhood is represented by indirection: the glory of the "martial step and lofty mien" is represented as the authentic English character that is violated when the English violate the Jews.[21]

The poem begins with an epigraph from one of Byron's "Hebrew Melodies," as I mentioned. But I believe that the poem to which "The Massacre" alludes more prominently is Byron's "The Prisoner of Chillon: A Fable." It was written in 1816, and despite its subtitle—fable—it is in fact based on the true history of Francois Bonivard. A Genevese priest whose views clashed with Duke Charles III of Savoy's, who imprisoned him in the Castle of Chillon, Bonivard offers a kind of dramatic monologue, beginning with a description of his degradation:

> My hair is grey, but not with years,
> Nor grew it white,
> In a single night.
> As men's have grown from sudden fears. (ll. 1–4)

In the Moss poem, "men with care, not age, grown white, / Meet in York castle hall to-night." In "Chillon," the speaker laments, "But this was for my father's faith, / I suffered chains and courted death," just as the Moss poem's martyrs are told, "This night doth Jehovah command us to die / The death of the brave, for the laws that he gave." But Bonivard does not die. He becomes one of Byron's archetypal Romantic sufferers because of the longevity of his suffering and his refusal to succumb to isolation and deprivation. When the last of his two brothers, imprisoned with him, dies, he notes, "I had no earthly hope—but faith, / And that forbade a selfish death" (229–230). The Jews of York are taught by their rabbi that their death will not be a selfish repudiation of faith: "There have been times, and this is such a time, / When even suicide is not a crime." The poem pauses to record the rabbi's judgment that their death would not constitute the grave Jewish sin of self-slaughter so as to emphasize that they die refusing to apostatize themselves, which in Jewish law signifies that they die *al kiddush Hashem*, in "the sanctification of God's name." And later in the poem, they are reminded:

> When the Israelites echoed the Maccabees' cry
> As they raised the Asmonean banner on high,
> They stayed not to think upon danger or death,
> But glorified God with their last fainting breath,
> And left in their country's annals a name
> That will ne'er be erased from the record of fame. (p. 16)

The Mosses' *Early Efforts* qualifies Byron's "Prisoner of Chillon" even as it assumes its proud defiance. The death of their heroes "will ne'er be erased from the record of fame" precisely because "their last fainting breath" "glorified God." In this respect, a historical poem of England "echoe[s] the Maccabees' cry." The literary and historical continuity implicitly claimed here is one that inherits the Maccabees as much as it inherits English high Romanticism and the British nationalist tale. To make a literary narrative out of English Jewish history is to make coherent a tale of belonging that is simultaneously about a history of rejection.

Didacticism and Inverting Nature

It is by embracing such seeming paradoxes that the Mosses are able to negotiate the multiple inflections of their own hybridity, which marks them as unblinking in their efforts to position their authority within a public sphere that would perforce challenge their subjectivity. The poem about the York massacre, then, does not simply describe their belonging: it *constitutes* the sphere of their belonging. In the preface to their 1840 prose publication, *The Romance of Jewish History*, they again quote Milman's *History of the Jews* in establishing again the heroism of the Maccabees. They do not cite any of the Jewish historians; their authority on the subject of the Maccabees is again a direct quotation from the Very Reverend Milman: "Among those lofty spirits who have asserted the liberty of their native land, against wanton and cruel oppression, none have surpassed the ablest of the Maccabees in accomplishing a great end with inadequate means—none have ever united more generous valour in a better cause"[22] (p. viii). *The Romance of Jewish History* blends romance with history in its retelling of selected moments of Jewish history, with the specific aim of bringing Jewish history into the realm of English consciousness. Having established that no less an authority than the Canon of Westminster applauds the unsurpassed valor and good cause of Judas Maccabeus, they declare their reasons for writing *The Romance*, which is to remedy the disconnect between Jewish life and English awareness:

> Namely, the fact that the English people generally, although mixing with the Jews in their daily duties, are as unacquainted with their history, religion, and customs, as if they still dwelt in their own land, and were known to them but by name.
> With this view, we have endeavoured to pourtray the Jews as they were while yet an independent people—to mark the most interesting events that took place after Judea became a kingdom. (pp. viii–ix)

For the Mosses, still notably young in 1840, only one year after the publication of *Early Efforts*, English ignorance is a source of undisguised frustration. And Jewish diffidence in the face of English ignorance is another source of frustration. In the dedicatory epistle to the volume, the Mosses explain that in their view, Jewish authors have confined their work to the more serious genres for fear of bringing dishonor to the Jewish community.

> That we have Authors of some eminence and celebrity among our people, we believe is generally acknowledged; but our men of genius have neglected the lighter branches of literature, directing their attention almost exclusively to theology, metaphysics, and philosophy.
>
> Even those who have desired to tread the more flowery paths of romance, have been prevented from appearing before the public, from a fear that however much they might excel, the prejudice existing against us as a nation, might reflect an odium on their work, and consign it to immediate oblivion.
>
> We have allowed no such feelings to deter us; for we think otherwise. The time is now arrived, or rapidly approaching, when such narrow-mindedness, the growth of a barbarous and priest-ridden age, will disappear. (pp. iv–v)

For the Mosses, aesthetic mastery from the pen of Jewish authors has been, until recently, no guarantee of literary recognition. They boldly declare that the English time is right for them because they have confidence in the prospective English reception of their work;[23] on the other hand, in the same prefatory pages they have declared that the English have no sense of the Jews among them as real flesh-and-blood human beings existing in common space. Their "romance" is in the service of a didacticism, but one intended to charm its audience into further study, or at least to a recognition of the real human beings before them: "We do not intend this production to be considered in the light of a history; our wish is to call the attention of the reader to the records of our people; to awaken curiosity—not to satisfy it." The Jews, that is, are a people with a complex past, some of whom have now come to share the condition of England. In this, the Mosses join aesthetic mastery and literary artifice to the subject of Jewish subjectivity within a nation that has not yet learned how to recognize them.

It is against such abstracting of the Jew out of flesh-and-blood existence, as it were, to which *Early Efforts* addresses itself. If "The Faded Flower" had thrown into sharp relief the complexity of the Mosses' struggle against competing definitions of femininity within the context of Jewish patriarchal expectations, then "The Moss Rose" reminds us that its authors are self-consciously manipulating the forms of subjectivity taken up within a lyric self-positioning. Here the foundational subject of the pastoral and its implications in Anglo-Jewish lyric are again brought to bear sharply. Like "The Faded Flower," "The Moss Rose," obviously playing on the poets' name, is a fair flower that suffers decay.

Like Wordsworth's Lucy, this beautiful maiden likened to the natural world fades inexplicably. The Moss Rose is "the queen of the garden, a brilliant moss rose," but it relinquishes its beauty in the course of organic change. Wordsworth's most haunting of Lucy poems, "A Slumber Did my Spirit Seal," abstracts the feminine beauty as a thing of nature who, before being absorbed into the vegetable and mineral world, "seemed a thing that could not feel / the touch of human years" (ll. 3–4). In "She Dwelt Among the Untrodden Ways," Wordsworth's designation of Lucy as part of the dynamic of metaphoric substitution highlights not a rose, but a violet by a *mossy* stone whose resistance to full visualization is also the condition of her metaphoric rendering as a lone—and highly visible—star:

> A violet by a mossy stone
> Half hidden from the eye!
> Fair as a star, when only one
> Is shining in the sky. (ll. 5–8)

Wordsworth's mossy stone obscures the violet: the *moss* half hides the violet. The Moss poets are plainly playing with the association, in ways that would privilege the transformative power of a lyric voice—their own lyric voice. In Wordsworth's poem, the moss obscures the girl/star/flower. In the Mosses' poem, the Moss Rose succumbs to natural decay, but only after "I saw in the pride of its beauty unclose." "I saw": it is the Moss author who performs the lyric seeing, and it is therefore the Moss author who reveals, rather than half hides, the beautiful flower.

What looks initially like a crisis in confidence in the later part of the poem—as if the Mosses do not yet have Wordsworth's control or confidence in metaphoric language—in fact would function as an assertion of lyric mastery. Their faded flower in "The Moss Rose" is offered explicitly in analogy to "a fair girl" in line 8 of the sonnet with the transitional designation of "Just so":

> Just so have I seen a fair girl in her spring,
> E're care had flapp'd o'er her its cold blighting wing,
> Oh! she was a bright and a beautiful thing,
> And no grief her fair forehead was shading,
> But long ere the summer could ripen her bloom
> Untimely she sank to the cold silent tomb,
> Like the rose she was brilliant but fading. (p. 47)

Do our young poets worry that their readers will fail to grasp the significance of the analogy? Do we really need the "Just so"? Why so obtrusive the lyrical finger-pointing? Throughout this volume, the Mosses assume various personae, including those of men instructing women in the worth of men who are undeserving of their affections. The brilliant moss rose of this poem, however, is not offered as the brilliant Moss who penned the sonnet. The moss rose of the poem is watched by a lyric "I" who sees the inevitable dynamic of decomposition in nature ("I saw in the pride of its beauty unclose, / But long e're the ev'ning sun sunk to repose, / The sweet crimson flower had faded away"); but "just so" is an unidentified "fair girl" the tenor of the moss rose's vehicle. The reader cannot but notice the obtrusiveness of the pun on "Moss," especially its beauty and brilliance. The displacement to an unexplained death momentarily undermines readerly expectations for lyric analogy, as the barely disguised assertion of self-sufficiency and mastery of the Moss author becomes an elegy for an unnamed girl cut down "ere the summer could ripen her bloom." This occurs despite the fact that, like Wordsworth's unnamed girl who could not feel the touch of human years, "no grief her fair forehead was shading." We never learn why Wordsworth's Lucy dies, in any of the Lucy poems. We do know that her absorption within the landscape offers only a qualified consolation, one that, in "She Dwelt Among the Untrodden Ways," registers a "difference" in the lyric mourner:

> She lived unknown, and few could know
> When Lucy ceased to be;
> But she is in her grave, and oh,
> The difference to me! (ll. 9–12)

Here are the final two lines of "The Moss Rose":

> Untimely she sank to the cold silent tomb,
> Like the rose she was brilliant but fading.

If Wordsworth's Lucy is a narcissistic extension of one aspect of her author's subjectivity, then the Mosses' moss rose is both subject and object of the lyric gaze. In "The Moss Rose," a brilliant Moss poet mourns the brilliant but fading moss rose. In Wordsworth, the moss obscures the subject flower even as the feminine flower is naturalized out of human existence. If the Mosses project themselves into the feminine role of brilliant but fading flower, they do so in ways that make them the lyric master of the natural dynamic. This is emphatically not a play on a projected suicide or loss of self-integrity. It is the recognition, by the poets, of the long-held association of the feminine with the weak of nature, and the assertion finally of control over it. They are not *merely* fading flowers, naturally decomposing aspects of the natural world. It is the Moss poets' initial assertion, after all, that the moss rose is the "queen of the garden." This is a dynamic controlled by the subjectivity of the lyric poets.

Control, however, is not always equal to absolute mastery, nor to ultimate triumph over adversity. Can a Jewish poet, can a Jewish woman poet especially, remain "queen of the garden" in post-Romantic England? Whatever their claims throughout the volume about asserting the integrity of their voice, the ambivalence over the certainty of their place within the public cultural sphere is still notable. These are, after all, "early efforts," but they are efforts all the same, and the nascent character of their self-positioning itself becomes a feature of self-understanding within the poetry. The familiar ambivalent refraction of the pastoral asserts itself in their poetry in ways that qualify again their inheritance of a dominant English literary heritage. Qualify, but not diminish: in "Autumn Is Coming," for example, we have a poem of three quatrains, each with rhymed couplets. In this poem we have the Mosses gesturing in the direction of Wordsworth's correspondent breezes, perhaps, but more obtrusively toward both Milton's "Lycidas" and Shelley's wild west wind, which Shelley allegorizes in political terms. For Shelley in "Ode to the West Wind," the wild wind is the "breath of Autumn's being" from whom the "leaves dead" "are driven, like ghosts from an enchanter fleeing." The ferocious menace of Shelley's west wind is imputed in his first stanza, and the leaves are almost immediately established as "pestilence stricken multitudes." It becomes a force for the poet's animation only because Shelley's speaker rises to the demand, which is the demand of the urgency of the historical occasion. The Moss poem hints at historical urgency, but it remains an intimation only. I quote the Moss poem in full:

Autumn Is Coming

Autumn is coming, the foliage is sear,
Sadly denoting the fall of the year,
The summer birds all have forsaken the spray
And its beautiful flow'rs are faded away.

Autumn is coming, and chill blows the blast,
Telling a sorrowful tale of the past;
Thus like summer, the bright hours of childhood will fleet,
And Autumn's decay mark them transient as sweet.

Autumn is coming, its fruits will repay,
For desolate gardens that late were so gay,
Completing the harvest that summer began,
And the seasons present a true emblem of man. (p. 47)

As in "The Moss Rose," the poem is careful to delineate its figurative significance. It takes no chances with readerly interpretation; or rather, it boldly presumes to direct its reader's interpretation, as well as its reader's recognition of its daringly allusive points of reference. Line 2 spells out the equation: "Sadly denoting the fall of the year." The year is falling because the "foliage is sear," and so our poets gesture toward, even as they modestly disclaim, the Miltonic opening of "Lycidas," whose poet plucks the laurels and myrtles with "ivy never sere" (l. 2) with his "forced fingers rude" (4).

The Mosses' "Autumn Is Coming" is an elegy not for another poet, such as "Lycidas" had been for Milton's Edward King, but rather an elegiac recognition of decay in human existence, a subject which "Lycidas" also takes up. The Mosses' "foliage is sear" because, though these are indeed "early efforts," they begin with a recognition of the reality of immedicable pain in the empirical world. If "The Moss Rose" concludes with the acknowledgment that even the "queen of the garden" was "brilliant but fading," "Autumn Is Coming" begins in diminishment, which of necessity contrasts itself with the figuring of loss in Milton's "Lycidas." The foliage is sear, as opposed to Milton's ivy that is "never sere." Both Milton and the Mosses represent themselves as working with a still developing poetic identity (Milton's "forced fingers rude"), but the Mosses resist Milton's ultimate theological equations, in part because as Jews negotiating their cultural inheritance in England, they must. Unable to affiliate themselves with a Protestant poetics of redemption, especially one linked to a presumed stable connection to the landscape, "Autumn Is Coming" remains stubbornly within the realm of immediate empirical reality. The seasons of the last stanza "present a true emblem of man," whereas the loss of Edward King to stormy weather is rendered in Christian terms as the figurative transcendence of organic phenomena: "So Lycidas sunk low, but mounted high, / Through the dear might of him that walked the waves"

(172–173). "*So* Lycidas": Milton clarifies the direction of his figurative meaning, which absorbs the pastoral and Christian redemption into one another. For the Mosses, "the seasons present a true emblem of man," not God, and not man in his interaction with the divine. The seasons do indeed become not subject, but the vehicle to humanity-as-tenor; however, the rendering still obtrusively resists Milton's high theological analogy. We are closer to the grieving Shelley of "Adonais," the one who resists the redemptions of cyclical regeneration and with it the consolations of its own great predecessors: "Winter is come and gone, / But grief returns with the revolving year" (154–155). This is the Shelley answering his own injunctions in the earlier "Ode to the West Wind." The consolation at the conclusion of the Mosses' poem is not supernatural, to be sure, but neither is it simply pastoral. The fruits of autumn are said to "repay, / For desolate gardens that late were so gay," but here the consolation in the cyclical reassurances of the natural world are primarily *about* figurative signification. Keats's 1819 ode "To Autumn" attributes to Autumn herself the integrity of elegiac consolation, one that inheres in her very being: "Where are the songs of spring? Ay, where are they? / Think not of them, thou hast thy music too" (23–24). The Mosses are trying out, as it were, a form of elegiac consolation by asserting that the seasons are not simply consolatory, but more importantly are emblematic: "And the seasons present a true emblem of man." If the seasons are the "true" emblem of man, then the foliage that is sear at the beginning of the poem is where the cycle repeats. Autumn is *always* coming, and that is precisely the point. The queen of the garden *always* fades. If winter comes, spring will not be far behind, as Shelley had it in "Ode to the West Wind," but neither will the end of another harvest be too distant. If the Mosses' autumn has its own music, then it is not one that, like Keats's, observes the red-breast whistling "with treble soft" (31). Nature provides for the Mosses a highly qualified consolation, one that emphasizes not recuperation but the gifts of linguistic naming: nature in the hands of skilled poets becomes an emblem, an image fit for poetic rendering. Closure in "Autumn Is Coming" is decidedly not premised on the idea that the seasons provide a haven *in which* humanity may find refuge; instead, it is the poetic equation between humanity and the seasons which is the poem's accomplishment and triumphant declaration. "Autumn Is Coming," then, is a self-reflexive exercise about their status as poets. In this, it is also a declaration of their right to strive for poetic mastery and, more crucially, cultural belonging in the land whose literary heritage they would render. This poem's presumption of cultural mastery is inflected by its belonging to a volume in which its authors also insistently seek self-definition as specifically Jewish poets with a particular gloss on the meaning of English as well as Jewish nationhood.

Indeed, poetic rendering—the insistence upon one's right to attribute meaning—is presented in the second stanza in ways that cannot but qualify the putatively happy assertions of recuperation in the third stanza. In the second quatrain of "Autumn Is Coming," autumn's chill wind is positively a "blast." Not quite yet Shelley's "trumpet of a prophecy," the autumn wind under description is still only anticipated; it has not *yet* come. Again, this stanza too directs its reader's figurative equations: "*Thus* like summer, the bright hours of childhood will fleet" (italics mine). Indeed, the Moss sisters are still children. Their fingers are still "rude." But the blast of autumn wind tells of something beyond the cyclical decay in nature, or the passing of childhood only. This poem of natural process, so familiar to English poetics, also has a tale to tell of *history*, and it is sorrowful. Here we have Shelley's west wind as unmistakable antecedent, where the west wind that destroys is also the preserver; the past never quite dies, as its catastrophe, hinted at by the poets, becomes the poet's tale of perseverance. Here is Shelley addressing the wind in the second section:

> Thou on whose stream, 'mid the steep sky's commotion,
> Loose clouds like Earth's decaying leaves are shed,
> Shook from the tangled boughs of Heaven and Ocean,
>
> Angels of rain and lightning: there are spread
> On the blue surface of thine aery surge,
> Like the bright hair uplifted from the head
>
> Of some fierce Maenad, even from the dim verge
> Of the horizon to the zenith's height,
> The locks of the approaching storm. Thou Dirge
>
> Of the dying year, to which this closing night
> Will be the dome of a vast sepulchre,
> Vaulted with all thy congregated might
>
> Of vapours, from whose solid atmosphere
> Black rain, and fire, and hail will burst: oh hear! (ll. 15–28)

Shelley's wind is the dirge of a dying year, just as the Mosses' wind denotes the fall of the year. The Mosses do not take up Shelley's bold stance as the harnesser of the autumn wind. They call it to their reader's attention only to turn from its presumptions. Their fingers actually remain, to a degree, "rude," nascent. As we have seen, their conclusion is to offer nature as fitting emblem of man. We will soon observe in Aguilar's poem "Dialogue Stanzas: Composed for, and Repeated by, Two Dear Little Animated Girls, at a Family Celebration of the Festival of Purim" that nature, even the nature that signifies so clearly in canonical British Romanticism, sometimes has a tale that is about life and death in a manner that is not at all universalist in its import. Nature's tale can also become the tale of a very specific history, but such rendering of the natural world depends very clearly on the specificity of the poet's historicity. Where Aguilar will directly confront this dynamic in "Dialogue Stanzas" by directly referring to the historical threats of violence against the Jews, the Moss sisters simply assert, in line 6—the very center of this twelve-line poem—that the wild west wind of autumn is "Telling a sorrowful tale of the past." Is this a specifically Jewish past, one to which they have been alluding or directly signifying throughout the volume? Or is it the past of Shelley's west wind, which is also a historical past whose political significance Shelley presumes to confront with the breath of revolutionary poetic language? Shelley harnesses the wild wind to establish the efficacy and integrity of his voice, and while the Mosses recognize that their "bright hours of childhood will fleet," the Moss poem concludes only with a further assertion of allegorical significance: "And the seasons present a true emblem of man." The consolation of the final stanza, if conceived in terms of pastoral conventions, is unearned; the "fruits will repay, / For desolate gardens." The Mosses' harvest is one that presents a "desolate" landscape. The plenitude of fruit exists, of necessity, in tandem with the desolate gardens. Is this any answer to the sorrowful tale of the past? Is this "true emblem of man" a reassuring image? This poem calls up the specter of Shelley's west wind precisely to acknowledge that it cannot follow where it leads. Shelley's conclusion makes of the wind not a quietest call for complacent reassurance, but rather a histrionics of power:

> Drive my dead thoughts over the universe
> Like withered leaves to quicken a new birth!
> And, by the incantation of this verse,

Scatter, as from an unextinguished hearth
Ashes and sparks, my words among mankind!
Be through my lips to unawakened earth

The trumpet of a prophecy! O Wind,
If Winter comes, can Spring be far behind? (ll. 63–70)

The restraint of the Moss sisters is not merely the reflex of youth's diffidence. In negotiating the natural world and its emblematic rendering in poetry, they come not to Shelley's prophetic future, not to the trumpet of a prophecy, but rather to the dark past of history that cannot be recuperated. The Mosses answer the multivalence of their allusiveness with still a further allusion to Coleridge's "Dejection: An Ode," in which the wind for the dejected Coleridge comes to be a "mighty Poet" telling tales of pain and groans and tremulous shudderings. Finally, the tale becomes one "of less affright," but one that the Mosses likely had in mind, as Coleridge's still-horrifying wind/poet tells a tale of a frightened girl whose only hope is to be heard:

'Tis of a little child
Upon a lonesome wild,
Not far from home, but she hath lost her way:
And now moans low in bitter grief and fear,
And now screams loud, and hopes to make her mother hear.
    (ll. 121–125)

A young girl who has lost her way and is screaming for succor, unsure if she will be heard: this is the tale that Coleridge's wind tells in section 7 of the Dejection Ode. The Mosses do not elaborate on the "sorrowful tale of the past" that their wind "blast" tells; what is significant is that it is a tale of the past that is sorrowful. The tale of the past becomes emblematic of the future insofar as the cycle of regenerative nature is being presented as the apt figurative representation of man. The past leads to a future where the plentitude of the harvest itself signals the desolation of the landscape even as it signals the availability, for the moment, of sweet fruit. It may well be named as recompense, but there is no necessary redemption here. Benjamin's angel of history is situated at the crossroads of a movement forward, but the gaze to the past is never erased.[24]

The Propriety of Elegy and the Fundamentals of Loyalty

Indeed, the two volumes to which the Mosses turned after publishing *Early Efforts* are specifically Jewish histories. *Tales of Jewish History* (1843) and *The Romance of Jewish History* (1840) are narratives intended to remedy the ignorance of the English public about the Jewish distant past. Though the volumes do not extend their reach to the Jewish diaspora in England, they do include long tales of diasporic wandering and of the self-experience of individuals who negotiate its challenges. In fact, they preface each narrative in *The Romance of Jewish History* with an "historical summary," the better to ensure that history is being accurately served in their tales. Further, the last line of the preface to *Romance* assures its readers that this is a specifically *Jewish* history, and from a Jewish perspective, that is being told: "It is almost needless to observe, that we have followed the Jewish historians in our chronology" (x). In fact, it is not needless to observe; the qualification is precisely the point. The Jews hold sorrowful tales of the past, ones that are inextricably entwined in any self-fashioning. It is important that any historical narrative be differentiated from its embellishments, and from its refractions in alternative story-telling." The "tale of the past" is a motif and an idiom that figures powerfully in Celia's tale about Herod Agrippa in "The Romance of Jewish History" (1840). In "The Fortunes of Herod Agrippa," the title character is writing a letter to his son on his deathbed, which occasions his reflections on the meaning of history:

> The Past! How much of gladness and gloom these two short words convey to the human breast! Who can look upon the history of his youth, without feeling that he has thrown away the golden moments of existence, and wasted precious opportunities that can never be recalled?—The Past! How many a tale it tells, of broken resolutions, vows never kept, and hopes scathed and blighted; of pride, passion, vanity, and love; of the good thrown from us, the evil cherished, until the goodly seed of virtue is choked up, and the poison of vice is all that remains!
> (p. 5)

The past tells many a tale indeed, and the one that Autumn tells must also be emblematic of man's propensity to suffer and to cause suffering.

"Autumn Is Coming" only hints at a past that is neither identified, nor even allegorically classifiable. But the point is made all the same: a sorrowful tale of the past haunts the representation of the seasons as it haunts the poets' own self-reflexivity. The elegiac insistence of "Weep no more" in the poem of the same name comes closer to an identification of the great canonical themes of patriotism and love, even as it too hints at the haunting ghost of an unnamed history. In this poem, the speaker enjoins a maiden to stop pining for a man who is unworthy of her devotion; he is unworthy because he is not among those "who die combatting with their country's foe." The speaker assumes the authority to instruct a "maiden" in the decorum of lamentation and in the even more essential requirements of patriotic valor. "Weep no more" is a familiar injunction in English elegy, most illustriously exemplified in Milton's "Weep no more, woeful shepherds" in "Lycidas" and Shelley's "mourn not for Adonais" (l. 362). What we have in the Mosses' "Weep No More," however, is a startling reversal. The maiden is instructed to cease her weeping not because her lost love has been "mounted high," nor because, as in "Adonais," he has "awakened from the dream of life," or that he "he has been made one with nature." Instead, the familiar refrain of "Weep no more" identifies the weeping maiden as lost, as it were, in the wrong genre: she is shedding tears over a lost love who retreats from patriotic duty. She ought to weep no more not because he has been mounted high through the dear might of him who walked the waves, but rather because the poem's speaker insists that he is not a fitting subject for elegy. It is as if the Felicia Hemans of "England's Dead" (1822) has adapted a Miltonic voice to school the young Jewesses in the propriety of how—and for whom—to write elegy. In "England's Dead," Hemans' English "mighty dead" may rest in alien lands or sea, but only as a mark of their awe-inspiring patriotic valor that knows no bounds in imperial England. *These* are the men who warrant commemoration in verse; indeed, language is the only marker of their lives, as their watery foreign graves are marked only figuratively: "Wave may not foam, nor wild wind sweep, / Where rest not England's dead."[25] The Moss speaker counsels against mourning, then, also by appropriating the rhetorical conventions of the patriotic poems of loss that had been regarded as the special talent of women poets: "No tears the lustre of thine eyes should dim, / Save 'twere in mourning for the glorious dead." The object of the Moss maiden's lament may not be counted among the glorious dead or mighty dead. He seems to have been someone who shirked battle, whose cowardly behavior makes him unworthy of the "Beauty" who ought instead to deplore only the loss of the brave, "Who die combatting with their country's foe." Again Hemans is a likely point of allusive reference, as "Casabianca" (1826) celebrates even a child of France whose loyalty to country is expressed as his loyalty to family honor, as, unable to secure his dead father's permission to escape the burning ship, young Casabianca dies refusing to leave his post. He too is worthy of tears: "But the noblest thing which perish'd there / Was that young faithful heart" (39–40). In the Mosses' "Weep No More," the authoritative speaker schooling the young lady knows the parameters of elegy; she knows what constitutes patriotism as well as its spoilage, and she knows about mourning gone awry. She knows, in other words, her history, both literary and political, and she knows the idioms by which that history is conventionally expressed in verse. The poem, whose title announces itself as elegy, gains power precisely because its English cultural sweep is called up only to be redirected. But the dynamic staged for the poem is one in which the object of address, the "maiden," still needs to be schooled in the propriety of elegy and in the fundamentals of loyalty. In the logic of the reader's experience, it is the Moss poets who perform these instructions. Indeed, this is an apologetic poem, as the lyric speaker seeks to distance herself from the very position by which Jewish authors are vulnerable to be characterized. The Mosses will not be situated exclusively within the cultural stereotype of an exotic other pining only for the lost Jerusalem, nor will they be seen as willing to weep for those who dishonor England. They too know the stakes of elegiac mourning: that it announces an affiliation with a cultural norm as much as it proclaims a metaphysical position upon which the claims of elegiac consolation rest. On the other hand, as they illustrate in "The Jewish Girl's Song" and in other poems similarly situated, they are also willing to assume the personae of exilic Jews in mourning for whom exile is their master narrative. In their poem "Weep No More," they are staging the tension that pervades the volume. Given the urgency of the politically charged debates over Jewish loyalty to England, and in light of the counter-emancipationist argument that the Jews will always recognize among foreign coreligionists a closer affiliation than among any non-Jewish native-born Englishman, the poem "Weep No more" reminds us of the historical dynamic, of the "sorrowful tale of the past," in the language of "Autumn Is Coming," which always echoes.

Multiple but Not Divided Loyalties

Thomas Macaulay's 1831 speech in parliament about the civil disabilities suffered by the Jews in England, offered in the wake of the defeat of the 1830

Jewish Relief bill, provides a particularly helpful gauge of the common rhetoric:

> The English Jews, we are told, are not Englishmen. They are a separate people, living locally in this island, but living morally and politically in communion with their brethren who are scattered over all the world. An English Jew looks on a Dutch or a Portuguese Jew as his countryman, and on an English Christian as a stranger. This want of patriotic feeling, it is said, renders a Jew unfit to exercise political functions.
>
> The argument has in it something plausible; but a close examination shows it to be quite unsound. Even if the alleged facts are admitted, still the Jews are not the only people who have preferred their sect to their country. The feeling of patriotism, when society is in a healthful state, springs up by a natural and inevitable association, in the minds of citizens who know that they owe all their comforts and pleasures to the bond which unites them in one community. But under a partial and oppressive government, these associations cannot acquire that strength which they have in a better state of things. Men are compelled to seek from their party that protection which they ought to receive from their country, and they, by a natural consequence, transfer to their party that affection which they would otherwise have felt for their country.[26]

In "Weep No More," the rhetoric of patriotic valor is unmistakable, even as the country is not named. In fact, Shelley's "Ozymandias" resonates in the conclusion. Where the king of kings would have his subjects look on his works with reverence and awe, his statue in fact rests in a landscape in which "boundless and bare / the lone and level sands stretch far away" (13–14). What marks him is "two vast and trunkless legs of stone" (2) that "stand in the desart" (3). The object of the maiden's lament in "Weep No More" is said to deserve no more than "a wide mound of leafless barren sand" which "Alone should mark where rests the coward slave." The monument for Ozymandias is trunkless, and the injunction to look on his works is ironic precisely because the poem is anti-commemorative. We do not weep for Ozymandias any more than we revere him. "Weep No More" is anti-commemorative too, but only because its maiden has erred in her affiliation:

> Weep no more maiden, weep no more,
> 'Tis not for such as him thy tears should flow,
> Beauty should for the brave alone deplore,
> Who die combatting with their country's foe;
> Not for the Serf who did not dare to die,
> Not for the recreant should'st thou repine,
> He who to save a worthless life could fly,
> Is all unworthy of a heart like thine.
>   Weep no more.
>
> Weep not for him, maiden, weep not for him,
> Vainly are those bright drops of sorrow shed;
> No tears the lustre of thine eyes should dim,
> Save 'twere in mourning for the glorious dead;
> No flow'res nurtur'd by affection's hand,
> Shall ever bloom above the dastard's grave,
> But a wide mound of leafless barren sand,
> Alone should mark where rests the coward slave.
>   Weep not for him. (pp. 80–81)

In Milton's "Lycidas," the shepherds learn a different kind of truth:

> Weep no more, woeful shepherds, weep no more,
> For Lycidas your sorrow is not dead,
> Sunk though he be beneath the wat'ry floor,
> So sinks the day-star in the ocean bed,
> And yet anon repairs his drooping head. (ll. 165–169)

Earlier Milton's poem asks, "Who would not sing for Lycidas?" (10). The Mosses seem to ask, who would dare sing for the unpatriotic? Their implicit answer: *not* the Jews. The country itself is never named, however. Here another ambiguity is opened: the country for which the "Serf" "did not dare to die" in the Moss poem could well be generalized as England, and certainly its cultural references are unambiguously situated within English literary history. In this regard, it functions as a reminder of the Jews' oft-proclaimed allegiance to England, especially in the midst of the emancipationist debates. But the poem could also potentially be seen as belonging among those lyrics situated in a specifically Jewish exile, where valor on behalf of Jerusalem is the dominant ethic of value. After all, the allusion to Shelley's "Ozymanidas" reminds us not only of hubris, but also of the ironic demand for misplaced allegiance. As Macaulay states in the speech cited above, "The feeling of patriotism, when society is in a healthful state, springs up by a natural and inevitable association." For Macaulay, the perpetuation of civil disabilities for the Jews is decidedly unhealthy. If "Weep No More" is finally a poem about the need to detach one's elegiac impulses from the politically and culturally unsuitable, then it is also a poem that gestures toward the more difficult question of what constitutes appropriate patriotism. Does "Weep No More" address more than one perspective, one which includes the prospect of an injunction to weep no more for those who forsake Jerusalem? Ozymanidas is the potentate from "an *antique* land" whose power is not only ineffectual, but also inappropriate, and we do well to recall that the maiden's "coward slave" of the Moss poem rests in "barren sand" that clearly alludes to the final line of Shelley's famous sonnet. This very volume, *Early Efforts*, then, throws into sharp relief the tensions inherent in multiple loyalties whose divisions many Jews would prefer to finesse. The allusive nature of the poems, referring as they do to failed and misplaced allegiances even within the contexts of canonical English literary tradition, offer up a recognition of the precarious cultural positioning of Jewish authors.

The Jewish Englishwoman who constitutes herself as a Jewish exile longing for Jerusalem is the same persona in the volume celebrating England as queen of the waves, even as she is situated in the same cultural position that would presume, as "The Massacre of the Jews at York" does, that she may school the English mainstream about their past of violence and inhospitality toward the Jews. This tension is never far from the political reality that the allegiance and patriotism of the Jews in England are among the defining rallying points—at least those spoken publicly—among those Englishmen opposed to Jewish emancipation. The political reality becomes tantamount to a cultural reality, and to a reality about the nuances of self-definition. Nine years before publication of this volume, the 1830 Jewish Relief bill was defeated. *The Spectator* for May 8, 1830, describes some of the objections leading up to its defeat: "It is alleged, in the second place, that the Jews are unworthy of sitting in Parliament, because they are aliens, and must ever remain so, not only in England, but in every other country under heaven. A Jew may be born in England—he may be bred there—he may speak the language, obey the laws, conform to the customs of an Englishman; he may cigar it, drink it, game it, race it, box it, as naturally as the most genuine bit of John Bull extant—and be an alien to all intents and purposes notwithstanding."²⁷ The specter of the political alien joins hands with the struggle against cultural alienation and self-alienation. The speaker of "Weep No More" appropriates a rhetoric that defines her as embracing the ethic and the very heart of the country in which she resides. If there is any ambiguity about England as the obvious point of reference, it is subtle. As in Hemans's "Casabianca," loyalty and patriotism are the defining standards of value which may be recognized even among the enemy. In "Weep No More," England seems to be the home of "the glorious dead" to which allegiance is owed, but the subtler hints of an alternative can stand without undermining the superficial, most accessible thematic point of the poem.

The poem's superficial thematic point is one matter; it is situated within the context not only of Jewish allegiance to England as a pressing political issue, but also the immediacy of the relationship between England's national Christianity and the cultural affiliation of the self-identified Jew who all the same labors within the grand tradition of English lyric. "Weep No More" establishes the Mosses as attentive to the demands of English genre and the English cultural and social sphere, but the subject of belonging is still often allied in their poetry to the subject of mourning. These are poems that negotiate the existential, as opposed to merely the political, challenges of the Jewish poet who at once understands herself as both loyal Englishwoman and exilic Jew. In commenting on Psalm 137 ("How can we sing the Lord's song in a foreign land") in his *History of the Jews*, Henry Hart Milman points out that during the Babylonian exile, the Jews presumably *did* sing their songs in a foreign land, however much it challenged their identity. Having cited Psalm 137, he observes: "Of their general treatment as captives we know little. The Psalm above quoted seems to intimate that the Babylonians had tasted enough to appreciate the poetical and musical talent of the exiles, and that they were summoned occasionally to amuse the banquets of their masters, though it was much against their will that they sang the songs of Zion in a strange land."²⁸ It is not against the will of the Mosses that they sing in England, as it were. But singing in exile is also a convention that the Mosses inherit from Jewish biblical and diasporic tradition, and it is one that complicates their relationship to English national culture, and to the way in which they inherit English national culture.

One poem that takes up the question of mourning and patriotism, "Thou Sittest Alone, Like a Widow'd Bride," explicitly situates the speaker as mourning the fall of Jerusalem, figured as "a widow'd bride," from a vantage point that is plainly exilic, "In the land of the far-off stranger." The fallen Jerusalem is now the lovely maiden being addressed, but the right to mourn is boldly assumed. This poem might well recall us to Hyman Hurwitz's elegy for Princess Charlotte, in which the poet appropriates the convention of Israel lamenting the fall of Jerusalem as a widowed bride pining for her lost love. Hurwitz appropriates the image to convey the depth of English Jewry's identification with the English princess and with England as a nation in which Jews may take their rightful place, both politically and culturally. For Hurwitz, it is their legitimate right to mourn Princess Charlotte, to proclaim consolation for such loss as the rightful prerogative of the Jews, who are loyal both to England and to their inheritance as Jews singing in a land at once foreign and their much-appreciated home. The Mosses' "Thou Sittest Alone, Like a Widow'd Bride," is an elegy whose propriety requires no special pleading; this is the elegy of the Jewish exile lamenting the fall of Jerusalem. However, the placement of such poems within a volume that also includes lyrics such as "Weep No More" reminds us of the dynamic tension of the volume's representations of subjectivity. If we read "Weep No More" as gesturing toward English Jewry's understanding of its obligations of loyalty, then the weeping for Jerusalem in the land of the "stranger" is still offered in the form of a twelve-line English sonnet lacking only the concluding couplet. Such dynamic tensions, then, represent internal divisions, self-representations that reflect the deep importance to their subjectivity both of their self-positioning as exilic Jews and as English poetesses who define themselves within English rhetorical and formal structures.

> Thous sittest alone like a widow'd bride,
> In the midst of thy fallen grandeur,
> And wound thee is scatter'd far and wide
> The remnants of by-gone splendour.
>
> The trampl'd shrine, the deserted bowers
> Of Israel's beautiful daughters,
> The fortress'd hills, the ruin'd towers,
> The blue unruffled waters.
>
> Thy sons are like Ishmael's wand'ring race,
> And their tents are pitch'd in danger,
> Away from their father's dwelling place,
> In the land of the far-off stranger.

If the Israelites have now become like "Ishmael's wand'ring race," it is because the exilic wandering issues in a self-alienation wherein being far "from their father's dwelling place" means that "their tents are pitch'd in danger," but also that the forms which contain them rest on alien ground. It is not that the Mosses are identifying themselves as under threat for their lives; it is that their volume emphasizes the condition of the Israelite's exile with a consistency and fervour that establishes exile as one condition of their cultural inheritance. That cultural inheritance is also the twin of a political reality in which England sometimes stands as "the land of the far-off stranger," as the land in which they still do not have political rights even if they still live in relative peace with their neighbors. That this is expressed within English cultural idioms, within the full range of an unmistakable English allusiveness, further complicates the scenario of vexed self-experience.

The themes of exile and national affiliation, of course, are common in mid-century England. The very epigraph to *The Romance of Jewish History* includes a quotation from Byron resonant of the general cultural fascination with ruins and national longing. The author is identified as Byron, but the title of the poem itself is not identified in the epigraph. The stanza is extracted from "The Isles of Greece," but as transplanted by the Mosses, and especially as unnamed, it stands as a proxy for a lament for Jerusalem:

> And where are they? and where art thou,
> My country? On thy voiceless shore
> The heroic lay is tuneless now—
> The heroic bosom beats no more!
> And must thy lyre, so long divine,
> Degenerate into hands like mine?

Byron appropriates Psalm 137 ("How can we sing the Lord's song in a foreign land") only for it to be appropriated right back by the Mosses as a gesture of their own authority. It stands as a cultural stamp of approval for the *Romance of Jewish History*; the Mosses inherit the lyre of their ancient land (Jerusalem), but it is one implicitly sanctioned for English public consumption by their refraction of it through the great canonical English poet.

A few stanzas later in "The Isles of Greece," Byron imagines the voice of the dead urging the living to break their silence. This is a stanza not included as part of the epigraph, but which stands all the same as an injunction heard and echoed by the Mosses, even if the nationalist reference point is implicitly altered:

> What, silent still? and silent all?
> Ah! no;— the voices of the dead
> Sound like a distant torrent's fall,
> And answer, 'Let one living head,
> But one, arise— we come, we come!'
> 'Tis but the living who are dumb. (ll. 43–48)

The "Emigrant's Song" by the Mosses recalls Byron's "The Isles of Greece" even as it provides yet another example of their self-definition as exiles. They leave a "lovely Isle"—possibly England, possibly one of Byron's Greek isles—to establish home yet again among "the stranger." The last two stanzas are most resonant:

> Far, far from your beautiful bowers must I roam,
> Farewell the bright landscape, the streamlet, the tree,
> For the land of the stranger is henceforth my home,
> But my heart is nigh broken at parting from thee.
>
> How fast from my sight, lovely Isle, thou'rt receding,
> Blest land of my sires, must I see thee no more;
> 'Tis at that bitter thought my bosom is bleeding,
> Farewell, O farewell, to thy beautiful shore! (p. 122)

For the Mosses, the ambiguity of the emigrant's homeland is precisely the point. This is a volume in which national displacement and nationalist loyalties are joined, not always easily, to Jewish exilic longing. For Byron, "the voices of the dead / Sound like a distant torrent's fall"; just so, "the sorrowful tale of the past" of Jewish history echoes in the lamentation of "farewell" and the detailing of the forsaken land's splendors even though the emigrant's homeland is unnamed. Where neither country nor affiliation is directly identified, the force of the absent referent becomes all the more potent. If the voices of the dead call upon us to speak, to lament in a voice that may be heard from the land that we have lost, then a lament for an unnamed land by an unnamed people can only over-signify. Lamentation for Zion is the biblical convention that the Mosses have made conventional in their volume of poetry. In instances where real ambiguity exists—such as in "The Emigrant's Song"—it also becomes joined to a more generalized declaration about the meaning of loyalty and loss. The "Emigrant's Song," after all, sounds also like the Romantic wanderer's recollection of the pastoral riches of England, "the bright landscape, the streamlet, the tree." This is the tradition to which Browning will famously contribute "Home Thoughts, from Abroad" in 1845. This is not a universalizing of the longing for Zion so much as it becomes, over the course of the volume, a palimpsest: the Mosses are not only or exclusively singing the Lord's song in a foreign land. They are singing of the longing for Zion and they are singing of England in the cultural idioms of English verse. The "Emigrant's Song" is the song of Jewish poetesses who have inherited the idioms of both English and Jewish biblical lament. Neither sit with unqualified stability in an English volume written by young Jewish woman in England in 1839.

It is for this reason that their laments for Poland are particularly resonant. Though Poland in the early to mid-nineteenth century was hardly a sheltering haven for the Jews, the Mosses seem to superimpose onto it the Poland of the eleventh to sixteenth centuries, when Poland was known as *paradisus Iudaeorum,* Paradise for the Jews. Its late eighteenth- and early nineteenth-century struggles for sovereignty against Russia, Austria, and Prussia are, for the Moss sisters, struggles that articulate not only their own identification with a geographical and cultural boundary, but also their sense of witnessing England's—and the rest of Europe's—impotence and unwillingness to intervene in a legitimate struggle for freedom and sovereignty. In 1795, the Kingdom of Poland was blighted. The famous November Uprising of 1830–1831 of young Polish patriots against Russia was brutally crushed, precipitating general resentment against Russia.[29] When the Mosses ask, for example, "Where shall liberty now find a shrine / Since the spirit of Poland is broke?" the question redounds on England, often perceived as impuissant in the cause of Polish sovereignty. It reflects also on themselves, subjects who elsewhere define England both as liberating and as the land of the stranger. Especially since the Polish November Uprising began in 1830, the same year as the defeat of the 1830 Jewish Relief bill in England, the identification with Poland signals considerable nuance in the Mosses' engagement with nationalist aspiration as it meets the formation of identity. To engage this geographical, religious, and existential boundary is to define, in part, the ironic status of Jewish cultural subjectivity.

The Mosses were not the only poets in England paying special attention to Poland in verse. Poland serves as a fine rallying point for nineteenth-century poets of many nations; seen sometimes as the "Messiah of the nations,"[30] Poland was a cause taken up by, for example, Tennyson, who published sonnets on Poland as early as his volume of 1832. The following sonnet was probably read by the Mosses:

> How long, O God, shall men be ridden down,
> And trampled under by the last and least
> Of men? The heart of Poland hath not ceased
> To quiver, tho' her sacred blood doth drown
> The fields; and out of every smouldering town
> Cries to Thee, lest brute Power be increased,
> Till that o'ergrown Barbarian in the East
> Transgress his ample bound to some new crown:
> Cries to thee, "Lord, how long shall these things be?
> How long this icy-hearted Muscovite
> Oppress the region?" Us, O Just and Good,
> Forgive, who smiled when she was torn in three;
> Us, who stand now, when we should aid the right
> A matter to be wept with tears of blood!³¹

Tennyson directly turns to England and calls for her "tears of blood" to expiate her indifference. The Mosses would not dare venture to wag a finger at the heart of the land of the stranger; still, didacticism comes in many guises. The Mosses offer two poems for Poland. "Lament for Poland," which indicates as a subtitle that it was "Composed at the early age of 13 years," is a fairly conventional but still spirited recognition of the pain of exile. It begins with an earnest consolation about the prospective claims of history:

> Brave Poland! Thy struggle for freedom is o'er
> Thy patriots are exil'd—thy power is no more,
> Fallen are thy heroes who fought to be free,
> And the laurels they won wave not o'er their graves;
> Yet their names are recorded in history's page,
> And their deeds will outlive them thro' many an age. (ll. 1–6)

If history will tell the tale of Poland, then history will also tell the tale that Tennyson tells of Poland in England; that England stood indifferent to the cause of freedom in an oppressed nation. "Polander's Song" is a subtler affair, for it more maturely appropriates the voice of a Polander lamenting the defeat of the nation. We will see, however, that appropriating the elegiac voice of the other is, for the Mosses, a recognition of the limits of sympathetic identification even as it serves as a recognition of its compelling allure, which is the temptation to recognize in another's rejection the threat of one's own. And I use the term "temptation" precisely because, as I will soon argue, it is a cultural dynamic they know they should resist. The first-person narrative is one that resonates with those poems throughout the volume lamenting the fall of Jerusalem and the defiling of the Temple. Indeed, were it not for the title, a reader could well read the first four stanzas of the poem's seven quatrains without realizing that it is *not* a lament for Jerusalem. The third and fourth stanzas subtly echo also the first lines of Tennyson's sonnet above:

> The standard of freedom is low,
> And drench'd in the blood of the slain;
> The foot of the merciless foe
> Our homes and our altars profane.
>
> O God, that such things should e'er be,
> And our patriots sleep in their graves,
> That the land of the noble and free
> Should be conquered by tyrants and slaves. (pp. 89–90)

Where Tennyson takes up the myth of Poland as crucified Messiah ("her sacred blood"), the Moss poem takes up the image of "the blood of the slain" as a profanation of holiness ("Our homes and our altars profane"). Where Tennyson moves on to reproach the inaction of England, the Mosses have the Polander crying out in confusion, asking where freedom may now rest. The implicit answer would seem to be, not even in England:

> Where shall liberty now find a shrine,
> Since the spirit of Poland is broke;
> Where shall freedom her laurels entwine
> Since Poland has bowed to the yoke.
>
> The last glorious struggle is o'er,
> The struggle for freedom or death;
> Our power, our might is no more,
> And the sword may now rust in its sheath.
>
> Our hearth-stones with blood are defiled,
> Not even our religion remains;

> Our warriors are dead or exiled,
> And our little ones weeping in chains.

The November Polish Uprising had been waged in the name of freedom and inclusivity. Its defeat could not but echo with the defeat of the 1830 Jewish Relief bill in England. The lament for profaned altars, for an exiled people, grafts Israel in exile—a recurrent motif throughout the volume—onto the vanquished Pole. And the vanquished Pole is the victim unaided by England. But this is no simple allegory, and here is no simple identification of the dynamics of the sympathetic imagination. The sympathetic Jewish imagination takes up the voice of the vanquished Pole forsaken by England, the martyr of the nations rejected by England, and even with the intended resonance of the defeat of the Jewish Relief Bill, the Mosses know that their poetic geography is the no-man's land of sympathy spurned. They may well presume to appropriate the voice of the Polander in their monologue, and yes, they may well gesture toward the well-worn tactic of displacing their (Jewish) voice onto one with easier cultural sanction, but their appropriation of the Polander's voice is one that they write also—subtly, implicitly—as necessarily impossible. "Where shall liberty now find a shrine?" Perhaps liberty never fully found a shrine, not even in Poland, the Romantic darling in exile. There had been real hesitation in accepting Polish Jews into the Uprising, and though there was Jewish participation in support of the Uprising, it was limited. In fact, in the years after the defeat, some editorialists even speculated that Polish defeat had been abetted by the hesitation in enabling the Jews to join the rebellion.[32] I argue that the echo of the volume's other poems addressed to Zion, and poems assuming the posture of Jewish mourning over the destruction of the Temple and of specifically Jewish exilic wandering, is precisely the point: to appropriate the voice of the Polander is to speak the language of self-alienation, their alienation, the one rejected too even by the Messiah of the nations. On what ground does this place them? In a way, the Polander's lament, which in fact can never be entirely the Mosses' lament, puts them right back in England, where the wanderer, the exile and the elegist are figures of cultural honor even if they can also function as signs of disenfranchisement, both political and existential. To lament in the voice of a Polander lamenting is to encounter the limits of sympathetic identification, which here becomes the boundary of the Jewish poet's freedom to stand ultimately as herself, in her own voice, which is all the same a voice that must always situate itself on ever-shifting ground.

Belonging as Estrangement

No one knows what kind of poetry Marion and Celia Moss might have produced had either of them turned her attention to another volume. They both continued to write and to publish poetry in periodicals, but not enough to make up a volume's worth. They turned their attention mainly to prose, and to family, and to work as educators. In 1847, Marion, as Mrs. M. Hartog, published "Song of the Expatriated" in *The Occident and American Jewish Advocate*, an American periodical in which both sisters would continue to publish. The lyric addresses England, and the poet's own deficient love, in ways that the earlier poems never could:

> Oh, land of mine adoption,
> Much loveliness is thine;
> Tho' thy fruitful vales produce not
> The olive, fig, and vine;
> Yet thy beauties are unheeded,
> Or coldly viewed by me,
> Thou land of western loveliness,
> Fair daughter of the sea.
>
> For I turn to my distant land,
> Now rendered lone and wild,
> With the deep and passionate yearning
> Of one from home exiled;
> For tho' she sits forsaken,
> And her children are in thrall,
> Yet Zion's sorrowing daughter
> Is beautiful withal.

It may be that English pastoral is a present and immediate enticement, but the figuring of Zion's real tactile splendors—its "olive, fig, and vine"—is what releases the poet from strangeness, alienation. And yet, the "land of western loveliness," the land in which lyric instantiates the subjectivity of the alienated poet, is the land that has supplied the poet with the expressive forum in which to articulate and to know her longing.

In "Up, Up with the Anchor," a poem from *Early Efforts*, the speaker leaves behind "the land of the stranger," but it stops just short of explicitly identifying it as England:

> Then up with the anchor and let us away,
> Spread the sails 'tis a favouring wind,
> And long ere the break of the morning we'll leave,
> The land of the stranger behind. (p. 81)

The longing for freedom in these poems is a longing that defines the subjectivity of the poets; they know themselves as ultimately estranged even as they define their voice as the space of their belonging. The "land of the stranger," after all, remains the ground beneath their feet.

CHAPTER 4

Grace Aguilar and the Demands of Lyric

> It is only within the last few years that the Jews, as a body, have been known beyond the circle of curious and abstruse readers. Their pursuits and capacities, it was supposed, were limited to stock-jobbing, money-lending, and orange-stalls; but few believed them to be a people of vigorous intellect, of unrivalled diligence in study, with a long list of ancient and modern writers, whose works—though oftentimes mixed with matter, much of which is useless, and much pernicious, and calculated far more to sharpen than to enrich the understanding—bespeak most singular perseverance and ability.
>
> —Lord Ashley, "State and Prospects of the Jews,"
> *London Quarterly Review* (1839)

What would it mean to "know" the Jews as Lord Ashley imagines such a scenario? If they are to be recognized beyond the confines of a degraded commerce—the "money-lending" or "orange-stalls"—what is to be made of the surprise over their "vigorous intellect" or "unrivalled diligence in study"? Can their "useless" or "pernicious" learning truly be contained within a parenthetical aside on the way to acknowledging a "most singular perseverance and ability"? Grace Aguilar indeed could serve as the very model catalyzing Ashley's bewilderment, for her work presents a Judaism and a Jewish people that refuse to be regarded merely within a circle of curious and abstruse readers. Hailing from a tradition in which the furtiveness of Jewish practice was a matter of life and death, her work is acutely sensitive to the constituents of her audience, and therefore vividly aware of such sentiments as Ashley's. Aguilar was born in 1816, and she died in 1847 after a lifetime of ill health. Her parents, practicing Portuguese Jews, came to England in flight from the Inquisition, not an uncommon situation at the time. She was born in London, where the family was active in the Sephardic Jewish community, her father even taking a leadership role in the Spanish and Portuguese synagogue. Aguilar thus took her place as the English child of Portuguese parents who had once been so-called crypto-Jews, Jews who hid their religious identity from public scrutiny, but who continued secretly to practice and to identify themselves as Jewish. England was recognized as the place where, at least superficially, they could be themselves. The veracity and significance of such claims would be explored by Aguilar throughout her short life in poems, historical fiction, fictional romance, polemical essays, and historical articles. She was a voracious reader in both secular and Jewish texts, and educated by her parents in the oral traditions of the crypto-Jews. Despite her life-long ill health, she was a remarkably industrious and prolific writer, and an insightful observer of the subtler forms of alienation. She gained an audience in both America and Britain, and her death at the age of 31 was mourned in England as well as America by Jewish readers especially who recognized the singularity of her achievements.[1]

Expostulation and Reply

Aguilar's poetry, coming somewhat later in the long Romanticism that I have designated for this study, has enough distance from Romantic antecedents for her to take the full, critically reflective measure of its meaning to her. She is also well enough situated within a Victorian matrix to be able to respond to mid-nineteenth-century ideological formations with a complexity that, I argue, is reflected in her poetic self-fashioning. In 1845 Aguilar published "Dialogue Stanzas: Composed for, and Repeated by, Two Dear Little Animated Girls, at a Family Celebration of the Festival of Purim."[2] This is a deceptively simple poem that illustrates its author's canny sense of the bearings of the Jews in England, and her own place within its culture. I discussed this holiday in the chapter on Hyman Hurwitz, for Hurwitz also alludes to it in his elegy for George III. Purim is a festival that often occurs in early spring. It is a holiday marked by a reading of the Book of Esther, which tells the story of the Jews' escape from King Ahasuerus's evil minister, Haman. The holiday occurs in the Hebrew month of Adar, a month during which, because of the festival of Purim, Jews are positively commanded to be happy. Traditionally such happiness is expressed in raucous exuberance, and during the reading of the Book of Esther in synagogue, the name of Haman is symbolically drowned out in a cacophony produced by noise-making objects. In the Book of Esther, the titular character is chosen to marry King Ahasuerus. He does not yet know that she is Jewish.

Esther's cousin Mordechai refuses to bow down to Haman, usually interpreted as his avowal that Jews bow only to God, never to temporal potentates. Haman vows to murder all the Jews in the kingdom, but Esther intercedes, and reveals her heretofore concealed Jewish identity to the king, who subsequently has Haman hanged on one of the very gallows he built for Mordechai. King Ahasuerus, one of the minor villains in the Purim story, shares a name with Ahasuerus the Wandering Jew, perhaps more familiar to Romanticists (the romanization of the spelling varies somewhat, as do the various literary legends associated with the name).[3] Aguilar's choice of this story to engage elegiacally with Wordsworth is no coincidence. Her "Dialogue Stanzas" has the two little girls debating the relative merits of frolicking in the early spring pastoral scene, on the one hand, and the persistent need, on the other, to read about a "cruel foe" who "swore vengeance on our race" (l. 11). The two girls end up convincing one another, and the poem ends on a relatively facile note, in keeping with the youthful prattle of two girls who cannot quite fathom their history. The final two stanzas are spoken by alternating girls:

> "Yes, yes, sweet sister, you are right, not only is to-day
> For idle mirth, and noisy games, and merry thoughtless play.
> We'll love our mother more and more, and all our dear kind friends,
> And grateful be that hours of dread, no more our Father sends;
> That we may sport amid the flowers as happy as a bee,
> And cruel foes can never come, to mar our childish glee."
>
> "See, see! I'm ready, sister dear—I've put the book away;
> Come while the sun so brightly shines, we'll weave our garland gay.
> What joy!—what joy! this happy day shall see us all together,
> E'en those dear friends, whom time and space so long from us did sever;
> Oh! many, many happy years, still spare us to each other.
> Sweet sister, come! I'm ready now—the garland for our mother."
> (ll. 25–36)

The "garland for our mother" motif pervades the poem: the frolicking girl—the girl who would at first turn from the text and forget history—wishes to celebrate the season and celebrate the Jewish commemorative festival by weaving a garland for their mother, a gift to the mother of mother nature's bounty from the very earth that sheltered our mothers.

The gift of Nature here has become the signature of History. This is a poem that virtually ingests and then regurgitates Wordsworth's "Expostulation and Reply" and "The Tables Turned": Aguilar's engagement with them is at once deeply vexed and directly explicit. In fact, it is the thematic center of a poem that is not quite sure if it wants to be ironic. Wordsworth's Matthew and William debate the relative merits of reading and quiet contemplation against the splendors of pastoral frolicking and of wise passiveness in the bosom of nature, not because the contemplation of human nature is less worthy than exultation in physical nature, but because "one impulse from a vernal wood / May teach you more of man, / Of moral evil and of good, / Than all the sages can" ("The Tables Turned," ll. 21–24). So says William, sure of the ethical ground of the landscape, sure that the throstle singing is no mean preacher, answering Matthew's indignation about his booklessness:

> "Where are your books?—that light bequeathed
> To Beings else forlorn and blind!
> Up! up! and drink the spirit breathed
> From dead men to their kind."
> ("Expostulation and Reply," ll. 5–8)

The next stanza haunts Aguilar's 1845 poem most directly:

> "You look round on your mother earth,
> As if she for no purpose bore you;
> As if you were her first-born birth,
> And none had lived before you!" (ll. 9–12)

Aguilar's dialogue with Wordsworth is elegiac insofar as it mourns the self-canceling gestures of her own expressive resources. Her Purim girls, scholar and frolicker both, enter a landscape that functions as trapdoor, as it were: the scene of pastoral merriment becomes a site of warning that is freighted with local historical resonances. The joy commanded in the Jewish festival is a reveling in the text. It admits no disjunction between *carpe diem* and the book.

The studious one of Aguilar's poem must warn the merrymaker: "A little while and I will come,—I only want to know / What pass'd upon this very day—a long time ago" (ll. 7–8). Upon this day passed a man with power who had sworn death to the marginalized Jewish population of ancient Persia. Not murdering to dissect—not reading the right book—might well mean being murdered. It is not simply the relative merits of nature learning and book learning that are at stake here: what is at stake for the girls of the poem is the historical memory figured by the landscape, and the landscape is at once threat of exile and/or death and the dream of tranquil restoration putatively supplied by its soothing qualities, its moral anchorage. If Wordsworth's is the poem's Romantic antecedent, then what passes here—here in a conjured scene of pastoral harmony—is a nostalgia for a harmony under threat already for Wordsworth, under threat enough to warrant a nostalgia insisting on its rights.[4] Aguilar cannot cleave to the healing thoughts of a land that writes also the story of her renunciation, even though she plays with the seductive allure of instantiating her subjectivity within it. Aguilar responds ironically to what in Wordsworth is already wistfully ironic.

All the same, this scenario composes, for Aguilar, an alienation from expressive resources that she would still claim, at least in part. The figuring of her own estrangement from her own familiar, her own soil, her own English literary history that is neither her only familiar nor only history, is the ultimate and most powerful source of the elegiac aspects of the poem's dialogue with Wordsworth. This is the Jew who would well rather claim all sorts of drops of bucolic blood in her veins, to cite the quotation from Amy Levy that began this book, but the author of the first *History of the Jews in England* written by a Jew also knows that she can poorly digest the English sustenance she has swallowed.

When one girl convinces the other, the gratitude for deliverance from Haman clearly rings with other sources of deliverance that still carry a bad taste:

"Yes, yes, sweet sister, you are right, not only is to-day
For idle mirth, and noisy games, and merry thoughtless play.
We'll love our mother more and more, and all our dear kind friends,
And grateful be that hours of dread, no more our Father sends."
(ll. 25–28)

The Romantic pastoral, however conceived, figures both a longing for inclusion and the sign of a persistent alienation. The self-alienation that is the yield of such self-contradiction relies precisely on the inaccessibility to Aguilar of the spring-like *carpe diem*, the pastoral nostalgia that Wordsworth himself may well partly ironize, but which becomes the dislocated specter Aguilar cannot fully embrace. Purim is often an early spring festival, but it is one commemorated precisely by recitation of a book. In fact, it is a specific positive commandment that the entire Book of Esther be read publicly twice, and that every word be heard by all Jews. Purim is a festival that demands that history be heard, and that commands merriment in the book as religious duty. The distant nightmare that threatens the girls' ease in their outdoor scene is the focus of their dialogue about the relative merits of playing in the landscape and reading the book. It is a dialogue that Matthew and William do not have because they have never needed to have it. This is the pathos of Aguilar's poem. Her dialogue about the ease of the landscape, and her implicit dialogue with the poetic precursors that structure it, are burdened with the history that must, of necessity, ironize it once and for all. Aguilar's "Dialogue Stanzas" signals the death of the symbolic value of a landscape that was never hers anyway.[5] The history book—the Book of Esther—that commands her to rejoice in an escape from death commands her to understand a dialogue between history and poetry. And that is a dialogue, finally, that plays itself out in her own efforts at self-definition.

This is a self-definition, to be sure, that is situated against a recognizable cultural type. Aguilar likely also has in mind Wordsworth's 1828 poem "A Jewish Family," which also describes two little Jewish girls. I cite the concluding two stanzas:

> Two lovely Sisters, still and sweet
> As flowers, stand side by side;
> Their soul-subduing looks might cheat
> The Christian of his pride:
> Such beauty hath the Eternal poured
> Upon them not forlorn,
> Though of a lineage once abhorred,
> Nor yet redeemed from scorn.
>
> Mysterious safeguard, that, in spite
> Of poverty and wrong,
> Doth here preserve a living light,
> From Hebrew fountains sprung;
> That gives this ragged group to cast

Around the dell a gleam
Of Palestine, of glory past,
And proud Jerusalem. (ll. 30–48)

Judith Page observes that "the Jews are acceptable here because they represent and endorse a Christian aesthetics of the beautiful, which in a paradoxical way domesticates and naturalizes their history of wandering."⁶ Aguilar's poem gives voice to the girls, one in which they are reclaimed from such abstractions of "glory past." Their dialogue is one in which they are facing one another in a recognizably English scene, and thereby engaging their author's dialogue with the weight of her cultural patrimony.

Neither Guest nor Full Citizen: Exile and Refuge

If Aguilar's stance with respect to England betrays signs of ambivalence, her remembering of the great golden age of the Spanish Jews makes of that am bivalence a potent anxiety; if even their beloved Spain turned so utterly against the Jews, what real stability could even England secure? The poem is entitled "Song of the Spanish Jews, During their 'Golden Age.'" It was written in 1843, four years before her death. It is prefaced by a quotation from Milman's *History of the Jews*, a text that had been very important to Marion and Celia Moss, as discussed in the previous chapter: "It was in Spain that the golden age of the Jews shone with the brightest and most enduring splendour. In emulation of their Moslemite brethren, they began to cultivate their long disused and neglected poetry; the harp of Judah was heard to sound again, though with something of a foreign tone."⁷ The poem itself is written in quatrains consisting of rhyming couplets. It follows an eleven-beat line, its generally iambic beat interrupted often and obtrusively by trochaic substitutions, with many lines demonstrating a hypercatalectic ending. The metrical discord makes contact with an almost aggressive ironizing of at least one Romantic credo of place, which in fact joins hands with the belief in England as refuge. The poem can only function as dramatic monologue insofar as it is an encomium to Spain's generous sheltering of the Jews, its ability to secure them with a long horizon of stable rootedness. Under Spanish auspices the Jews indeed produced a literary and musical heritage of remarkable distinction. The golden age of the Jews in Spain ended, of course: first vicious persecution, and then total expulsion in 1492. In Aguilar's poem, the hymnic encomium to the Spanish land as dramatic monologue becomes an ironic elegy, one that marks an ethical conundrum. She begins not simply with praise for Spain's sheltering generosity, nor even with praise for the beautiful landscape. Neither does she begin directly with an exhortation for those sheltered Jews to appreciate their bounty. Instead, the poem begins with ominous foreboding, as it chastens any withholding of Jewish gratitude owing to the host country:

> Oh, dark is the spirit that loves not the land
> Whose breezes his brow have in infancy fann'd,
> That feels not his bosom responsively thrill
> To the voice of her forest, the gush of her rill. (ll. 1–4)

If Coleridge in "Dejection: An Ode," having seen but not felt the delicate beauties of the horizon, finally learns that "we receive but what we give" (l. 47), Aguilar ups the ante: the peril of nonresponsiveness becomes tinged with the shadow of exile, real physical exile. The aggressively ironic stance of the poem transforms it into elegy not so much for the land of Spain lost to the Jews when they were expelled from this once paradise, but for the Jews' alienation from the expressive resources that define Romantic standards of value. Given the retrospective, what would meeting nature halfway here possibly mean? As she continues with the hymn-like praise of the particularities of the landscape, so she sustains an imagined castigation of those who refuse the immersion within the culture of Spanish pastoral tranquility, or more precisely, the culture that knows to praise the pastoral.

> Who hails not the flowers that bloom on his way,
> As blessings there scattered his love to repay;
> Who loves not to wander o'er mountain and vale,
> Where echoes the voice of the loud rushing gale. (ll. 5–8)

In other words, if you cannot feel the power of the pastoral assertion, if it does not make you feel "that in this moment there is life and food / For future years" (Wordsworth, "Tintern Abbey," ll. 64–65), if you cannot accept that this is the "green isle" that "needs must be / In the deep wide sea of Misery" (as Shelley has it in "Lines Written among the Euganean Hills," ll. 1–2), then you are defective, cold, ungrateful, in short, responding to the land in an unethical fashion. The point here is that the poet's longing to appropriate the pastoral hymn becomes a longing to instantiate a subjectivity defined precisely by the very expressive resources from which the Jew is alienated. It may well be a dark spirit whose bosom will not responsively thrill to the voice of the forest, but the Jews of England were almost never in the forest. The unstable hospitality that is being alluded to here by Aguilar, in the midst of an ironic but still wistful encomium to the Spanish landscape, itself complicates even the irony. If the wandering Jew and the Romantic peripatetic share anything in common, then the figure in which they meet is the horizon. For the Jew of this poem, the longer view of the horizon figures expulsion and exile. Walking is not the same as running away, and we should not forget that Aguilar's parents came to England on the run from the Inquisition, which was not officially extinguished in Portugal until 1821. In this sense, land becomes transformed, for the cosmopolitan Jew, from landscape into a concern about the historical exclusivity of land and of hospitality within foreign lands. It thereby speaks also to the ethical implications of how we figure the relationship to the land in which we dwell.

In 1844, Aguilar wrote a poem more direct in its anguish and less vexed in its ethical import, "The Hebrew's Appeal, on Occasion of the Late Fearful Ukase Promulgated by the Emperor of Russia." There had been many ukases, or decrees against the Jews by Russian emperors, beginning with Catherine the Great's in the 1790s. Aguilar's poem responds directly to Nicholas I's dissolution of all Jewish communal organizations and exiling of the Jews into the Pale, which was on the border of Russia and Poland. Alluding to England's abolition of the slave trade in 1807, and to the fact that England in 1837 ended all slavery throughout the British Empire, she asks:

> Will she who gave to Liberty the slave,
> For God's own people not one effort make?
> Will she not rise once more, in mercy clad,
> And heal the bleeding heart, and Sorrow's sons make glad?
> (ll. 27–30)

And from a later stanza: "Oh England! Thou hast call'd us to thy breast / And done to orphans all a mother's part" (ll. 37–38). What are the ethical imperatives of mother to child? Adapting a common Romantic nostalgic maneuver, and perhaps thinking directly of Wordsworth's "Tintern Abbey," whereby the beloved land, in its obtrusive stability, becomes the correlative of the very mother who first conferred the child's security and locus of identity, Aguilar tilts the trajectory. Will the mild mother, the gentle breast to starving orphans, please not take to her bed? Will she please become the firm but loving rebuker, "send her voice all thrillingly afar" (l. 32), especially "when her rebuke might shake / With shame and terror, e'en the tyrant Czar?" (ll. 33–34). Aguilar's call to the mother here is a call that she knows will go unheeded, and it is in the very unheeding, in the clear foreknowledge of the unheeding, that the arrogation of England as maternal figure to the wandering Jew is called in question. Aguilar's speaker is alienated from the very imagery she would appropriate, indeed alienated from the very rhetorical repertoire that is all the same her natural point of reference, her natural point of departure. The worrying of the natural here is precisely the point.

> Will England sleep, when Justice bids her wake,
> And send her voice all thrillingly afar?
> Will England sleep, when her rebuke might shake
> With shame and terror, e'en the tyrant Czar,
> And 'neath the magic of her mild appeal,
> Move Russia's frozen soul for Israel to feel? (ll. 31–36)

Neither guest nor full citizen, neither pastoral poet nor cosmopolitan citizen peripatetic, the Jew inhabits a space between, which here is the space of a longing that cannot be properly named.

Indeed, for Aguilar, the ethical response to the landscape runs a perilous course between genuine sympathetic regard and ironic inflection. Such ironic reflection, of course, itself is continuous with mainstream Romantic irony; however, we have seen that to ironize Romanticism from its margins, no matter how subtly, is a complicated venture, and certainly Aguilar is persistently conscious of her vulnerability to the charge of ingratitude. Indeed, her sensitivity to her reception by the mainstream English public has sometimes led to the charge of Aguilar as "Jewish Protestant."[8] Very few of the Jewish authors in this study have escaped this charge of overmuch pandering to a Christian public possessed of limited understanding of their peculiar positions as Jews; still, the author of multiple volumes in the public domain about Jewish history, Jewish faith, Jewish women, and sundry other explicitly Jewish themes pulls back before she has crossed an imaginary line. Her Jewish particularism tends, paradoxically, to have a universalist cast; there is very little in Aguilar's published prose about Jewish particularity that could be perceived as directly threatening to a Protestant mainstream. Even in her 1847 "History of the Jews in England," Aguilar concludes on a note extolling the virtues of English toleration of the Jews as she looks forward to complete Jewish emancipation, an accomplishment that was still several years in the future. The point she insists upon in this conclusion is the very same one insisted upon by many Anglo-Jewish authors of the nineteenth century: the Jews love and are grateful to England as much as they could love any place. Jewish emancipation is the natural end for a country that recognizes its common cause with its Jewish population. And the history of the Jews in England, for Aguilar, is a history of exile and trauma whose telos might almost be designated as the present moment of glorious acceptance—"almost" because the Jewish civil disabilities have not yet been fully abrogated in 1847:

> Now, however, the British empire has given the exiles of Judea a home of peace and freedom, and that they feel towards her an affection and reverence as strong and undying as any of her native sons, it is to be hoped that the prejudice against the Jews will ultimately disappear with the dawn of an era in which all Englishmen, however differently they may pray to the Great Father of all, shall yet, so long as they fail not in duty to their country and to each other, be regarded as the common children of one soil.[9] (p. 353)

This is the Aguilar of public prose: proud Jew, proud Englishwoman, and putatively at one with her public pronouncements. The "common children of one soil" are the children whose communings with nature proceed from the same wellspring of love, or even the same wellspring of regard that knows how to qualify that love. The poetry, however, is consistently Aguilar's forum for exploring the nuances of the fiction that we are all, in the end, children of one soil.

Conversion and Stalwart Nature

If "Song of the Spanish Jews" reminds its readers of the paradoxes of gratitude for the soil of one's land, Aguilar's poem "The Evergreen," part of her series entitled "Communings with Nature,"[10] reminds us that fidelity to the soil can sometimes be figured as fidelity to the common dwellers on the soil; and since love of the land does not always proceed smoothly, neither does love of man. The evergreen is "sad and lone," even "mid nature's bloom." The faithful evergreen, tenacious in the face of danger and unmoved by nature's threatening menace, stands finally for "meek endurance." Perhaps too meek: its meek tenacity becomes the means of its invisibility, its disregard by an unappreciative humanity:

> And still thou smilest,—man's neglect,
> Rude storm, and blighting blast,
> Thine upward growth have never checked,
> Nor lain thee with the past.
>
> Thou'rt ever present,—ever nigh,
> In meek endurance still,
> Oh, ingrate man, to pass thee by,
> Till life grows changed and chill!

Like the "Song of the Spanish Jews," this poem contemplates the meaning of ingratitude for nature's bounties, but here the ingratitude proceeds from misunderstanding. The poetic apostrophe to the evergreen opens, in fact, by pondering the evergreen in its status as unworthy of poetry:

> Thou art so changeless, that we deem
> No poesy dwells in thee,
> No vision'd love, no shadowy dream
> Shrin'd in thy leaves may be.

By the end of the poem, the poet reverses her position on whether poetry dwells in the evergreen. Contemplating its rude neglect by the individuals who are accustomed only "To garner in our wayward heart / The beauty that must die," the speaker addresses the lone evergreen as in fact the *most* poetic of natural subjects. In so doing, however, this most poetic of nature's bounties, having been understood first as unsuitable to the muse, becomes enveloped in the vocabulary of recognizably Jewish representation:

> Emblem of God's omnific love,
> His never-changing care!
> Fair shrub, His faithfulness to prove,
> Thou'rt scatter'd ev'ry where.

The Jew scattered over the face of the globe, despised for his constancy to an alien God, is one of the dominant images of Jewish representation. As we move forward in the century, however, positive regard and even admiration for such obduracy begins to mix with frustration: In 1840, *The Church of England Quarterly Review* observes in a review essay, "There is something peculiarly appealing in the fixedness of the Jewish character, as a proverbial reproach, during a career of bondage so protracted and enduring."[11] Indeed, the Jews' "stubborn" refusal to accept Christian conversion, the constancy of the Jews in their tenacious adherence to their faith despite remarkable obstacles throughout the lands, was very much a part of the vocabulary of antisemitism, even of philosemitism in England (whose principal goal was conversion of the Jews). Frank Felsenstein has elaborated the context in which, especially "for Christian conversionists . . . Jews are considered stiffnecked in their inability or refusal to recognize in Jesus the true Messiah."[12] In Aguilar's poem "The Evergreen," the rhetoric of tenacious constancy against all odds, and the rhetoric of being despised for such constancy, is given to the unpoetic evergreen even as it resonates with the vocabulary assigned to the condition of the Jew in history. As Cynthia Scheinberg observes, "'The Evergreen' becomes a symbol of the 'changeless' nature of Jewish identity through the ages; as such, this poem works to recast negative Christian stereotypes of Judaism, and to claim the natural world as rich with Jewish meaning."[13] The evergreen's meekness is transformed, at the poem's end, into dignified defiance that brings it closer to God:

> Constant in every varied scene,
> Of Nature's joy and grief,
> For this I bless thee, evergreen,
> And love thy fadeless leaf.
>
> And feel how much of poesy lies
> In thy still changeless shrine;
> Unto the heart thy voice replies,
> With whisperings divine!

The evergreen now has God—the divine whisperings—as well as the muse. By poem's end, the identification of the Jew with the evergreen is unmistakable. The steadfast evergreen, who all the same has no choice but to be "scatter'd ev'ry where," in fact is a "shrine" to "poesy." If the Jew is to be equated with the evergreen, however, it is an appropriation of natural imagery whose metaphoric significance is not about nature at all; it is about the contrivance of poetic principles of equivalence. Furthermore, the metonymic logic is decidedly not deciduous; as always green, the unchanging tree is not conventionally appropriated to image forth ideals about rejuvenation or regeneration, ideals typically appropriated in pastoral elegy in establishing solace within the cyclical generation of nature. As an image of that which transcends cyclical change, or at least the obvious iterations of it (changing color and losing leaves), however, its promise of steadfastness marks it as the extreme example of an almost quirky resoluteness. In this, the children of one soil may all, universally, take shelter in it.

One soil, however, is no source of reconciliation for all interested parties. The children of one soil are also the children of one inheritance, a fact that crosses paths with the more dominant image of the Jews as a nation apart. As Felsenstein remarks, "Defying the unecumenical sentiments of those who would prefer that it were otherwise, the roots of Judaism and Christianity continue to be fed by a common soil. However, a prominent doctrinal distinction that remains to this day fundamental to the ultimate separation of the two religions rests in their respective attitudes to conversion."[14] Felsenstein goes on to chronicle the conversionist stance of Christians toward Jews in England, a situation that is deeply registered by Jewish writers of the period. Aguilar's particular concern in *Women of Israel*, a collection of tales about Jewish and biblical women of historical significance, in fact takes up the subject of Judaism's treatment of women precisely in relation to the Christian conversionist effort to offer greater equality to Jewish women if only they will adopt Christianity's more tolerant privileges. Her introduction to the volume situates the anti-conversionist stance of "Women of Israel" adamantly, as she summarizes the specious conversionist view that "to Christianity alone [women] owe their present station in the world: their influence, their equality with man, their spiritual provision in this life, and hopes of immortality in the next. Nay more, that the value and dignity of woman's character would never have been known, but for the religion of Jesus; that pure, loving, self-denying doctrines, were unknown to woman; she knew not even her relation to the Eternal."[15] This summary, plainly brimming with the author's frustration, takes on a tone of muted outrage when Aguilar addresses the view, again popular with Christian conversionist missions to Jewish women, that Judaism is in its essence discriminatory toward women:

> How or whence originated the charge that the law of Moses sank the Hebrew female to the lowest state of degradation, placed her on a level with slaves or heathen, and denied her all mental and spiritual enjoyment, we know not: yet certain it is that this most extraordinary

and unfounded idea obtains credence even in this enlightened age. The word of God at once proves its falsity; for it is impossible to read the Mosaic law without the true and touching conviction, that the female Hebrew was even more an object of the tender and soothing care of the Eternal than the male. (pp. 248–249)

Aguilar's tenacity on behalf of Jewish women, and her insistence upon the misguided claims of Christian conversionists, is still the twin of her complicated efforts to represent a Judaism that is compatible with English life and English sensibility, even in the face of the existential challenges that accompany such efforts. It is also joined with her efforts to showcase a feminine sensibility that is unthreatening, even as it is conscious of distinctively Jewish modes of difference. The children of one land and the children originating from one book (the Bible), after all, sometimes dig the soil in markedly different ways. Again, we see in the poetry Aguilar's negotiations of the subtler complications of this dynamic. "An Infant's Smile," written in 1845,[16] begins on a note that, like many of the poems of the Moss sisters, signals the poet's feminine sensibility in the most stereotypical of scenes: delight over an infant. The poet addresses the baby, whose captivating and unprovoked smile is a source of pleasure and mystery to the speaker. This pleasing, apparently innocent meditation is also responsive to Aguilar's negotiation of her Romantic inheritance. The latter half of the poem makes of the infant a Wordsworthian character trailing clouds of glory, a potent contrast to the adult who, plainly echoing Wordsworth's "Immortality Ode," is destined to forget his glories. Wordsworth's ode hails the child:

> But trailing clouds of glory do we come
> From God, who is our home:
> Heaven lies about us in our infancy! (ll. 64–66)

Aguilar's lyric, less ecstatic than Wordsworth's, asserts:

> Thou art immortal! God hath placed
> The breath of life in thee, and traced
> His Image, babe, on thine!

To Wordsworth's "Our birth is but a sleep and a forgetting," Aguilar's speaker acknowledges "Vainly wouldst thou the past recall, / What did thine infancy befall." Wordsworth famously addresses the infant as

> Mighty Prophet! Seer blest!
> On whom those truths do rest,
> Which we are toiling all our lives to find. (ll. 114–116)

Aguilar also addresses the infant before her:

> And in thine innocence, art twined
> With purer beings of soul and mind?
> That fly, when thou wilt know
> This earth's o'erclouded tale of life.

Aguilar's expressive Romanticism is also the assertion of a universalism, as she showcases a shared sensibility and even assigns to the infant a nascent spirituality that is more Wordsworthian than Jewish. It is the third stanza of this ten-stanza poem, however, that gives the reader pause. Referring to the infant's smile, the speaker addresses the infant:

> Whence came it? tho' thy mother bends
> Caressing, as thy wants she tends,
> Thou dost not know her voice;
> A stranger's arm might softly hold thee,
> A stranger's breast in love enfold thee,
> And yet thou wouldst rejoice.

For the poet who has elsewhere championed Jewish education as the prerequisite to Jewish continuity, the recognition that this infant, this immortal being who stands as the supposed universal representation of blessed infancy, is indifferent to its own mother, is potentially startling. The child is easily swayed by "A stranger's arm" and "A stranger's breast" in which he all the same "rejoice[s]." The vocabulary of such seduction shares a rhetoric in common with one of Aguilar's central concerns: the education of the Jewish child, even from infancy, so that he/she will be equipped to recognize and counter the threat of assimilation and the temptations of Christian conversionists. It is a concern that also underlies one of the very foundations of Jewish self-identity. As Michel Galchinsky has persuasively argued, many of the romance novels written by Jewish women during the middle of the nineteenth century were positioned against the dominant Christian conversionist romance, in which the Jewish woman is wooed by the promise of Christian spiritual comforts and the most desirable of Christian suitors.¹⁷ Aguilar's own fiction functions as, in part, a response to this familiar narrative, one in which the influence of the stranger's breast can be rejected by the Jewish woman who chooses Jewish continuity over the seductive allures of Christian solicitation. For Aguilar in the poem "An Infant's Smile," the infant's *tabula rasa* serves as a warning and perhaps an implicit plea for Jewish education. In this, it joins the great subject of identity to the motif of mistrust. The infant's acquiescence in the stranger's arm and the stranger's breast shares some of the vocabulary of Aguilar's exhortations about the education of youth in *The Jewish Faith*: "Our youth indeed need help and guidance, or they are likely to be lost in the fearful vortex of contending opinions around them. To rest indifferent and unenquiring, always unnatural to youth, would actually be impossible now; and more than ever books are needed on which the mind and heart may rest; and more especially for our FEMALE YOUTH."¹⁸ In "Tintern Abbey," the banks of the River Wye and the Tintern Abbey environment become the stabilizing measure against which the poet's maturation may be measured. It is in this respect that the natural scene becomes for Wordsworth "the anchor of my purest thoughts, the nurse, / The guide, the guardian of my heart, and soul / Of all my moral being" (108–111). What the Jews need, according to Aguilar, is an educational resource that would in fact function like the evergreen in her poem of the same name. This is a matter of Jewish life and death, of Jewish survival in England and elsewhere. The locus of stability is not the mind's mediation of the natural environment, as it is for Wordsworth; the heart and mind of Jewish youth must "rest" on the locus of permanence that is defined by "books" that in her current moment are needed "more than ever." For Aguilar, the soul of the moral being is the evergreen power of Jewish learning.

The infant's Wordsworthian capacities lead inexorably, as they do in the "Immortality Ode," to a life of forgetting her celestial origins. Wordsworth's "little Actor cons another part" (102), while Aguilar's infant is still viewed from the perspective of the hapless babe: "Thou wilt look back, in vain,—no dream, / Of what thou wert, will faintly gleam, / Thro' more awakened power." For Wordsworth as for Aguilar, we forget our infant ministrations of "the glories [we] hath known." But for Aguilar, the mother—not mother nature, but the human mother—becomes implicitly the figure for remedying the condition. If Aguilar's poem reminds its readers that the mother who "bends caressing" could easily be lost to the arms and breast of the stranger, then the poem's conclusion is the affirmation that the mother, and only the mother, reiterates until it becomes internalized as faith:

> Smile! While we clasp thee, gentle one,
> Whom such sweet prayers are whisper'd on
> Smile in thy baby glee!
> One lovely thought that smile expresseth.
> Babe as thou art, a FATHER blesseth,
> A GOD hath love for thee!

We might well ask: Whence comes this assurance? How does the conclusion that a God has love for the infant proceed from a poem detailing the child's forgetfulness and malleability? The babe's unknowing smile is a reminder to the adults who encircle it. In *The Spirit of Judaism*, a meditation on the Hebrew prayer entitled the *Shema*, Aguilar emphasizes the place of its recital even in early infancy. The *Shema* is Judaism's central affirmation of faith and announcement of monotheism, and every Jew is commanded to recite it twice a day. It derives from Deuteronomy 6:4: "Hear O Israel, the Lord our God, the Lord is One." The declaration begins the first of three paragraphs recited in the synagogue service: Deuteronomy 6:4–9, Deuteronomy 11:13–21, and Numbers 15:37–41. Of the prayer, Aguilar insists: "It is right to learn this prayer in our earliest childhood; it would be wrong to wait till we could understand its importance to attain the words. . . . The faith we receive merely as an inheritance, will not enable us to defend it from insidious attack or open warfare, will not satisfy the cravings of our nature, will not give us a rock whereon to cling in hope and such deep love, that we could be strengthened even to die for it, if it were needed" (215). Later in the volume, she goes on to recite the injunction to pass on the significance of the *Shema* to our children: "'And thou shalt teach them diligently unto thy children,'—ie. The love of God all that is therein comprised" (222). For mothers, the primary source of religious knowledge for young children, a special task is enjoined. It may well be, as in "An Infant's Smile," that the mother is not distinguished yet from the stranger, but it is the mother whose task it is to lead the smiles of infancy to the conclusion of the poem's logic: "GOD hath love for thee." *The Spirit of Judaism* insists:

> To speak of God, to teach the child His will, to instil His love into the infant heart should never be looked on as a daily task, nor associated with all the dreaded paraphernalia of books and lessons. . . . The Hebrew mother who desires her offspring to say their prayers morning and evening, to abstain from writing, working, or cutting

on the Sabbath, to adhere to particular forms and observe particular days, as she does, has yet not wholly fulfilled her solemn duty. This will not be enough to make the Hebrew child love his God or his religion; not enough to restrain him in manhood from becoming a Christian if it favour his interest or ambition so to do.

   Far more depends on Hebrew parents than on Christian; the latter have their places of public worship wherever they may dwell, their ministers whose whole lives are devoted to the service of their God, to the moral and religious welfare of their fellow-creatures. . . . To his mother alone the Hebrew child must look, on his mother alone depend for the spirit of religion, the inculcation of that faith which must follow him through life. (pp. 222–223)

So much depends on "Hebrew parents." The infant's smile must be a call to pedagogical arms; the flexibility of the infant's affections, however adorable, is the Hebrew parents' most urgent warning.

Transcending the Nature It Surveys

Whatever Aguilar's investments in making Judaism palatable to the English mainstream, then, she does not conceive of an unthreatening Judaism as one that shrouds itself in an apparent obliteration of difference. The particularism of her understanding of Judaism is one with which English Protestants especially could easily identify: an unswerving faith in and reliance upon the Bible; a strong commitment to ancestral heritage; and a commitment to the English nation that ought to recognize in Jewish practice no incommensurability with English deportment. This commitment is not challenged by Aguilar's ironic reversals or recognition of the inherent threats to Jewish survival. They do, however, exert pressure on her self-identification as inheritor not only of Jewish tradition, with all of its particular challenges to women, but of Romantic lyric effusion. In poems such as I discussed earlier in this chapter, such pressure may clearly be discerned. In other poems, such as "An Infant's Smile," the lyrics gesture more subtly to the sources of their anxiety. Another such poem is the remarkable "Autumn Winds," the fifth poem in the "Communings with Nature" series.[19] It is all the more remarkable for following on "Autumn Leaves," the fourth poem in the series and an effusion that hardly rises above the clichéd admiration for the "gorgeous hue and shade" of the leaves, which are finally transformed into a religious lesson about God's love. One hint of the more challenging poem that is to follow, though, is perhaps contained in the stanza which gives voice to the autumn leaves:

> "Fear not! the Hand which robes the tree
> In glory e'er it fade,
> Hath dearer mercy, man, for thee,
> E'en in death's gloomy shade."

The leaves proclaim that God's love is greater for man than for the leaves. The speaker effaces its voice, or at least gladly takes second place in the hierarchy it proclaims. The leaves declare themselves a symbol for that which transcends nature.

"Autumn Winds" finally gives pride of place to God's benevolence in the world; however, unlike "Autumn Leaves," it presents a view of nature that is multifaceted and implicitly in dialogue with Aguilar's Romantic inheritance of nature poetry. The poem begins with a headnote:

> The most casual observer of nature must, we think, have noticed the peculiar tones of melancholy wailing borne on the wings of the wind at the commencement or middle of autumn—not the wild terrific gusts of threatening winter, but a low sobbing wail, not loud enough to disturb or alarm, but just sufficient to impress its melancholy on the most thoughtless heart. Its wail having been one evening universally noticed, the following poem was the consequence.

What is "universally noticed" is not the sublime; it is the low wail "not loud enough to disturb or alarm" which Aguilar seeks both to allegorize and interpret. Acknowledging that the voice of autumn is "sad," the speaker asks if the "wailing tone" proceeds from the knowledge that "mother Earth a robe must wear / Of Bliss o'erthrown?" The second stanza continues the interrogation, asking if the peculiar moaning of the wind proceeds from her knowledge "That Nature is but one wide tomb / O'er loveliness and mirth?" The recognition of Nature's fickleness and capacity to serve as shroud here is still fully within the bounds of Romantic nature conventions, even if its language of nature as a "wide tomb" is more aggressive than the norm. Still, Shelley's "Ode to the West Wind" is clearly echoing in the background, especially when the speaker of Aguilar's poem seeks to console the melancholy wind:

> Oh! check thy moanings; but a while
> Is hid sweet Nature's glowing smile:
> 'Twill wake again, and Earth beguile
> Of tear and sigh!

Shelley's poem concludes on a triumphant note of the power of cyclical renewal: "O Wind, / If Winter comes, can Spring be far behind?" (69–70). Neither Shelley nor Aguilar ornament an autumn wind which, in Shelley's language, blows the leaves as "pestilence stricken multitudes," a sign also to his readers of the political subtext of the poem. Both Shelley and Aguilar apostrophize the western wind, but Shelley is not addressing an autumn wind who, in the language of Aguilar's headnote, is "a low sobbing wail, not loud enough to disturb or alarm." His is "wild," and the leaves flee it "like ghosts from an enchanter fleeing" (3). Shelley's wind is aggressive, fierce, and unyielding; its relationship to the world of social action is unmistakable, all the more so because Shelley in addressing it insists on an identification with the poet's voice, and the poet's voice longs to be the wind's "lyre" (57), longs for it to "Be through my lips to unawakened Earth / The trumpet of a prophecy!" (68–69). We recall that in "Autumn Leaves," the lyric immediately preceding "Autumn Winds" in Aguilar's chronology, the leaves are much more complacent. They mark a tomb, but "with smiles of trusting love, ye gild / The pathway to the tomb." In "Autumn Winds," the speaker does indeed ask the wind if "Mourn'st the wreck thy pinions find—/ Leaves brown, and bare, and strewn." Still, here there is no wild ecstasy; where Shelley's wind is a tempest with whom the speaker identifies, Aguilar's wind shifts its point of symbolic reference.

It is this shift in symbolic reference that is most noteworthy. Both Shelley and Aguilar begin their poems as apostrophes. Only Aguilar transforms an apostrophe into a dialogue, and that dialogue transforms nature into an image of that which transcends the very nature that it surveys. In "Autumn Winds," the wind speaks back. We have been following Aguilar's voice addressing the wind and assigning to it the conventional associations: it weeps with sad voice because it learns that nature is a tomb, or that the "laughing sunshine" has evaporated in its midst. The speaker consoles the wind and reminds it of a lesson that is not incompatible with that of Shelley's speaker in his address to the wind: "but a while / Is hid sweet Nature's glowing smile: / 'Twill wake again, and Earth beguile / Of tear and sigh!" Finally, the apostrophe becomes a dialogue and the wind corrects its speaker's complacent and platitudinous assumptions. The wind insists that it does not mourn the decay of nature. He already knew, in fact, that such glories are "A brief while pass'd away." The wind is speaking back to the poet of nature and demanding that her imagistic associations are simply mistaken. The final six stanzas of the wind's response are worth quoting in their entirety:

> "But there are lovelier blossoms,
> Now shrin'd in love and mirth,
> In whose rich smiles and silver laugh
> No dream of wo hath birth.
>
> "I see—I see them passing;
> I mark the shrouding pall;
> The loving and the blessing—
> Like leaves, I see them fall!
>
> "I weep the broken-hearted—
> The spirits left to moan—
> The bounding hope—the trusting love—
> The springy joyance flown.
>
> "I weep the young hopes blighted,
> That may not bloom again;
> The stars that love hath lighted,
> Quench'd 'neath pale sorrow's rain.
>
> "I mourn the heavy anguish
> That winter's cold touch brings;
> The fireless hearth—the scanty board—
> The pangs that hunger wrings.
>
> "The famish'd babe and mother—
> The strong man chafed to sin.
> Oh! help'd ye one another,
> Such woes had never been!"

If Aguilar's speaker had hoped that the wind would become a trumpet of a prophecy for regeneration even as it took solace in the confidence that spring is soon to follow in the natural world, the wind itself is conceived as refuting such conventional hope as not only naive, but misguided, an essential misunderstanding of the real meaning of nature. In fact, what the wind in Aguilar's poem gives voice to is precisely the misconceptions of consolation in the bosom of nature. The speaker of Shelley's "Ode to the West Wind" follows a shift in its speaker's affective range: imploring the wind to complete his self-identification with it and thereby lift him "as a wave, a leaf, a cloud!" he laments that "I fall upon the thorns of life! I bleed!" (53–54), before boldly beseeching, "Be thou, Spirit fierce, / My spirit!" (61–62). The identification complete, his emotional valence turns from the thorns of life that wound him to the trumpet of a prophecy by which his words—so he continues to implore the wind—are scattered, "as from an unextinguished hearth / Ashes and sparks, my words among mankind!" (66–67). Aguilar instead refuses conventionalized identification with natural force. The identification with the landscape and consolation within the landscape are refuted by the wind itself, who never did mourn for natural decay anyway. The speaker, so it avers, got it wrong. The audaciousness of Aguilar's vision has its own potency, as her wind insists that it will not be transformed into a metaphoric equivalent of the abstraction of revivification, political or otherwise. In fact, the wind denounces its transformation into trope altogether, and this is the real force of Aguilar making of this poem a dialogue instead of an apostrophe. It refuses to stand merely as symbol. This wind, cold and unrelenting, brings a "cold touch" and "fireless hearth" to the poor. Of "young hopes blighted," the wind baldly notes that they "may not bloom again." We are here in the realm of "the scanty board," in a cold autumn that, so the wind reminds us, marks "the pangs that hunger wrings." These are not metaphoric pangs from falling on the thorns of life because they are not metaphorical thorns that cause bleeding; they are real hunger pangs—not tropes—that proceed from the "scanty board" brought on by "winter's cold touch." When the wind blows, it may make poets image forth fantasies of regeneration and grandiose visions of self-identification with powerful forces. Aguilar's speaker herself indulges in this when apostrophizing the wind in the first half of the poem. But when Aguilar's wind is given voice, it dismantles the voice of the nature poet. The voice of the wind is not triumphantly transformative. The thorns of life in Aguilar's poem belong to the empirical world, and they cannot be abstracted out of consciousness.

It is not that Aguilar is rejecting associations with nature altogether, nor is she necessarily criticizing Shelley nor any of her predecessors in their well-worn appropriations of landscape imagery. Shelley too is signaling the presence of human need, after all, and he is obviously calling for remedy. Aguilar's poem, however, reminds us of the tangible necessities of that which transcends lyric. The anthropomorphized wind transforms the decay of nature into an admonition to humanity for blights that take precedence over lyric effusion. The final stanza aggressively takes up the familiar image of the "babe and mother" as the wind points out that it witnesses and laments a "*famish'd* babe and mother" (italics mine). The wind finally becomes a scold: not the scold that wonders, like Wordsworth's Derwent, "was it for this" when the poet fails to make nature his primary theme. Aguilar's wind scolds about human neglect of the human: "Oh! Help'd ye one another, / Such woes had never been!" Published by a Jewish poet in 1846, and published in the Jewish venue *The Occident and American Jewish Advocate*, this effusion resonates with Aguilar's other thematic preoccupation: the condition of the Jews in England who face an English public that will not take the Jews' cultural integration for granted.

I would not strenuously argue for this poem as an assertion of Jewish frustration over Jewish alienation; I would, however, point out that an alternative sensibility, aware of its points of obtrusive difference, undergirds this poem. When the wind is given voice in the later part, it is talking back to the conventionalized poetic appropriation of the wind. It is responding, that is, to a tradition in which nature is not yet red in tooth and claw, and which looks forward to the telos of consolation. This is a tradition that the poet clearly is not willing entirely to relinquish; the poem, after all, is a dialogue, and the wind's response, however startling, could serve equally as a response to some of Aguilar's other poems, especially in the "Communings with Nature" series. In "Autumn Winds," the poet is willing to take on and invert some of the central tenets of her inherited Romanticism, and to do so by way of a poem that concludes on a note of rebuke directed at those who disregard the needs of their fellow human beings as much as at those who believe that nature will remain a panacea. Still, it is a poem that does not utterly reject Shelley and the other Romantics so much as it qualifies the sensibility from which they speak. If at first Aguilar's wind seems less strident than Shelley's, we do well to remember that the wind of her poem is still "weeping," still scolding, and tenaciously participant in the poetic tradition by which nature is animated, its anthropomorphic transformation an especially potent example of such connection to traditional expression. Aguilar's poem conveys its own aggressive agenda, but its stridency is restrained by its self-reflexive resistance to over-valorizing the voice of nature's consolation. It too yearns for a trumpet to prophesy the means of remediation, but the trumpet itself—the poetic voice—is not its primary concern. It is in this spirit that the poem's concluding couplet, offered immediately after the wind concludes its eight-stanza response, acknowledges the import of the wind's "song":

> And so the mournful wind went murmuring along,
> And thrilling truths were breathing in its sad and solemn song!

These are truths no less "thrilling" than those imagined by Shelley's "wild west wind." The faith in the aesthetic resolutions, however, is diluted by the poem's recognition that our human "woes had never been" had we but "help'd . . . one another."

From Flower to Soul

Aguilar challenges received notions of the aesthetic integrity of pastoral resolution in subtle ways throughout her poetry. In "I Never Loved a Flower," subtlety does not mask her misgivings, but neither does she have the full strength of her convictions to offer her apprehensions as anything other than self-mockery. The poem is subtitled, "Stanzas Written in a moment of extreme hilarity." There is really no need for the hilarity, however, as the poet proceeds to dismantle straightforwardly the various pieties about nature and its succor. I quote the first two stanzas:

> I never lov'd a flow'r
> And cherish'd it with pride
> But it wither'd in its home of love
> And bow'd its head and died.
>
> I never lov'd a star
> And dream'd it gave reply
> To my spirit's deep imaginings
> But it faded from on high. (ll. 1–8)

The point is made with facile ease, but this moment of "hilarity" still speaks to the tensions inherent in Aguilar's self-contradictory commitments both to nature and to the recognition of its limitations. Nature is not merely cyclical or regenerative. It foregrounds decay; it challenges our faith in renewal; it allegorizes our disappointments in love and sensibility too. Flowers do wither and stars do fade. Aguilar is surely not assigning to Romantic lyric the facile view that nature is simple panacea to all earthly woes. She is assigning to herself, perhaps, an exaggeration of her own longing to be at one with a valorization of the natural world. The cult of sensibility has long passed by Aguilar's time, but the expectations of human kindness are no less a requirement for ease of being. The subsequent stanza raises the stakes of disappointment:

> I never lov'd a friend,
> But parting's fiat came,
> And sympathies were sever'd, that
> Ne'er seem'd again the same. (ll. 9–12)

The fourth stanza recalls the flower imagery:

> I never felt deep gladness
> But a silent shadow stole,
> E'en 'mid the laughing flow'rs that twin'd
> A moment o'er my soul.

The friendship does not simply wither like the flower or fade like the star. Parting is a "fiat," and its decree is irreversible. From nature to an allusion to legal directive, what is at stake in acknowledging such withering of flowers may well be a slippery slope. I quote the fourth stanza again:

> I never felt deep gladness,
> But a silent shadow stole,
> E'en 'mid the laughing flow'rs that twin'd
> A moment o'er my soul.

We have moved, in the first four stanzas, from flower, to star, to friend, and now to soul. There is an escalation in the gravity and the consequence of each stanza. We do not expect flowers to do anything *but* wither, after all, and we already know that stars fade from view. We could reasonably hope for friendship's endurance, and we could most emphatically demand that our very souls remain constant. As each exemplary Romantic image fails to sustain a correspondence with its intended glory, so the soul itself betrays its might. In the "Immortality Ode" Wordsworth concludes his narrative of disappointment in nature's enduring nourishment by affirming the value of his soul's enduring responsiveness: "To me, the meanest flower that blows can give / Thoughts that do often lie too deep for tears" (202–203). This exemplifies Wordsworth's recognition of the "strength" that "remains behind" (179–180) as he grows older. Aguilar's title, "I Never Loved a Flower," alludes to Wordsworth's poem even as it qualifies its significance to her, and though "hilarity" may well be the putative origin of the stanzas, the disclaimer only serves to counterpoint the poet's points of difference from the pastoral that she both inherits and struggles against.

If the poet cannot find repose in the natural world or in the Romantic remedies, then what she turns to for relief is precisely the recognition of faith. She does not name it as the Jewish faith, but she does not need to do so. The poem was published in *The Occident* in 1844, by which time Aguilar was well recognized as a specifically *Jewish* author. When the Romantic natural pieties fail her, she seeks and finds peace in religion. Addressing her "spirit," she concludes on a note that emphasizes "safety" in the soul's ultimate dwelling:

> Oh come back to thy stillness,
> And dwell there with thy God;
> His blessed paths of quietness
> Securely thou hast trod.
>
> And tho' no dazzling flow'rs
> May there breathe tales of glee,
> And mirth's light laugh no echo finds:
> In safety thou wilt be.
>
> Our Father's smile will lead thee,
> His love will go before—
> Return! Return, my spirit—Oh
> Come to thy God once more.

There is indeed perhaps something disturbing in Aguilar equating a return of the soul to God with the cessation of "mirth's light laugh" or the absence of "dazzling flowers." Such deprivation is offered in the name of "safety," and figured finally in terms of a familiar and canonical Jewish motif: that of the "return." The longing to "Return, Return, my spirit" clearly echoes the liturgical Jewish lyrics of longing to return to Zion and to God. The *Amidah* prayer, discussed in Chapters 1 and 2 of this book, includes in its section about repentance the prayer to "return us to your Torah." Lamentations 5:21 is one of the more recognizable biblical quotations in Jewish liturgy emphasizing return and spiritual renewal: "Turn thou us unto thee, O Lord, and we shall be turned; renew our days as of old" (KJV). Lamentations, the book of elegies for the destruction of the first Temple and the exile of the Jews, is recited on Tisha B'Av. Lamentations 5 begins with the equally suggestive recognition: "Remember, O Lord, what is come upon us: consider, and behold our reproach. Our inheritance is turned to strangers, our houses to aliens" (5:1–2). The allusive points of reference recall the "Dialogue Stanzas," discussed earlier, in which Aguilar engages directly with Wordsworth as she presents two girls debating the relative merits of nature and The Book of Esther. There, she had presented the debate between nature and books as portending life or death, a motif that does not belong to Wordsworth's "Expostulation and Reply" or "The Tables Turned." Here too, the turning away from nature and from the Romantic pieties is the prerequisite for the soul's stillness. It is a matter of safety in a condition of exile, one that recalls the foreboding of the earlier poem, but also the foreboding of the first stanzas of "I Never Loved a Flower": recalled from the retrospect especially of the concluding lines, there is surely no "hilarity" to be found. The soul is starved, friends are estranged by "fiat," and there is no solace in the landscape. The allusions to Wordsworth are suggestive of a wistful dream that counterpoint her knowing flight to faith. There is no safety in the domain in which she is most manifestly situated. Her call for "return" is not a call to the returns supplied by cyclical nature, but the restoration to a fuller expression of faith whose endurance is the only guarantee of spiritual survival in the land whose cultural definition is given, in part, by the very nature repudiated in this poem.

Whatever her lyrical explorations of safety, Aguilar continues to cherish the aesthetic, and she takes deep pleasure in her Romantic and English inheritance even when they threaten the repose of direct devotion. She turns to sources she acknowledges as alienating as much as to the safer forums, but she does so with a highly qualified—even a somewhat suspicious—confidence in the solace of the landscape and of natural beauty. This connects well with the theme of "Autumn Winds," discussed above, which concludes with the lament that had human beings "help'd ye one another," the woes of the world had never been.

Hearing the Lord's Song in a Strange Shrine

Helping one another is indeed a leitmotif of both Romantic and religious writing. For Aguilar, the spirit of cooperation is a fundamental virtue in the exercise of religious freedom. Although she is careful to recognize in England a source of gratitude for the Jews, she does not forget its long record of inhospitality either. Her aesthetic sensibilities are sometimes in conflict with her recognition of the need to qualify the meaning of an aesthetic sensibility beholden to its Romantic precursors. The tension is displayed boldly in a poem of 1844, "A Vision of Jerusalem," a lyric prefaced by a significant subtitle: "While Listening to a Beautiful Organ in One of the Gentile Shrines." The vision of Jerusalem is intended to be juxtaposed with the vision of the Gentile shrine, and yet it is the Gentile shrine that gives rise to such longing. The poet subverts our expectations in the opening lines further still, which follow the poet as she is imaginatively transported to ancient Jerusalem, drawing, as Michael Galchinsky has noted, on an allusion to Ezekiel's vision of the Resurrection of the House of Israel in Ezekiel 37:1–4;[20]

> I saw thee, oh, my fatherland, beautiful, my own!
> As if thy God had raised thee from the dust where thou art strewn,
> His glory cast around thee, and thy children bound to Him,
> In link so brightly woven, no sin their light could dim.
>
> Methought the cymbal's sacred sound came softly on my ear,
> The timbrel, and the psaltery, and the harp's full notes were near;
> And thousand voices chaunted, his glory to upraise,
> More heavenly and thrillingly, than e'en in David's days.[21]

The speaker is moved to see her "fatherland" while in a Christian church. Aguilar sometimes visited Christian worship services, in part because, as a non-fluent Hebrew speaker, she could better appreciate the language of the Hebrew Bible as recited during the Anglican service in English. Her ecumenicalism also played a part. In an 1837 essay, published as one of her "Sabbath Thoughts," Aguilar defends the practice of joining with other faiths in worship:

> There is nothing, in my opinion, that enlarges an unprejudiced mind more, than joining with those of another faith in their religious ceremonies; but then it *must* be an unprejudiced mind, a

charitable and kindly spirit, otherwise just the contrary of liberality and enlargement of ideas must be the consequence. Let no Jew who has a contempt of the Christian, enter into a place of worship belonging to the latter. . . . I thank God, He has, in His mercy, permitted me to be so firmly convinced of the truth and holiness of my own belief, that it *is* a pleasure to me to join with Christians in their religious forms. If we *look* for it, we shall find in almost, nay, in every lecture whose foundation is religion, somewhat that comes home to our own hearts, somewhat that will strike the inmost recesses of the soul, even though it be addressed to the followers of Christ, and their Saviour be the principal subject; even then may the mind of a liberal and pious Jew be enlarged, for he will know why and what a Christian does believe.[22]

Aguilar, then, proclaims the sympathetic enlargement of her imagination and of her knowledge in ways that ought to lead, perhaps, to a perfect symmetry between her religious faith and her residence in England. The above effusion is especially resonant of the stance she takes in her prose fiction, which combats the various myths of conversionist narratives. Similarly, it serves as the answer to her anxieties about the place of education for Jewish children in particular, who must be strengthened in their belief even as infants, as she observes in *The Spirit of Judaism*, or "they are likely to be lost in the fearful vortex of contending opinions around them." Aguilar's assertions in "Sabbath Thoughts" would situate her as among those who imbibed the spirit of Judaism sufficiently even from infancy, so much so, in fact, that she can take pleasure in Christian church services. Such enlargement of mind, such a cooperative spirit with the dominant culture, however, is not, *pace* her effusion above, a pure pleasure. In the poem, her vision of the fatherland—Jerusalem—comes to a close and is replaced by a heightened consciousness of profound alienation:

> I stood ALONE 'mid thronging crowds who filled that stranger shrine,
> For there were none who kept the faith I hold so dearly mine:
> An exile felt I, in that house, from Israel's native sod,—
> An exile yearning for my *home*,—yet loved still by my God.

Her present locale—a church in England—renders her "alone" even among "thronging crowds." She feels herself an "exile" not only from the synagogue, not only from her family, but indeed from "Israel's native sod." The felt experience of communal estrangement leads to a longing not simply to rejoin her Jewish community; she recognizes herself and declares herself an "exile" from "Israel's native *sod*." She figures herself as alienated from the landscape that she defines as "home," even as her primary point of reference is the condition of the Jews in England in the mid-1840s, tolerated but not yet fully emancipated, a foreign race still in the eyes of the majority.

What is significant here is the choice she makes to attend the church service in the first place. The subtitle would remind us that however alienated our speaker may feel, she has come to church for the aesthetic experience that she still acknowledges as "beautiful." She may well be a stranger in church, in England, in her diasporic world; however, her soul finds a sure echo in the music of the church service which all the same leads to a recognition of profound alienation. I would suggest that such alienation is "profound" because, like many of the authors studied in this volume, Aguilar comprehends a self-alienation from which there is no simple relief. Hers is the love of Christian organ music; hers is the frustration and dissatisfaction with the synagogue service and Jewish learning in England; hers is the appreciation of the dedication of Christian worshippers and their easy access to the Bible in a language they understand. And hers is the revulsion she experiences in their midst. In *The Spirit of Judaism*, Aguilar descries the Jewish neglect of the Bible by Jews and the poverty of aspects of the synagogue service:

> But the great evil under which the Hebrew nation is still suffering, is not so much the *denial* as the *neglect* of this precious word. We are in general perfectly satisfied with reading the Parasha and the Haftorahs marked out as our Sabbath portions. The other parts of the Bible rest utterly unknown. Brought out on the Sabbath for the brief space of half an hour, the portions are read, and hastily dismissed, as a completed task, bringing with it no pleasure and little profit. Even this is but too often neglected, and we adhere to the forms and ceremonies of our ancestors, scarcely knowing wherefore; and we permit our Bibles to rest undisturbed on their shelves not even seeking them, to know the meaning of what we do.[23]

The book, as we have earlier observed, figures matters of life and death. Aguilar urges a firmer grasp of Hebrew scripture within a rehabilitated synagogue service that brings content "to the forms and ceremonies of our ancestors." In this, she joins her advocacy for Jewish education to her reliance upon aesthetic criteria. The complaint about the meager experience of the Bible on the Sabbath is that it is performed as a "task," a labor that must be completed, one that brings "no pleasure." For pleasure in "A Vision of Jerusalem," Aguilar heads to church. There she is in no danger of conversion or of disavowal of her Jewish faith; she *is* in danger of the stark recognition that the ground beneath her feet is unstable, and that stability will not be reinstated even when she flees to the synagogue, or to her home in England. In fact, *home* has been redefined in this poem as "Israel's native sod." Her faith is the one defining feature of her identity that anchors her, but it is an anchor set down in stormy seas.

> No exile from his love! No, no; tho' captive I may be,
> And I must weep, whene'er I think, my fatherland, on thee!
> Jerusalem! My beautiful! my own! I feel thee still,
> Though for our sins thy tainted sod the Moslem strangers fill.

Aguilar here conflates her sense of alienation in the church, wakened rudely from her reverie about Jerusalem in Temple times, with her sense of alienation in England as well as her alienation from the Jewish people who, according to the prophets, "for our sins" are responsible for the present condition of exile.

If she wakes to the condition of exile, she also wakes to the realization that at least she is no exile form God's love. Her "captivity" is not merely a continuation of reverie, though. If she identifies home with Jerusalem, exile with the sins of her coreligionists, and aesthetic pleasure with the church that is a "Stranger shrine," then the dream of "home" is the obverse of the apprehension that "home" is a dream. Where has she conceived her vision of home? In church. And it is in church that she awakens to the meaning of having only God as the one source from which she does not feel estranged. Aguilar figures this dynamic finally in the terms of the past and of the landscape:

> Alas, my country! Thou must yet deserted rest and lone,
> Thy glory, loveliness, and life, a Father's gifts, are flown!
> Oh! that my prayers could raise thee radiant from the sod,
> And turn from Judah's exiled sons their God's avenging rod!
>
> And like an oak thou standest, of leaves and branches shorn;
> And we are like the withered leaves by autumn tempests torn

> From parent stems, and scattered wide o'er hill, and vale, and sea,
> And known as Judah's ingrate race wherever we may be.

The exilic scattering into diaspora reaches up to Aguilar's present, a Jew who finds herself in a foreign land, in Christian England, a child of parents who landed here in flight from the Portuguese Inquisition. Aguilar is fond of the conventional image of autumn leaves tossed by the tempest. Here, they are in contrast to the oak of Jerusalem, the "parent" solidity helpless to prevent its progeny from becoming "scattered wide o'er hill, and vale, and sea." Over the sea to Portugal, over the sea to England: in England, not only Judah's ingrate race, but ungrateful to the home country that serves as haven. This ingratitude is marked with some annoyance in *The Church of England Quarterly*, in the same article noted above, where the author observes with some astonishment, "Those who associate nobility with love of country will also regard the Jews; the descendants of Abraham never forget 'the pleasant land,' and maintain, under every variety of outward circumstance, the same unperishing attachment to their ancient mountains"[24] (130).

"A Vision of Jerusalem" is more hymn than ode. It admits of no synthesis or resolution. It begins in a church in England and ends with a messianic yearning to leave England altogether for a rebuilt, redeemed Jerusalem.

> Oh! blessed was that visioned light that flash'd before mine eye;
> But, oh, the quick awakening check'd my soul's ecstatic sigh!
> Yet still, still wilt thou rise again, my beautiful, my home,
> Our God will bring thy children back, ne'er, ne'er again to roam!

The poet has still not physically left the church, not even while dreaming that her people might yet "ne'er again" need "roam." In the opening situation of the poem, she is listening to the beautiful organ, secure in her own faith, and enlarged sufficiently in sympathy to be transported to a vision that would affirm her faith. This is where she has the vision of Jerusalem in the days of its Temple glory, where she hears the beautiful music of Jerusalem as inspired by the beautiful music of the Anglican church service. Waking from this reverie, she may well recognize that she is a stranger on alien ground, but we may not forget that the foundation of her vision is the aesthetic pleasure in the church service. Having passed through the struggle of her sensation of estrangements and its implications, she concludes not by circling back to the church with a corrected vision, but by displacing herself from both her reverie and the comfort of her familiars.

The "visioned light" that she imagined in church may well have been "blessed," but her assertion of the value of "my home" proceeds from the "quick awakening" that "check'd my soul's ecstatic sigh!" If God will bring His children back "ne'er again to roam," then the poem concludes affirming that home, for the Jews, is not in England. Home exists in some millennial future constructed on a vision of the past, which is as much to say that home is a textual construction. England is where the Jews "roam."

England, however, is also where the Jews long to be recognized as loyal subjects. The dream of the return to Jerusalem is not yet a plan actually to journey to the Middle East; it is acknowledged consistently and self-consciously as imaginative vision, or at least as millennial prayer. England is the domain in which Aguilar and the Anglo-Jews roam and is therefore the sheltering habitation; existentially, the master narrative of her self-identification is as a Jew. Unlike her English precursors, then, she cannot put an anchor into the landscape of Christian England by which to define her subjectivity, at least not without self-contradiction. Her primary locus of objectivity is her master narrative of her life as a Jew in England, which must also be the narrative of the very tensions that define her.

The Rocks of Elim

"The Rocks of Elim"[25] illustrates some of the tensions inherent in "A Vision of Jerusalem," but is more aggressive on behalf of Aguilar's implicit claim to authority than it is attentive to her sense of self-alienation. The poem contains a subtitle orienting its reader: "Suggested by a Perusal of Lord Lyndsey's Letters on the Holy Land, &C. Vol 1, Pages 260–1." Lord Lindsay—as it is properly spelled—(1812–1880) is today best known as an art historian responsible for *Sketches of the History of Christian Art* (1847). As a young man, in 1837–1838, he traveled to the Middle East, which resulted in *Letters on Egypt, Edom and the Holy Land*, published in 1838. It was reviewed in *The London Quarterly Review* for January–April 1839, as part of a section entitled "State and Prospects of the Jews."[26] The review and article were authored anonymously, though we now know that it was Anthony Ashley Cooper, Lord Ashley (later seventh Earl of Shaftesbury), who wrote it. Ashley was a major proponent of Christian Zionism, and his essay advocates the return of the Jews to Palestine. For Ashley, this was both politically and economically strategic, and was also in keeping with his restorationist views that the return of the Jews to the

Holy Land is the will of God. Mere pages after recounting the scene in Lindsay's *Letters* which Aguilar is to appropriate in her poem, the reviewer offers a philosemitic Christian conversionist discussion of the state of the Jews as he regards them:

> But a mighty change has come over the hearts of the Gentiles; they seek now the temporal and eternal peace of the Hebrew people; societies are established in England and Germany to diffuse among them the light of the Gospel; and the increasing accessions to the Parent Institution in London attest the public estimation of its principles and services.
>
> Encouraged by these proofs of a bettered condition, and the sympathy of the Gentiles who so lately despised them, the children of Israel have become far more open to Christian intercourse and inquiry.[27]

Aguilar's poem was written in 1840, and the section in Lindsay to which she refers concerns his travels across the desert and his conjecture that a particular spot is near the site of an oasis that had served as camp for the Israelites in their wanderings through the desert:

> Between Beer Howara and Wady Gharendel, the country becomes more mountainous, and assumes a more picturesque character. Two divisions of the Waled Said were encamped near the Wady; one of the Bedouins quitted us, and disappeared, diving down a small ravine that seemed to end in nothing. One could scarcely fancy human inhabitants of such wilds. We halted among the tarfa-bushes under one of the hills of Wady Gharendel, but at too great a distance from the wells to admit of our visiting them. This, probably, is the Elim of scripture.[28]

As in "A Vision of Jerusalem," the poet begins in the domain of Christian identity; travel narratives to the Holy Land were popular in the nineteenth century, and though some Anglo-Jews did visit, it was primarily a Christian activity. Lindsay's astonishment that the Bedouins could actually survive in such harsh wilds certainly joins hands with orientalist discourse even as it might well have served to remind Aguilar of the contexts of exilic wandering as they occur not in a distant past or in the "civilized" world of England, but in the present world of present-day Palestine. Lindsay's subsequent mention of Elim occurs when he is leaving the area, and I believe that it is the passage to which Aguilar specifically refers in her subtitle:

> It was the stillest hour of the day; the sun shone brightly, descending to his "palace in the Occident,"—the tide was coming in with its peaceful pensive murmur, wave after wave;—It was in this plain, broad and perfectly smooth from the mountains to the sea, that the children of Israel encamped after leaving Elim; what a glorious scene it must then have presented, and how nobly those rocks, now so silent, must have re-echoed the song of Moses and its ever returning chorus, "Sing ye to the Lord, for he hath triumphed gloriously; the horse and his rider hath he thrown into the sea!"[29]

Aguilar's opening lines follow Lindsay with remarkable fidelity:

> The sun was sinking slowly in the west,
> Yet filling that fair scene with golden light,
> Which, soft and mellow'd, heat intense suppress'd,
> Yet gilded rock and wave with radiance bright;
> And o'er the lovely azure of the sky,
> Clouds, gold and crimson, gorgeously swept by,
> But all breathed peace and stillness.

This identification with Lindsay's text is all the more remarkable given that "The Rocks of Elim" appropriates the descriptive rendering, appropriates Lindsay's detailing of the physical prospect, but assigns to it an alternative signification. The poet's visual range of apprehension of Elim is actually Lindsay's, though their sensibilities and religious visions are in no way congruous. For Aguilar as for Lindsay, the hour is still; the sun is slowly sinking; and the rocks are gilded with radiance. Later in the poem, Aguilar too will recall the songs of the Israelites to the Lord, though Aguilar will not neglect an allusion to Miriam's song as well. Strangely, Aguilar's poem praises not the oasis of Elim, but the "rocks," which according to Lindsay must have echoed the songs of Exodus 15. Aguilar would appropriate the song not only of Moses, Miriam, and the ancient Israelites, but more audaciously she would appropriate the Protestant refraction of it. In so doing, she does not turn Lindsay's patronizing sensibilities on their head so much as she reclaims the landscape and the voice by which she would identify herself. Aguilar renders Lindsay's descriptions as her opportunity for asserting proprietary ownership of the real meaning of vision within Elim. The travel narrative, the local descriptions, are his. Aguilar redefines vision of the space and, most crucially, articulation of its meaning.

She begins with the sense of sight provided to her by Lindsay's *Letters*; she proceeds to the sense of hearing, just as Lindsay does; however, unlike Lindsay, who imagines immediately the silent rocks echoing with song, Aguilar dwells for a while on the silence, and from there imagines an absence of all sentient life: "not a sound / Broke the full silence" (7–8); "No sea-bird clave the soft yet breezy air; / No note of life, from the huge mountains there" (11–12); the plain is "bearing no stain / Of man's disturbing step" (14–15). "The Rocks of Elim" was written four years before "A Vision of Jerusalem," and like the later poem, it experiments with a locus outside of her immediate community in her search for a self-defining voice. She is doubly displaced from Elim: she experiences it through someone else's travel narrative, and the narrative's author is an established member of the upper echelons of Anglican England, one whose rendering of the scene resonates with the full range of Christian conversionist polemic. The endnote to Lindsay's introduction to Elim quotes Michael Syncellus on the significance of the landscape: "The twelve fountains, and the seventy palm-trees of Elim, are emblems of the twelve apostles of our saviour and the seventy disciples, sent forth to scatter the sweet waters of the Gospel over the World."[30] If Aguilar is struggling to articulate a subjectivity defined by mastery of voice, then her challenge remains consistent across her oeuvre; that is, she establishes the tensions in her lyric poetry that define her existence, even as she recognizes and forecasts at once that the construction of "voice" is partly constitutive of her subjectivity. For it to rely on a displaced center of gravity, as it were, is to acknowledge the meaning of a partial self-alienation by which she would also define her voice. She transforms Lindsay's echoing landscape into one that is quiet, bereft of human and beast alike; but she does so, I would argue, in order to gain the space of the landscape itself, as if to reclaim it for an alternative reflection. This landscape as reread by Aguilar is neither one of pastoral ease, nor of sublime obscurity, nor of Lindsay's Christian allegorizing. Lindsay's animated writing barely slows down; Aguilar insists on a space of pause. The silent landscape for Aguilar signifies "mighty memories" (17) that are conjured "E'en in the thrilling stillness" (18). Those are the memories of biblical salvation as much as they are about the wandering in the desert of the Israelites.

When a "voice" is finally introduced into this landscape, it still is not yet the echoing voice of the song of Moses. The sound finally audible beyond the earlier "low murmur of the rippling wave" (9) is still one of natural, not human, force:

> A voice was cradled in that soft blue sky,
> Whisp'ring that the same God of love was nigh,
> Who in that heaven had set his shadowy cloud,
> And fiery pillar, his beloved to shroud;—
> Darkness to Mitzraim's host—but radiant light
> To them He saved from slavery's starless night. (ll. 23–28)

The voice belongs to the waters that had once parted to let pass the Israelites as they fled Egypt and which became the watery grave of the Egyptian army of Pharaoh as they pursued them. "A voice had those blue waters, now so still" (29), she reminds us, just as the poet reminds us of the biblical story of God guiding the Israelites by night with a fiery pillar and by day with a cloud.

Aguilar cannot claim possession of Lindsay's actual footsteps through the landscape; she is staking a claim to the landscape and to its interpretive import. In this dynamic, nature does have a voice, but she is the one who reads it correctly. She may do so in part because she also lays proprietary claim to the biblical narrative itself. The echo she claims to hear in the verse quoted below is an echo possibly of the past but possibly also of the shofar ("the silver clarion's blast")—the ram's horn blown in Jewish ritual to mark the Jewish New Year and the conclusion of the Day of Atonement—which announces present momentousness:

> Oh! was it but the phantom of the past,
> Or did once more the silver clarion's blast
> Sound in mine ears, and mount and rock and plain,
> 'Neath those full notes, are quiv'ring again?
> The Jewish hosts are marshalling the ground
> From mount to sea— (ll. 49–54)

These are not "Israelites" but, anachronistically, "*Jewish* hosts," a term not employed in the Hebrew Bible to describe the Israelites wandering in the desert. The term "Jew" comes into use during the post-exilic period. For Aguilar to assert that "*Jewish* hosts" are marshaling the ground is for her implicitly to assert ownership of the narrative, in the sense of rightful inheritance of the text, figured as knowledge of how to read it. This is a dynamic that echoes the experiments of Hyman Hurwitz and Emma Lyon in negotiating the vagaries of translation. Lindsay's privilege and social standing may have paved the way for his travel and narrative, but Aguilar and her coreligionists are the Jewish hosts who, so she would have it, inherit its meaning and its hermeneutical complexities.

Now we finally move on to the echoing song of Mose that Lindsay mentions so early in his recounting of his experience of Elim. Aguilar notes that the people, saved from the encroaching Egyptian army by God's miraculous parting of the sea, sing praises to God, and that "rock and ridge, with sudden radiance bright, / Fling back the song of praise, of glory loud, / That wakes in chorus from the holy crowd" (58–60). Aguilar has delayed until now the outpouring of great sound because she has been preparing the ground for understanding that the songs of Moses, of Miriam, and of the people of Israel after crossing the sea are songs that she, as Jewish poet, has rightfully inherited within the narrative of her own self-definition. Lindsay remembers the song of Moses. Aguilar remembers too the song of Miriam:

> "Sing, sing ye to the Lord of Hosts, for He
> On Mitzraim's hosts hath triumphed gloriously,
> The horse and rider in the seas o'erthrown,
> The depths have cover'd them, they sank as stone!
> Sing, sing ye to the Lord!" (ll. 65–69)

These lines from "The Rocks of Elim" follow closely from Miriam's song in Exodus 15:21. Aguilar does not forget that not only Moses, but also Miriam the prophetess has a song and that "all the women went out after her with timbrels and with dances" (KJV, Exodus 15:20). The song is one inherited by Aguilar and situated in a poem in which Aguilar clarifies the authority by which she stands as one of "the women of Israel" to give voice to her yearning. Miriam's song having been sung, the poem returns to conclude on a note of silence. This is a silence, however, that does not signify the frustration of the incommunicado. The return of silence reminds of the space for interpretation which Aguilar established earlier in the poem, insisting upon the pause that becomes the voice of authoritative interpretation:

> The vision past! Hush'd was the glorious sound,
> The rocks in stillness, solemnly profound,
> Hung deepening shadows, on the sandy plain,
> And all was hush'd and desolate again.
> Spirit of truth! Thou didst my soul enfold,
> And wrapt it in thy robe—till scenes of old
> Embodied came, to thrill my yearning heart,
> And deeper love and thanksgiving impart!
> Oh! let the scorner, and the sceptic seek
> Where nature's self-inspired love can speak,
> Where rock and ocean, mount and moaning blast,
> Proclaim aloud the story of the past. (ll. 79–90)

Nature speaks for itself; it is "self-inspired" because it does not need an interpretive crutch. It "proclaims" the "story of the past." Its physical delineations could be told as easily by Lord Lindsay as by any visitor to the scene. The hermeneutics of the story itself, however, are mediated not by nature but by human agency, one that invokes the "Spirit of truth" to enfold the poet's soul. The rocks of Elim are self-inspired. Aguilar makes of the scene a marker of her continuity as singer of Israel, and when she inherits the song of Miriam she defines the authority of her voice, one that far surpasses any traveler. The pastoral scene that would be transformed into visionary song by her Romantic precursors is here too transformed into visionary song. The difference is that Aguilar marks it as the scene of her just inheritance, one that encompasses her claim to lyric as well as her claim to history. Lord Lindsay wrote the letter; Aguilar wrote the poem. The poem assumes the authority of lyric and its cultural associations with interpretive potency; beyond that, it asserts a claim about the Jewish reader's interpretive authority of Hebrew biblical narrative.

What I have referred to as gaining the space of the landscape itself is offered by way of situating Aguilar within the broader context of public consideration of the Jews in England. The *London Quarterly Review*'s article about Lindsay and "the state and prospects of the Jews" acknowledges that England has a singular place in the history of the Jews in Europe. This is a history acknowledged also by Aguilar in her *History of the Jews*, but one that still has power to surprise. Lord Ashley's philosemitic conversionist stance still finds room to recognize the Jews' gratitude to their host country:

England has attained the praise of being the first of the Gentile nations that has ceased to "*tread down* Jerusalem!" This is, indeed, no more than justice, since she was the first to set the evil and cruel example of banishing the whole people in a body from her inhospitable bosom. France next, and then Spain, aped our unchristian and foolish precedent. Spain may have exceeded us in barbarity; but we invented the oppression, and preceded her in the infliction of it. . . . We oftentimes express our surprise at the stubborn resistance they oppose to the reception of Christianity; but Christianity in their view is synonymous with image-worship, and its doctrines with persecution. . . . Though a people deep in their sentiments of hatred, they are accessible, even when beguiled by neological delusions, to those who address them on their national glory; and many persons living can attest the gratitude of the Hebrews, as of old, to those who seek the welfare of their nation. (p. 106)

England is indeed the first country to expel wholesale its entire Jewish population from all parts of the country. For Ashley, the real crime is that centuries of persecution have served as a poor model of Christian love and benevolence. The Jews are less likely to convert under the cruel conditions they have experienced by their Christian hosts. For Aguilar, the threat of the conversionist niceties is the threat of being defined against one's own peculiar self-image. Aguilar embraces the image of the stubborn Jew unbowed by kindness and cruelty alike, but she is not "accessible," to appropriate Ashley's terms, to the self-defeat of conversion. When Aguilar modulates the voice of her implicit authority, she does so knowing that such sentiments as Ashley's constitute the wider context of her world.

Other Exiles: Hagar and Ismael

Given Aguilar's preoccupation with voice, her poem "The Wanderers"[31] is daring in its appropriation of the voice of another. Subtitled "Genesis, xxi. 14–20," the poem traces the wandering of Hagar and her son Ismael after they are banished from Abraham's home. In the biblical narrative, Hagar the handmaid bears Abraham's first son because Sarah was infertile. Soon after Sarah, at the age of 91, gives birth to Isaac, she is disturbed by the presence of

Hagar and Ismael, and urges a reluctant Abraham to cast them out. Written in 1838 and published in 1845 in *The Occident*, "The Wanderers" is a mature engagement with some of the most complicated themes in the Aguilar oeuvre. For in its immediate advertising of the biblical story, offered as subtitle, it resonates with the familiar thematic preoccupations of cultural authority; in its appropriation of the voice of Hagar, wandering in exile, estranged from home but not estranged from God, it echoes the similarly familiar theme of heroines who situate themselves against the dominant norms, calling upon reserves of faith that forecast the tenacity of Jewish being. Several commentators have noted that in "The Wanderers" Aguilar identifies the Jewish exile with Hagar.[32] In context especially of Aguilar's body of work, it is indeed virtually impossible to not see in "The Wanderers" a parable of Jewish displacement. All the same, I would argue that Aguilar is alive to the tensions inherent in the very act of appropriating the voice of Hagar. By the time we arrive at the fourteenth line of Genesis 21—the first line in Aguilar's subtitle—Sarah has already finished complaining about Hagar. God has already assured Abraham that he ought to harken to the voice of his wife and cast out his "bondwoman," because Ismael too will be made into a nation, even though "Isaac shall thy seed be called" (21:12). Genesis 21:14 begins with Abraham rising early in the morning and furnishing Hagar with bread and water. Aguilar's poem may well strongly echo the Jews' exilic wandering, but it opens with Abraham, this time a concerned *father*, a man saddened to tears that he must part from his beloved son. Sarah is nowhere mentioned in this narrative, even though the biblical context requires that we have in mind Sarah's responsibility for this parting. Aguilar emphasizes God's promise to Abraham that Ismael will be saved:

> But God had spoken, and he knew His word was changeless truth,
> He could not doubt His blessing would protect the friendless youth;
> He bade him go, nor would he heed the anguish of his soul;
> He turned aside,—a father's woe in silence to control. (ll. 5–9)

This is the opening situation of the poem: not Hagar's suffering, not Sarah's jealousy, but Abraham's paternal anguish. The scene of Hagar's suffering and anxiety for Ismael is as poignant as any grief-stricken narrative of maternal distress. The son's solicitation and care for his beloved mother Hagar is equally heart-rending:

> "Oh, mother lay me down," he cried, "I know not what I feel,
> But something cold and rushing seems thro' all my limbs to steal—
> Oh kiss me, mother dear, and then ah, lay me down to sleep—
> Nay, do not look upon me thus—kiss me and do not weep!"
> (ll. 29–32)

Aguilar foregrounds a benevolence toward others that depends upon recognizing their alterity. Where Lord Ashley, in *The Church of England Quarterly*, praises the strangers in their midst by way of tolerating them well enough to convert them to versions of themselves, Aguilar in "The Wanderers" looks into the heart of the suffering Hagar and the suffering Ismael and recognizes them in their otherness. She looks also into the heart of the suffering Abraham, the figure with whom she identifies religiously, and acknowledges the depth of his agony over his parting from the other sufferers. Some identification between Hagar in her wanderings and Aguilar in her preoccupation with Jewish exile is, to be sure, resonant; however, the poet seems to be confronting Hagar not as she can be made over into an allegory for the Jew, or "converted," as it were, into the image of the very character (Sarah) who has caused her suffering. She is Hagar who has been banished. She is the mother of a son loved by his father Abraham. The son loves and comforts her, and God finally saves and cares for them. There is another narrative version—the Hebrew Bible—that tells the same story, and it serves for Aguilar as ultimate Truth. The embellishments added by Aguilar serve only to underline the depth of emotion experienced by the characters. The very subtitle is of the relevant biblical passage because Aguilar is emphasizing the truth value of the story, one in which God saves Abraham's "other" son. If this is a narrative that reminds its readers of the Jew in exile, then it must be one that also reminds us of the famous Jewish dictum, pronounced by Rabbi Hillel, "What is hateful unto you, do not do unto your neighbor. That is the whole Torah, all the rest is commentary."[33] If both Hagar and the Jew in exile share a repertoire of images, it is not because one can be collapsed into the other. Rather, it is because the cultural story of each of them is a story of suffering as well as a story of misunderstanding and resentment of the other in our midst. Aguilar would suggest that we can understand Hagar without making her into our own image. The poem began with Abraham's agony over the departure of his child. It concludes on a note of revival. God provides an oasis for Hagar and Ismael, and the mother is overwhelmed with gratitude and love:

> She held him to her throbbing breast, she gazed upon his face—
> The beaming features, one by one, in silent love to trace.
> She bade him kneel to bless the Hand that saved him in the wild—
> But oh! few words her lips could speak, save these—"My child, my child!"

This is the conventional image of the loving mother. Muslim, Christian and Jew share in this story as part of their common soil.

Sabbath Thoughts

A common soil, of course, is the soil most often subject to misinterpretation. If Aguilar sometimes takes up the tension in illustrating both the similarities of and differences between Judaism and Christianity, her series of poems, "Sabbath Thoughts," underline just how productive this tension is for her work. As Cynthia Scheinberg has pointed out, many of the poems include footnotes in which "Aguilar is able to make claims that resonate with both Jewish and Christian readers without relinquishing her commitment to Judaism. This footnoting strategy ensures that her Jewish readers will be able to claim her description of spirituality as explicitly Jewish, yet it also serves to assure a Christian reader that there are common themes that bind Jewish and Christian belief."[34] Thus, in "Sabbath Thoughts I,"[35] for example, Aguilar footnotes Psalms 91:4 and Isaiah 41:26, 60:16, and 63:8. This is offered in support of the stanza that emphasizes God's protection of humanity:

> No earthly forms the void can fill,
> Which thirsts to drink th'immortal spring—
> No earthly balm the heart can still,
> Which droops to clasp his Saviour's wing;
> Then blessed be that lonely hour
> Which first proclaims a Father's power.

The "Sabbath Thoughts"[36] poems repeatedly emphasize the impoverishment of temporal joys, in ways that are sometimes more recognizable as Christian in temperament than Jewish. In "Sabbath Thoughts III," the poet similarly emphasizes that God has filled "The craving void of suffering" (5), and that "this fair earth has never given, / To yearning hearts, one answering word"

(3–4). "Sabbath Thoughts IV" is tellingly titled "Parting From Friends,"[37] and the poet urges us to "seek our God in prayer" even "When friends on earth must part." The verse from Psalms footnoted in the first of the "Sabbath Thoughts" poem, cited above, supplies an entirely expected supplement to the entire series: "He shall cover thee with his feathers, and under wings shalt thou trust: His truth shall be thy shield and buckler" (91:4). As a note to the first of the six "Sabbath Thoughts," this verse is apt to be read in terms that are most compatible with Christian exegesis: the radical division between temporal and transcendent is emphasized, and God's protection of a debased humanity the primary focus. This understanding is made all the more striking for the poet's insistence that Sabbath rest is a respite from religious anxiety. "Sabbath Thoughts III" provides a good example of this dynamic:

Oh leave me not, forsake me not,
Unto my own rebellious will,
Whate'er of trial cloud my lot,
Let me but love Thee, trust Thee still!

Keep me but constant in my trust,
Father! Oh grant it fail not now,
Lest, sinking prostrate in the dust,
Despair and doubt should cloud my brow.

The religious anxiety broadcast by these verses is in apposition to the insistence, evident throughout "Sabbath Thoughts," that temporal life is a tempest of pain and unfulfilled longing: Aguilar is cleaving to God for dear life, both literally (attendant on the Bible, embodying her longing in her writing) and figuratively. The earlier footnote to Isaiah 41:26, then, seems to add another layer of complexity: "For he said, Surely they are my people, children that will not lie: so he was their Saviour." If Aguilar is reassuring both Christians and Jews about the appropriateness of her poetry, then referencing this line in a footnote to the first of the "Sabbath Thoughts" raises questions about truth and chosenness. The footnote itself gives only the citations, not the biblical lines themselves. For that, a reader must look it up, must have some facility with the Bible, and here we would do well to recall Aguilar's complaints in *The Spirit of Judaism* that Jews are insufficiently versed in the Bible. If the Jews are surely God's people—even if the Christians are too—then they would do well to determine the responsibilities conferred by such a condition while living in Christian England. The

Jews as the "Chosen People" was a difficult topic anyway for Anglo-Jews interested in mainstream acceptance. Moreover, the Jew as liar and thief was one of the dominant familiar aspersions cast upon Jews. The religious anxiety displayed in these poems underlies the poet's assertion of her temporal suffering; she needs to ensure that her path is straight to be assured of ultimate relief. The latter is a motif easily recognizable among Christians, even as the reference to the "Saviour" is bound to be interpreted by Christian exegetes typologically as a reference to Jesus. What is accumulating here is a hint of unease about the generalization of religious piety, an unease that is thrown into sharpest relief when the passage from Isaiah 60:16, also cited in the footnote, is recalled: "Thou shalt also suck the milk of the Gentiles, and shalt suck the breast of kings: and thou shalt know that I the Lord am thy Saviour and thy Redeemer, the mighty One of Jacob." The prophecy of Isaiah here refers to the promise of recompense.

What would sucking the milk of the Gentiles mean to Aguilar? I would suggest that in the context of this poetic series, it means engaging in fruitful exchange with a meaningful spirituality. It has subtler, darker undertones as well. Whatever the poet's commitment to valorizing a life beyond earthly concerns, she must still negotiate her safe passage, as it were, within Christian England. The historical resonance surely sounds as well, especially in the recognition that, writing in the 1840s, Aguilar is poised between an England that provides safe haven and an England still more than a decade away from full Jewish emancipation. The nourishment—the "milk" of the Gentiles—is unavoidable, and it does not flow as freely as the prophecy in Isaiah portends.

Aguilar is writing "Sabbath Thoughts" at a time when the difference between the Christian and Jewish Sabbath is one obvious point of difference between the two religions. Even though strict ritual observance of the Sabbath laws in Judaism was not widespread, especially among the rich and the poor,[38] it was still well known that the Jewish Sabbath is observed on Saturday, not Sunday, and that various restrictions on work are observed by the ritually observant. Many Jews who were not ritually observant went to work or to the theater, but Jews still understood that the Sabbath was intended as a day of peaceful rest. It was acknowledged even if not consistently observed with ritual precision. Again, the difference between the Jewish and Christian Sabbath was a marker of substantial difference, which makes Aguilar's tacit ecumenism all the more intriguing. To make of any Jewish poem a consistent affirmation both of Jewish particularism and of the qualities in Judaism compatible with Christianity is striking enough; to make of a poem about the specifically Jewish Sabbath an engagement with the universal qualities of Judaism is to speak directly to the idiosyncrasies involved in maintaining Jewish life in a Christian land, especially where that Christian land also plays host to the cultural inheritance that serves as one facet of the poet's defining inheritance. A passage from *The Intellectual Repository and New Jerusalem Magazine*, in an article of 1850 entitled "The Sabbath of the Jew," provides helpful context in understanding how Christians generally understood the difference:

> But there is a great difference between a Jewish celebration of the Sabbath and a Christian observance of the Lord's day; and it appears to us that much confusion and strife have arisen, especially at various periods in the history of the church, from the mistaken endeavour of introducing into the practice of Christian duties the strict ceremonial of the Jewish Sabbath. That ceremonial was, together with nearly all the rituals of the Jewish Church, entirely abolished and removed by the Lord when He came to establish the Christian dispensation as the grand result of his redeeming love. We have, therefore, now no more to do with the ceremonial of the church of the Jew in respect to the Sabbath, than we have with the ceremonial of sacrificing the lamb every morning and evening as the only condition of keeping up a sense of religion amongst us.[39]

There is indeed great difference, even if piety and gratitude are common contexts too. The author of the above quotation asserts that sacrificing a lamb every morning and every evening would be no less preposterous than observing Sabbath like the Jews. There is no presumption in Judaism that Christians should observe the Jewish Sabbath. The point is simply that the recognition of obtrusive difference is unavoidable, and that Christians of the period tend to find Jewish Sabbath observance, at best, an antiquarian oddity. This is the context against which Aguilar pens the "Sabbath Thoughts." In "Sabbath Thoughts III," then, Aguilar's epigraph opens up another set of complexities. She quotes, but does not reference, the following line: "I will never leave thee, nor forsake thee." These are the exact words used in the King James version of the New Testament, in Hebrews 13:5. There are similar phrases in the King James version of the Hebrew Bible, notably Deuteronomy 31:6, 8 and Joshua 1:5. These are often understood in Christian exegesis as typological foreshadowings of the New Testament. The sentiment itself is universal enough, but it is telling that Aguilar cites the New Testament line specifically. Why? Its placement in context provides a valuable source of understanding, both of this particular crux and of the series as a whole. The second of the "Sabbath Thoughts" poems is subtitled "Written on the Close of a Peculiarly Blessed Day of Rest."[40] It too begins with an epigraph, one from Leviticus 23:3: "Six days shall work be done, but the seventh day is the Sabbath of rest. It is the Sabbath of the Lord in all of your dwellings." The passage from Leviticus emphasizes the separateness of the Jews, one sign of their obtrusive otherness. The very next poem in the series is the one that begins with the quotation from the New Testament *Hebrews,* and it thereby provides not balance so much as acknowledgment of the poet's historicity. This is the poet, after all, who sometimes goes to church for its aesthetic appeal. This is the poet who asserts that attending places of worship belonging to other faiths is an acceptable form of spiritual exploration. And this is the poet who situates Jewish spirituality not in a context in which she hopes to see it diluted, but in the public sphere in which it is recognized as something other than a quaint antiquarianism. The Sabbath of the Jews may well be a marker of separation and of difference, but it is not like the difference between—to recall the quotation from *The New Jerusalem Magazine*—sacrificing lambs morning and evening and living a civilized life in the modern world. The Sabbath is both a common reference point for Jews and Christians even as it is the marker of obvious difference.

Aguilar inhabits a world in which she must be always alert to the tensions in her engagement with the majority culture as well as her own Jewish community. As she seeks out the solace of repose on the Sabbath, so she seeks out the solace of community within her larger world, and sanction within the general literary community. If this puts pressure on her own self-definitions, then the yield of such tension is the remarkable range of her writing.

CODA

Amy Levy's Impossible Modernity

In "Stanzas from the Grande Chartreuse," first published in 1855, Matthew Arnold summed up one of the effects of Victorian doubt and post-Romantic angst. Gazing with longing at the austere piety of the Carthusian monks, an order established in 1084 by St. Bruno, Arnold could only refract his observations of them through the prism of his own sense of dislocation, his alienation from the security of belief that the great monastery and its inmates represent. And so he cries out, "Wandering between two worlds, one dead, / the other powerless to be born" (85–86).¹ Herein we have the essential alienation described not only by the Victorians, but still by many fin-de-siècle poets in England. Neither belonging to a medieval world of chastened Christianity, nor to the distant future enlightened world of anticipated rational harmony and peace, Arnold sees himself as caught irreconcilably between one world vanished and the other he knew he would never live to see. A child, supposedly, of the Enlightenment, he could find no certain access to the conventional sources of consolation. The Romantic pieties too—however ironized by the Romantic poets themselves—have dwindled in value by now, and even though place still remains a value term, by the time we arrive at the middle of the nineteenth century, place holds an even less stable equation with pastoral than it did for the Romantics, and pastoral no longer holds its ground as the primary harbinger of the tranquil mind. The poets of the mid- and later nineteenth century are on the move, into the cities and in step with the urbanization of the later nineteenth century. Yet on the move does not always bring with it a clearly defined destination point. Wandering between two worlds gives way in "Stanzas from the Grande Chartreuse" to nostalgia for the austerity and perfect Christian faith that, so Arnold descries, was purged from his soul in the wake of post-enlightenment Victorian ideology:

> For rigorous teachers seized my youth,
> And purged its faith, and trimmed its fire,
> Showed me the high, white star of Truth,
> There bade me gaze, and there aspire.
> Even now their whispers pierce the gloom:
> *What dost thou in this living tomb?* (ll. 67–72)

He was to have dispensed with the severe religious exercises represented by the Carthusian monks in favor of Victorian modernity. Literature has been sacralized in the wake of the disenchantment of religion, but Arnold senses too that no aesthetic could be answerable to the spiritual vacancy against which he struggles.

At other times, the grind of the Victorian quotidian gives way to nostalgia for the arcadia that poets now can only dream of. And after all, Arnold is wandering between two worlds, ones that retain a wistful appeal for him. He does not fail to notice the monastery's overgrown, yet mild garden, with fragrant, flowering herbs from which the liqueur Chartreuse is made. What we have is a longing for pastoral ease precisely at the moment in which it seems most elusive, and a longing for safe haven in the older Christian pieties at the moment when pastoral ease is recognized as a cruel—cruel because inaccessible—fantasy. Still within the monastery, Arnold thinks of Byron and Shelley, and of the inefficacy of their poetic fictions. Again, in an age that would replace the religious pieties with the poetic, a recognition of the inefficacy of poetic fiction is tantamount to ultimate defeat. I quote again from "Stanzas from the Grande Chartreuse":

> What boots it, Shelley! That the breeze
> Carried thy lovely wail away,
> Musical through Italian trees
> Which fringe thy soft blue Spezzian bay?
> Inheritors of thy distress
> Have restless hearts one throb the less? (ll. 139–144)

I have begun this conclusion with Arnold who, like so many of the nineteenth-century Anglo-Jewish poets, knows that the consolations of Romanticism extend only so far. For Arnold, the inefficacy of literary solace is particularly salient when set against the already discredited succors of conventional religion. Arnold's is a context that provides a valuable point of contrast to Amy Levy, whose observations about the paucity of bucolic blood in the Jew began this book. A brief coda considering Levy reminds us that even when Victorianism is already in full swing, the forms of Jewish engagement with canonical measures still present modes of complex alterity. This is an alterity at once continuous with, and a variation of, Anglo-Jewish Romantic poetry. As such, it is indicative of the historical trajectory in which Anglo-Jewish poetry of the nineteenth century is situated.

I would suggest that Levy is denied even the comfort of an expressive resource in Arnold's well-crafted despair, for the paucity of consolation for her precludes even the nostalgia that comes so floridly to Arnold and to many of their literary peers. Nostalgia for an austere Christianity is not hers to aver. The fire and faith that Arnold's rigorous teachers purged from him are not points of loss for Levy. Her Judaism, though a central source of self-identification, retains only a highly diluted spiritual claim on her.

Amy Levy was a Jewish woman born in Clapham in 1861.[2] She committed suicide in 1889, a couple of months before she was to turn twenty-eight. In her brief life, she published poetry, fiction, and nonfictional prose, including several essays about Jewish authors and Jewish cultural life. Levy was heir to Victorian angst and doubt, to the predicament of an apparently immedicable pain no less than any of her contemporaries. But whereas Arnold, as my prime example here, expressed his dismay in the terms of alternatives that he knew to be inaccessible, to a nostalgia that he fully recognized as too fanciful to be taken seriously—he is not about to join the Carthusian monks, after all, and after all of Shelley's lovely wailing, the breeze still carried it away and restless hearts have not one throb the less—Levy was denied even the momentary comforts of a self-reflexive nostalgia; that is, her mode of lamentation often transforms itself into self-lament, into a form of mourning for the privations of her literary repertoire.

Levy harbors no nostalgia for the pastoral. She harbors no nostalgia for the old Christian pieties. She is not wandering between two worlds, as is Arnold, because Arnold's historical consciousness of a distant, sacred asceticism never was a world for her. His dream of the enlightened future, of a race "More fortunate, alas! than we, / Which without hardness will be sage; / And gay without frivolity" (158–160), is a dream in which Levy could only have an uneasy place.

Levy was the first Jewish woman to attend Cambridge University. Like many assimilated Jews who self-identified as Jewish, she also strongly self-identified as English, even in the full consciousness that British cultural and nationalist aspirations are founded on a history that already forecloses the authority of her efforts to claim straightforwardly membership in their lineage. Levy's most famous novel, *Reuben Sachs*, portrays a Jewish family whose eponymous hero is afflicted with the nervous condition that, his doctor advises him, is the mark of his race.³ It is still often (and unfairly) regarded today as an example of Jewish self-hatred, in its characterization of Jews unable fully to integrate with their Church of England, upper-class countrymen. For Levy, there is indeed much at stake in the forms of Jewish alienation.

When Matthew Arnold laments the inefficacy of lyric, he is responding to it as an ideal that slips through his fingers, as it were. The vanished succors of Romantic pastoral are foregrounded in its nostalgic evocation, much as he evokes the Carthusian piety for which he longs: for which he longs precisely because it is the sign of a vanished world he can claim in his remote past. Arnold can still claim membership, however lapsed, in a world whose passing he laments. Levy's defining other is neither pastoral nor religious succor. The poetic focus of her longing is to define the ground beneath her feet—both literally and existentially—even as she understands that the ground beneath her is always shifting. And to define such a space is to define, among other things, her literary inheritance. Her defining other is the very lamentation of poets whose mode of lament is also, in part, the signature of her alienation. She cannot lament loss the way Arnold does because Arnold's elegiac terms of reference are not hers. This is a question that has been asked of all of the poets in this study: if the Jew hath not a drop of bucolic blood in his veins, then what of the poet whose poetry depends upon a refraction of the British bucolic? What of the poet who, recognizing the inaccessibility of pastoral consolation, cannot turn to any of the conventional religious pieties either? Where the succors of Victorian hearth and home depend on nationalist history, and where Jewish history must be acknowledged as a narrative of exile, civil and political disabilities, and finally reluctant tolerance—with all the pejorative connotations implied by the term "tolerance"—Levy's yearning to be recognized as a poet is joined to her recognition that she cannot claim to be heir of the Romantic pastoral *or* of its Victorian rejection. The terms of reference are not hers. She will not evoke the pastoral only to undermine its efficacy because the pastoral cannot stand as the longed for object which refuses her. What we are left with, then, is a struggle to articulate a sense of loss that is finally ineffable because never easily identifiable.

The London Plane Tree is a volume of poetry that was published posthumously in 1889. The copyright page announces, "The proofs of this volume were corrected by the Author about a week before her death."⁴ The title poem, "A London Plane Tree," figures the poet as the plane tree in the city square, who is green even while "the other trees are brown; / They droop and pine for country air; / The plane-tree loves the town" (2–4). It is not that nature thrives in cities too; it is that it is a quirk of nature to witness the oddity of a living, breathing tree sustained by dun fog and grey curls of smoke. Here is no gentle breeze of Romantic salvation. "Among her branches, in and out, / The city breezes play" (9–10). But neither is there any hint of longing for the gentle breezes of an outmoded Romanticism: "Others the country take for choice, / And hold the town in scorn; / But she has listened to the voice / On city breezes borne" (13–16). The Jew hath not a drop of bucolic blood in his veins. For Levy, the city breezes conceal a voice. What follows in the volume is a struggle against the city, a stubborn insistence that it be seen as sufficient to its poet, an insistence that also thematizes the tenuous status of its promise of vitality, or vividness, or industry. We are presented, then, not with the wild west wind of autumn familiar to readers from Shelley's "Ode to the West Wind," but the east wind that Levy addresses in "A March Day in London." Shelley's "Ode to the West Wind" has indeed been a consistent point of reference throughout this study, and it is no less crucial as a counterpoint for Levy. Here is Shelley's first line: "O wild West Wind, thou breath of Autumn's being" (1). Here is Levy: "The east wind blows in the street to-day" (1). Like Shelley, she finds herself restless, wandering, a kind of madness in her breast. But where Shelley seeks solace in the fantasy of joining the vitality of the unyielding west wind, Levy seeks stasis. Shelley's drive to impersonate the wind also carries a political subtext, "the trumpet of a prophecy" that will revive "unawakened Earth," which is why he asks the wind to "drive my dead thoughts over the universe" (63).

Levy describes a real, defiantly literal wandering, one that she would, if she could, repel:

> From end to end, with aimless feet
> All day long have I paced the street.
> My limbs are weary, but in my breast
> Stirs the goad of a mad unrest.
> I would give anything to stay
> The little wheel that turns in my brain;
> The little wheel that turns all day,
> That turns all night with might and main. (ll. 7–14)

The pathetic fallacy offers the aimless hurrying to the freneticism of the mind, but there is almost a concealed humor in Levy's allusiveness, an assertion that her elegiac form lays bare the source of her true poetic authority, and that it is an authority from which she will not shrink. And I conjecture a sly humor because it is joined with a sort of defiance. Levy's wonderful line about the Jew not having a drop of bucolic blood in his veins comes, after all, in the midst of an essay on Jewish humor. The statement, which I cited in the introduction and have referred to throughout this study, bears repetition in this conclusion:

> [The Jew] hardly has left, when all is said, a drop of bucolic blood in his veins. He has been huddled in crowded quarters of towns, forced into close and continual contact with his fellow-creatures; he has learned to watch men's faces; to read men's thoughts; to be always ready for his opportunity. If he could raise a laugh at his neighbor's expense when his neighbor's demeanor was such a matter of importance to him, who will grudge him the solace and the vengeance.

If the authority of the bucolic is not hers to claim, then she will positively embrace the freneticism of the rootless cosmopolitan.[5] The point of defiance is competitive. The poem "London in July" tries out a highly qualified but effective form of solace, one that need not presume upon piety or redemption:

> And who cries out on crowd and mart?
> Who prates of stream and sea?
> The summer in the city's heart—
> That is enough for me. (ll. 13–16)

Shelley's "Ode to the West Wind" famously concludes with the hopeful question, "O Wind, / If Winter comes, can Spring be far behind?" (69–70). Levy's "A March Day in London" ends by noting that the east "wind has fallen with the night." The final stanza of this poem too manages to find fortitude:

> And o'er, at last, my spirit steals
> A weary peace; peace that conceals
> Within its inner depths that grain
> Of hopes that yet shall flower again. (ll. 24–27)

The breeze of the city—the voice of the city—is here the voice of belonging, and as such it is the voice of tenacity.

It is in such tenacity that the cosmopolite without a drop of bucolic blood in her veins finds a measure of solace. The prominent allusive counterpoint in the background is Wordsworth, but I cite him here as paradigmatic of the voice Levy could ultimately turn her back on, a gesture that earlier nineteenth-century Jewish poets would not so easily engage. Here are the opening lines of Wordsworth's 1805 *Prelude:*

> Oh there is blessing in this gentle breeze,
> That blows from the green fields and from the clouds
> And from the sky; it beats against my cheek,
> And seems half conscious of the joy it gives.
> O Welcome messenger! O welcome friend!
> A captive greets thee, coming from a house
> Of bondage, from yon city's walls set free,
> A prison where he hath been long immured.
> Now I am free, enfranchised and at large,
> May fix my habitation where I will. (ll. 1–10)

For Levy it is the east wind blowing, not the gentle breeze; it is the city breezes playing which can figure the animation of her spirit. Levy does fashion herself a "captive," but not because she dwells in the "city's walls." Her poem "The Village Garden" situates her as mourning an unnamed grief even while sitting amidst the "mixed delight of lavender and lilies."

> Fain would I bide, but ever in the distance
> A ceaseless voice is sounding clear and low;—
> The city calls me with old persistence,
> The city calls me—I arise and go.
>
> Of gentler souls this fragrant peace is guerdon;
> For me, the roar and hurry of the town,
> Wherein more lightly seems to press the burden
> Of individual life that weighs me down. (ll. 13–20)

Levy will not lament in the voice of her precursors. Nor will she pine the loss of consolations that were never hers. She does not wander between Arnold's two worlds because her own world does not include his past or his vision of the future. The individual life that weighs her down struggles for greater clarity, but remains ill-defined and tentatively expressed. But her voice will be the voice of the cosmopolite, insistently never blessed by the gentle breezes. In this, she subtly enacts her authority to claim the city, to claim London as the rightful ground beneath her feet.

In so doing, she also mobilizes her authority self-consciously to turn her back on the stable rootedness symbolized by splendid English landscapes or pastoral ease, and claim the very flux and uncertainty of cosmopolitanism as one sign of her just inheritance, for which the frenetic city is the rightful image. If London cannot quite be the certain ground beneath her feet that defines her stability, it will at least serve as the sign of her restless and still amorphous longing. In this, the city of London is established as a sign that she is fully entitled to appropriate: she lays claim to the cultural authority by which she may claim the city of London as her rightful metaphor *and* as her authentic space. Its freneticism is both the correct metaphoric equivalent to her mental being *and* the proper place of her physical boundaries.

The poets I have identified as Anglo-Jewish Romantics negotiate their cultural authority even as they tentatively define the ground from which they speak. They are not yet in a position to cherish, as Amy Levy could, the city qua city as a forum for self-possessed invigoration. In 1854, Marion Hartog (née Moss) published a commemorative tribute to Grace Aguilar, one that strikes a note of frustration about the cultural receptiveness of Jewish readers, even as it boldly stakes a claim to the enduring worth of the Anglo-Jewish voice. I quote the final three stanzas:

> Thine were the soft notes of the turtle-dove,
> That breathes a sweetness o'er the desert waste;
> And shall thy lessons of religious love
> Die with the brain that thought, the heart that traced?
>
> No; Israel long shall cherish Grace's name,
> All apathetic though her children be;
> Though living they neglected thee, O shame!
> In death they'll twine a myrtle wreath for thee.
>
> How long shall Israel's thoughtless great ones—say—
> (Who to be learning's patrons should be proud)

Let living genius hopeless pine away,
And waste their empty honours on a shroud.[6]

Marion Moss Hartog's encomium to the memory of Grace Aguilar offers the ultimate resistance to elegiac sentimentalism. She wishes to waste no empty honors on a shroud. She does not position herself as victim of an unheeding majority culture. Her adjuration for "Israel" to cherish Grace Aguilar is an appeal for Jewish self-identification with "living genius." The Mosses had found the mere English landscape insufficient as a ground for conferring honor; Amy Levy finds that the English city only partly mitigates the burden of "individual life that weighs [her] down." In the tribute to Aguilar, Moss Hartog has no illusions about "the desert waste." What she reads in her exemplary Jewish poet is its revelation: a poet who knows to breathe "a sweetness o'er the desert waste," a sweetness that is sustained in all the permutations and self-contradictions of its textual complexity.

NOTES

INTRODUCTION

1. Levy, "Jewish Humour," in Levy, *The Complete Novels and Selected Writings*, p. 523.
2. The term "pastoral" is still contested in contemporary scholarship, and I have chosen to use it more broadly than the "no shepherd, no pastoral" dictum of which Leo Marx famously complained ("Pastoralism in America," in Bercovitch and Jehlen, *Ideology and Classic American Literature*, p. 45). On the other hand, neither do I appropriate it in an "ungoverned inclusiveness," which Alpers describes as one of the unfortunate hallmarks of modern discussions of pastoral (*What Is Pastoral*, p. ix). I do use the term to designate engagements with nature that evoke the tone of Virgilian pastoral: community, hospitality, and a simplifying of the complexities of human nature within the beauty and ease of the landscape.
3. Hazlitt, *The Complete Works of William Hazlitt*, p. 462.
4. Ibid.
5. Lamb, "Imperfect Sympathies," in *Essays of Elia*, p. 72.
6. Ibid.
7. Shelley, *Shelley's Poetry and Prose*.
8. For a remarkably comprehensive discussion of the legend of the Wandering Jew, see the definitive work by Anderson, *The Legend of the Wandering Jew*.
9. For broad historical perspectives of the Jews in England, see Endelman, *The Jews of Britain, 1656 to 2000*, and Katz, *The Jews in the History of England, 1485–1850*.
10. Disraeli, *The Genius of Judaism*, p. 244.
11. See Endelman, *The Jews of Georgian England, 1714–1830*, esp. chap. 4.
12. See Godfrey and Godfrey, *Search out the Land*, pp. 16–17.
13. Vital, *A People Apart, 1789–1939*, p. 39.
14. For a helpful summary, see Michie, *On the Sacramental Test Act, the Catholic Relief Act, the Slavery Abolition Act, and the Factory Act*.
15. HC Deb, May 17, 1830, Vol. 24, cc. 784–814.
16. Clark, *Albion and Jerusalem*, p. 31.

17. Goldsmid, *Remarks on the Civil Disabilities of British Jews*, p. 34.
18. Perry, *Public Opinion, Propaganda, and Politics in Eighteenth-Century England*, p. 1.
19. Endelman, *The Jews of Britain*, p. 74.
20. Perry, *Public Opinion*, p. 3.
21. Endelman, *The Jews of Britain*, p. 76.
22. Valman, *The Jewess in Nineteenth-Century British Literary Culture*, p. 17.
23. The best history of the assimilation and acculturation of the Jews in England is Endelman, *Radical Assimilation in English Jewish History, 1656–1945*. For this discussion, see esp. chap. 1, "Sephardim, 1656–1837," and chap. 2, "Ashkenazim, 1690–1837."
24. I do not include the verse of Isaac Disraeli in this study because his poetry, which is the weaker work of his younger years, does not engage the concerns of this study.
25. Ruderman, *Jewish Enlightenment in an English Key*, p. 19.
26. Ibid., p. 61.
27. Ibid., p. 8.

CHAPTER 1

1. Bronson, *Facets of the Enlightenment*, p. 147.
2. Blake, "Annotations on Reynolds' Works, 1798–1809," p. 641.
3. For details on Lyon, see Cream, *Isaac Leo Lyon*. See also Scrivener, *Following the Muse*.
4. Lyon, *Miscellaneous Poems*. A fully accessible digitization of this text is available through the Davis British Women Romantic Poets Series, 2002, http://www.lib.ucdavis.edu/BWRP/Works/#L, p. viii. Text references are to page numbers of this edition.
5. Milton, *Paradise Lost*.
6. Ruderman, *Jewish Enlightenment*, p. 33.
7. Katz, *God's Last Word*, p. 210.
8. Hamlin, *Psalm Culture and Early Modern English Literature*.
9. Scrivener, *Following the Muse*, p. 117.
10. Wordsworth, *William Wordsworth*, p. 597.
11. Gillingham, *Psalms through the Centuries*, p. 216.
12. *Select Psalms in Verse, with Critical Remarks, By Bishop Lowth and Others*, p. xiii.
13. See Hannay, *Wisdome the Wordes'*.
14. Ibid., p. 66.
15. See the interesting discussion by Knowles, "'Now English Denizened, Though Hebrue Borne.'"
16. Gillingham, *Psalms Through the Centuries*, p. 230.
17. Backscheider, *Eighteenth-Century Women Poets and Their Poetry*, p. 126.
18. Ibid., p.135.
19. McCarthy, *Anna Letitia Barbauld*, p. 149.

20. White, *Early Romanticism and Religious Dissent*, p. 1.
21. Enfield, *Hymns for Public Worship*, p. 209.
22. Ruderman, *Jewish Enlightenment*, p. 33.
23. Bate, *The Scripture Meaning of Aleim and Berith Justified Against the Exceptions of Dr. Sharpe*.
24. Paine, "The Age of Reason," in *Thomas Paine: Political Writings*, p. 289.
25. Coleridge, *The Major Works, including Biographia Literaria*.
26. For a discussion of English conversionist philo-Semitism, see Endelman, *The Jews of Georgian England*, pp. 50–85.
27. For further clarification and details about these prayers, see Donin, *To Pray as a Jew*.
28. See the JPS translation and footnotes, pp. 1772, 1433.
29. Ruderman, *Jewish Enlightenment*, p. 76.
30. During the king's last illness, he even sustained delusions that Princess Amelia was alive and living in Hanover. See Hadlow, *A Royal Experiment*, p. 514ff.
31. Robinson, "Elegiac Sonnets."
32. Smith, *The Poems of Charlotte Smith*.
33. Milton, *Complete Poems and Major Prose*.
34. Levi, *A Succinct Account, of the Rites, and Ceremonies, of the Jews*, p. 52.
35. See Gray, "Jewish Ethics of Speech," in *The Oxford Handbook of Jewish Ethics and Morality*.
36. For more on the *vidui* of Yom Kippur and Yom Kippur liturgy, see Elbogen, *Jewish Liturgy*, pp. 124–128.
37. The most accessible source for this parable can be found in Goldberg, *Passover Hagaddah*, p. 20.
38. Endelman, *The Jews of Georgian England*, p. 71.
39. Ruderman, *Jewish Enlightenment*, p. 57.
40. Scrivener, "British-Jewish Writing of the Romantic Era and the Problem of Modernity," p. 167.
41. Levi, *Letters to Dr. Priestley, in Answer to Those He Addressed to the Jews*, p. 4.
42. See Heschel, *The Prophets*, esp. chap. 1, "What Manner of Man Is the Prophet?"
43. See Parens, *Maimonides and Spinoza: Their Conflicting Views of Human Nature*, p. 114.

CHAPTER 2

1. In Shaw, *Elegy and Paradox*, we have an excellent survey of the juxtapositions and paradoxes inherent in elegiac form. For Shaw, "often the most moving moments in an elegy occur when a poet juxtaposes the mourner's address to the dead person with a sympathetic but skeptical testing of that convention" (p. 9). On the long history of the complications of elegy, see essays in Weisman, ed., *The Oxford Handbook of the Elegy*.

2. Shelley, "Adonais," in *Shelley's Poetry and Prose*.

3. Milton, "Lycidas," in *The Complete Poetry*.

4. Geoffrey Hill is not Jewish, but his "September Song" supplies an excellent example of the ethical conundrums of elegiac poetry that addresses Jewish suffering. *The Collected Poems of Geoffrey Hill*, p. 67.

5. Wordsworth, *William Wordsworth: The Major Works*.

6. In his "Life of Milton," Samuel Johnson famously complains of Milton's "Lycidas" that "where there is leisure for fiction there is little grief," in Lonsdale, ed., *The Lives of the Most Eminent English Poets*, p. 278.

7. Behrendt, *Royal Mourning and Regency Culture: Elegies and Memorials of Princess Charlotte*. Behrendt is an excellent source of information about the public reaction to Princess Charlotte before and after her death, and I am much indebted to his research.

8. The best source of information on Hurwitz is Leonard Hyman, *Hyman Hurwitz: The First Anglo-English Professor*. On the *Hebrew Tales*, see Page, *Hyman Hurwitz's Hebrew Tales*.

9. I would like to thank Rabbi Professor David Novak for his generous assistance with the elegy to Princess Charlotte.

10. Roth, *The Great Synagogue, London, 1690–1940*, p. 217.

11. Hurwitz, [*Kinat Yeshurun*]: *A Hebrew Dirge, Chaunted . . . on the Day of the Funeral of Princess Charlotte*.

12. Rosenfeld, *Tisha B'Av Compendium*, pp. 175–176.

13. See Seidman, *Faithful Renderings*, pp. 37–72.

14. Genesis 15:13–18; translation of the Jewish Publication Society (2003). Unless otherwise stated, all scriptural translations are from this version.

15. *Yahrzeit* is a Yiddish term meaning anniversary time, but the requirement to commemorate yearly the death of a loved one is discussed in the Talmud, whose final redaction was in the fourth century CE.

16. Rosenfeld, *Tisha B'Av Compendium*, p. 129.

17. I cite both Hurwitz's poem and Coleridge's translation from J. C. C. Mays, ed., *The Collected Works of Samuel Taylor Coleridge: Poetical Works I, Part 2* (Bollingen edition). Mays offers extensive notes about the poem and its translation, and I am indebted to his commentary. I discuss some points of disagreement with Mays about the translation.

18. See ibid., p. 975.

19. See Singer, "Jews and Coronations," pp. 80–84.

20. Abrahams, "Hebrew Loyalty under the First Four Georges," p. 104.

21. Ibid., 107.

22. Adler, "Hebrew Elegies on English Monarchs."

23. Ibid., 146.

24. Ibid., 147.

25. Ibid., 143.

26. See Steinsaltz, *A Guide to Jewish Prayer*.

27. Shedlock, "Coronation Music."

28. See Gray, "Jewish Ethics of Speech."

29. Damrosch, "Nayler, James (1618–1660)."

30. Parl. Deb., H.C. (3d series), March 1, 1833, vol. 16, cc 10–7.

31. Adler, "Hebrew Elegies," p. 144.

32. Ibid., p. 145.

33. See Ditchfield, *George III: An Essay in Monarchy*, esp. chap. 6, "The Changing Nature of the British Monarch, 1784–1810," pp. 138–165.

34. Roth, *The Great Synagogue*, pp. 202–217.

35. Lord Byron, *The Major Works, including Don Juan and Childe Harold's Pilgrimage.*

36. Endelman, *The Jews of Georgian England*, p. 120.

37. Ibid., p. 122.

38. Levi, *A Succinct Account of the Rites and Ceremonies of the Jews.*

39. Ruderman, *Jewish Enlightenment*, p. 59.

40. Mays prints Hurwitz's poem in Hebrew, Coleridge's English translation, and the Bollingen translation into English of a discursive translation.

41. For a nuanced view of the more complicated religious views of George III, see Ditchfield, *George III*, chap. 4, "The Religion of George III," pp. 77–108.

42. Ruderman, *The Jewish Enlightenment*, p. 261.

43. Page, *Imperfect Sympathies*, p. 82.

44. See Ruderman, *The Jewish Enlightenment*, p. 261.

45. Ibid., p. 262.

46. Judith Page in *Imperfect Sympathies* argues that Hurwitz's project in *Hebrew Tales* "resembles the *Lyrical Ballads*, particularly in the way that Wordsworth theorized that project in his Preface and transmitted a literary version of traditional folk narratives in the poems. Because of Hurwitz's desire to redeem Judaism from scorn and to reconcile it with contemporary English culture his goal was even more complicated than Wordsworth's" (p. 83).

47. Hyman Hurwitz, "An Introductory Lecture Delivered in the University of London on Tuesday, November 11, 1828," p. 4.

48. Ibid., p. 29.

49. Ibid., p. 31.

50. JPS version.

51. See Bar-Yosef, *The Holy Land in English Culture, 1799–1917.*

52. For a fuller discussion of Cobbett's antisemitism, see Felsenstein, *Anti-Semitic Stereotypes*, pp. 231–238.

53. Hyman Hurwitz, "A Letter to Isaac L. Goldsmid, Esq. F.R.S."

54. Ibid., p. 3.

55. Ibid., p. 4.

56. Ibid., p. 8.

57. Ibid.

58. Ibid., p. 9.

59. Ibid.

60. Ibid., p. 13.

61. Hyman Hurwitz, *A Grammar of the Hebrew Language*, p. 272.
62. Hurwitz, "An Introductory Lecture," p. 27.
63. Blake, "Milton: A Poem in 2 Books," in *The Complete Poetry and Prose of William Blake*, p. 95.
64. See Kugel, *The Idea of Biblical Poetry*, p. 221.
65. "Cobbett and the Jews," p. 484.

CHAPTER 3

1. See Bossche, "On Chartism."
2. See Levin, *The Condition of England Question*, esp. pp. 26–29.
3. Carlyle, *"Chartism,"* p. 153.
4. See Feldman, *Englishmen and Jews*, esp. "Jewish Emancipation and Political Argument in Early Victorian England," pp. 28–47.
5. Alderman, "Hartog, Numa Edward (1846–1871)."
6. Levin, *The Condition of England Question*, p. 45.
7. Carlyle, "Chartism," p. 156.
8. See Endelman, *The Jews of Britain 1656 to 2000*, esp. "Poverty to Prosperity [1800–1870]," pp. 79–124.
9. Galchinsky, *The Origin of the Modern Jewish Woman Writer*, p. 107.
10. Ibid., pp. 107–108.
11. Celia Moss and Marion Moss, *Early Efforts*.
12. Mill, "Thoughts on Poetry and Its Varieties."
13. Coleridge, *The Major Works*.
14. Shakespeare, Sonnet 19.
15. Valman, *The Jewess in Nineteenth Century British Literary Culture*, p. 115.
16. On Charlotte Smith's "Beachy Head," see Labbe, *Charlotte Smith*, pp. 142–165.
17. Matthew, "Milman, Henry Hart (1791–1868)."
18. Trumpener, *Bardic Nationalism*, p. 132.
19. Nadia Valman, in *The Jewess in Nineteenth Century British Literary Culture*, also notes that the Mosses "in their enthusiasm for Jewish national liberty, bypassed the arguments about Jews which had been circulating in Parliament in the 1830s, and modelled their texts instead on the literature of Romantic nationalism" (p. 116).
20. Some thirteen years later, Benjamin Disraeli, who had been baptized in 1817, is to indulge in discourse that identifies the Jews as the very "trustees of tradition," though not without some rhetorical special pleading: "The Jews represent the Semitic principle; all that is spiritual in our nature. They are the trustees of tradition, and the conservators of the religious element." Disraeli, *Lord George Bentinck*, p. 496.
21. See Valman, *The Jewess in Nineteenth Century British Literary Culture*, who reads this poem and others in terms of the protector of liberty: "In appealing to Britain's identity as a nation which protects 'liberty,' the poem links British interests with these other

struggles for national liberation. In their poetry, the Mosses bring the biblical dispossession of the Jews and their persecution in medieval England into the compass of radical-liberal politics, claimed as a peculiarly British inheritance" (p. 120).

22. *The Romance of Jewish History, by the Misses C. And M. Moss.*

23. Valman, in *The Jewess in Nineteenth Century British Literary Culture,* points out that the preface, with its description of a "Priest-ridden age," is part of the anti-Catholic rhetoric that "links the Jews firmly with Protestantism, civilization and modernity" (p. 117).

24. I refer, of course, to Walter Benjamin's ninth essay in *Illuminations,* "Theses on the Philosophy of History."

25. Hemans, *Selected Poems, Prose and Letters by Felicia Hemans.*

26. Macaulay, *Civil Disabilities of Jews,* p. 229.

27. *The Spectator,* May 8, 1830, p. 8.

28. Milman, The *History of the Jews, from the Earliest Period down to Modern Times,* vol. 1, p. 453.

29. See Prazmowska, *A History of Poland,* esp. chap. 5, pp. 130–158.

30. The reference is to the Polish Romantic poet Krasinski. See Nance, *Literary and Cultural Images of a Nation Without a State,* p. 154.

31. Tennyson, *The Poems of Tennyson.*

32. See Porter, *When Nationalism Began to Hate,* p. 49.

CHAPTER 4

1. For a fuller biographical essay, see Galchinsky in Aguilar, *Grace Aguilar: Selected Writings,* pp. 17–30.

2. Aguilar, *Grace Aguilar: Selected Writings.* I cite poems both from this edition and from the journal *The Occident and American Jewish Advocate.* For ease of readerly reference, I make use of the Galchinsky edition unless otherwise noted.

3. For a wide-ranging examination of the myths of the Wandering Jew, see the essays in Hasan-Rokem and Dundes, eds., *The Wandering Jew.*

4. Simpson's *Wordsworth's Historical Imagination* is still one of the finest examinations of Wordsworth's historical consciousness engaging with his idealizations of nature.

5. Scheinberg argues that Aguilar's experience in rural England enabled her to appropriate nature traditions, especially in her poetic sequence "Communings with Nature," which I discuss below: "While other Anglo-Jewish women writers who followed her . . . tended to emphasize the importance of the urban setting in Jewish experience, perhaps in recognition of the Jewish exclusion from English pastoral traditions, Aguilar's somewhat unusual life experience in rural England allowed her to participate in the Romantic tradition of nature poetry, most clearly seen in her series of poems titled "'Communings with Nature.'" *Women's Poetry and Religion in Victorian England* , p. 163. As my argument makes clear, I do read Aguilar's nature poetry differently, but I want to acknowledge Scheinberg's important observations here.

6. Page, *Imperfect Sympathies*, p. 165.

7. Aguilar, *Selected Writings*, p. 195.

8. This is not exclusively about sensitivity to public reception, of course. In *The Origin of the Modern Jewish Woman Writer*, Galchinsky observes of Aguilar that "Conversionists could see her as a 'Jewish Protestant,' while Jews could laud her as a moderate reformer with strong traditional leanings" (p. 187). Valman, in discussing Aguilar's *Records of Israel*, notes that "the Jews, in Aguilar's vision, demonstrate the tolerant and inclusive scope of imperial Protestantism." *The Jewess in Nineteenth Century British Literary Culture*, p. 115.

9. I quote Aguilar's *History* from Galchinsky's accessible edition.

10. The "Communings with Nature" poems were published in *The Occident and American Jewish Advocate*, much of which has been recently professionally digitized and is available freely through the website of the *Historical Jewish Press*. http://web.nli.org.il/sites/JPress/English/Pages/The-Occident-and-American-Jewish-Advocate.aspx.

11. *The Church of England Quarterly Review*, p. 130.

12. Felsenstein, *Anti-Semitic Stereotypes*, p. 91.

13. Scheinberg, *Women's Poetry and Religion*, p. 163.

14. Felsenstein, *Anti-Semitic Stereotypes,* p. 90.

15. Aguilar, *Selected Writings*, p. 248. Wherever possible, I cite Aguilar's *Women of Israel* from Galchinsky's accessible collection. I indicate when I cite it from other sources.

16. *The Occident and American Jewish Advocate*, December 1845, pp. 440–441.

17. Galchinsky, *The Origin of the Modern Jewish Woman Writer*, esp. pp. 105–189.

18. Aguilar, *Selected Writings*, p. 301.

19. All the poems from "Communings with Nature" are cited from *The Occident and American Jewish Advocate*, as above.

20. Aguilar, *Selected Writings*, p. 196.

21. I cite this poem from Aguilar, *Selected Writings*, pp. 196–198.

22. Aguilar, *Sabbath Thoughts and Sacred Communings*, p. 1.

23. In Aguilar, *Selected Writings*, p. 217.

24. *The Church of England Quarterly Review*, p. 130.

25. In Aguilar, *Selected Writings*, pp. 206–209.

26. "State and Prospects of the Jews," pp. 93–107.

27. Ibid., p. 99.

28. Lindsay, *Letters on Egypt, Edom, and the Holy Land*, I, pp. 265–266.

29. Ibid., p. 268.

30. Ibid., p. 353.

31. In Aguilar, *Selected Writings*, pp. 204–206.

32. Harris, for example, argues that "Aguilar finds in Hagar her emblem for the Jew battered from place to place." "Hagar in Christian Britain: Grace Aguilar's 'The Wanderers,'" p. 144.

33. See Telushkin, *Hillel: If Not Now, When?*

34. Scheinberg, *Women's Poetry and Religion in Victorian England*, p. 170.

35. In *The Occident and American Jewish Advocate*, August 1843, pp. 236–238.

36. All of the "Sabbath Thoughts" poems were published in *The Occident and American Jewish Advocate*, and my reading text for "Sabbath Thoughts III" is Aguilar, *Selected Writings*. The others are from the journal, as above.

37. In *The Occident and American Jewish Advocate*, November 1845, pp. 379–380.

38. See Endelman, *The Jews of Britain, 1656–2000*, pp. 114–115.

39. "The Sabbath of the Jew," *The Intellectual Repository and New Jerusalem Magazine*, p. 282.

40. In *The Occident and American Jewish Advocate*, January 1844, pp. 484–486.

CODA

1. Arnold, *The Poems of Matthew Arnold*.

2. See Bernstein's introductory material in Levy, *Reuben Sachs*, pp. 11–47, and Levy, *The Romance of a Shop*, pp. 11–14.

3. "'More than half my nervous patients are recruited from the ranks of the Jews,' said the great physician whom Reuben consulted. 'You pay the penalty of too high a civilization.'" Levy, *Reuben Sachs*, p. 56.

4. Levy, *A London Plane Tree and Other Verse*.

5. Scheinberg, in *Women's Poetry,* observes that Levy represents a point of departure also because the terms of reference for women's work was also shifting: "By Levy's time, the separate spheres ideology which relegated women's lives and identities to the moral, spiritual, private, and domestic realms and assigned to men the theological, public, intellectual, and business realms, had begun to break down, offering some new possibilities for women in the worlds of work and education. Further, the previous generations of successful women poets and writers had also made the figure of the woman writer, if not equally respected by the critical patriarchy, far less of a cultural anomaly than in the earlier part of the century" (p. 196).

6. In Aguilar, *Grace Aguilar: Selected Writings*, "Appendix A," p. 359.

BIBLIOGRAPHY

Abrahams, I. "Hebrew Loyalty Under the First Four Georges." *Transactions of the Jewish Historical Society of England* 9 (1918), 103–130.
Adler, Elkan N. "Hebrew Elegies on English Monarchs." *Transactions of the Jewish Historical Society of England* 2 (1895), 141–148.
Aguilar, Grace. "Autumn Leaves." *The Occident and American Jewish Advocate* 2, 7 (Nov. 1844), 384–85.
———. "Autumn Winds." *The Occident and American Jewish Advocate* 3, 10 (Jan. 1846), 503–505.
———. "The Evergreen." *The Occident and American Jewish Advocate* 4, 2 (May 1846), 78–79.
———. *Grace Aguilar: Selected Writings*. Ed. Michael Galchinsky. Peterborough, ON: Broadview Press, 2003.
———. "I Never Loved a Flower." *The Occident and American Jewish Advocate* 2, 9 (Dec. 1844), 427–428.
———. "An Infant's Smile." *The Occident and American Jewish Advocate* 3, 9 (Dec. 1845), 440–441.
———. "Sabbath Thoughts." *The Occident and American Jewish Advocate* 1, 5 (Aug. 1843), 236–238.
———. *Sabbath Thoughts and Sacred Communings*. London: Groombridge and Sons, 1853.
———. "Sabbath Thoughts No. IV Parting from Friends." *The Occident and American Jewish Advocate* 3, 8 (Nov. 1845), 379–380.
———. "Sabbath Thoughts Written on the Close of a Peculiarly Blessed Day of Rest." *The Occident and American Jewish Advocate* 1, 10 (Jan. 1844), 484–486.
Alderman, Geoffrey. "Hartog, Numa Edward (1846–1871)." *Oxford Dictionary of National Biography*. Oxford: Oxford University Press, 2004. http://www.oxforddnb.com/index/12/101012501. Last accessed June 30, 2017.
Alpers, Paul. *What Is Pastoral*. Chicago: University of Chicago Press, 1996.
Anderson, George. *The Legend of the Wandering Jew*. 1965. Reprint. Hanover, NH: University Press of New England, 1991.
Arnold, Matthew. *The Poems of Matthew Arnold*. Ed. Kenneth Allott and Miriam Allott. London: Longman, 1979.
Backscheider, Paula R. *Eighteenth-Century Women Poets and Their Poetry: Inventing Agency, Inventing Genre*. Baltimore: Johns Hopkins University Press, 2008.

Bar-Yosef, Eitan. *The Holy Land in English Culture 1799–1917: Palestine and the Question of Orientalism*. Oxford: Oxford University Press, 2005.

Bate, Julius. *The Scripture Meaning of Aleim and Berith Justified Against the Exceptions of Dr. Sharpe*. London: Printed for E. Withers, 1751. Eighteenth Century Collections Online, ESTC Number T68496.

Behrendt, Stephen C. *Royal Mourning and Regency Culture: Elegies and Memorials of Princess Charlotte*. New York: Palgrave Macmillan, 1997.

Benjamin, Walter. *Illuminations*. Trans. Harry Zohn. New York: Schocken Books, 1969.

Bercovitch, Sacvan and, Jehlen, Myra, eds. *Ideology and Classic American Literature*. Cambridge: Cambridge University Press, 1986.

Blake, William. *The Complete Poetry and Prose of William Blake*. Ed. David Erdman. New York: Doubleday, 1988.

The Book of Common Prayer. Ed. James Wood. New York: Penguin Classics, 2012.

Bossche, Chris Vanden. "On Chartism." *BRANCH: Britain, Representation and Nineteenth-Century History*, ed. Dino Franco Felluga. *Extension of Romanticism and Victorianism on the Net*. http://www.branchcollective.org/?ps_articles=chris-r-vanden-bossche-on-chartism. Last accessed June 8, 2016.

Bronson, Bertrand. *Facets of the Enlightenment*. Berkeley: University of California Press, 1968.

Byron, Lord. *The Major Works, Including Don Juan and Childe Harold's Pilgrimage*. Ed. Jerome McGann. Oxford: Oxford University Press, 1986.

Carlyle, Thomas. *Selected Writings*. Ed. Alan Shelston. Harmondsworth: Penguin, 1971.

Cheyette, Bryan, and Nadia Valman, eds. *The Image of the Jew in European Liberal Culture 1789–1914*. London: Vallentine Mitchell, 2004.

Clark, Michael. *Albion and Jerusalem: The Anglo-Jewish Community in the Post-Emancipation Era*. Oxford: Oxford University Press, 2009.

"Cobbett and the Jews." *New Monthly Magazine and Literary Journal* (1833), 484–485.

Coleridge, Samuel Taylor. *The Collected Works of Samuel Taylor Coleridge: Poetical Works I, Part 2*. Ed. J. C. C. Mays. Princeton, NJ: Princeton University Press, 2001.

———. *The Major Works, Including Biographia Literaria*. Ed. H. J. Jackson. Oxford: Oxford University Press, 2009.

Cream, Naomi. "Isaac Leo Lyon: The First Free Jewish Migrant to Australia?" *Journal of the Australian Jewish Historical Society* 12, 1 (1993), 3–16.

———. "Revd Solomon Lyon of Cambridge, 1755–1820." *Jewish Historical Studies* 36 (1999–2001), 31–69.

Damrosch, Leo. "Nayler, James (1618–1660)." *Oxford Dictionary of National Biography*. Oxford: Oxford University Press, 2004. http://www.oxforddnb.com/view/article/19814. Last accessed June 9, 2016.

Disraeli, Benjamin. *Lord George Bentinck: A Political Biography*. 4th ed. London: Colburn, 1852.

Disraeli, Isaac. *The Genius of Judaism*. London: Edward Moxon, 1833.

Ditchfield, G. M. *George III: An Essay in Monarchy*. New York: Palgrave Macmillan, 2002.

Donin, Hayim H. *To Pray as a Jew: A Guide to the Prayerbook and Synagogue Service*. New York: Basic Books, 1991.
Elbogen, Ismar. *Jewish Liturgy: A Comprehensive History*. Philadelphia: Jewish Publication Society, 1993.
Endelman, Todd. *The Jews of Britain, 1656 to 2000*. Berkeley: University of California Press, 2002.
———. *The Jews of Georgian England, 1714–1830: Tradition and Change in a Liberal Society*. Philadelphia: Jewish Publication Society of America, 1979.
———. *Radical Assimilation in English Jewish History, 1656–1945*. Bloomington: Indiana University Press, 1990.
Enfield, William, ed. *Hymns for Public Worship: Selected from various Authors and Intended as a Supplement to Dr. Watts's Psalms*. Printed for the editor: Warrington, 1772.
Feldman, David. *Englishmen and Jews: Social Relations and Political Culture 1840–1914*. New Haven, CT: Yale University Press, 1994.
Felsenstein, Frank. *Anti-Semitic Stereotypes: A Paradigm of Otherness in English Popular Culture, 1660–1830*. Baltimore: Johns Hopkins University Press, 1995.
Galchinsky, Michael. *The Origin of the Modern Jewish Woman Writer: Romance and Reform in Victorian England*. Detroit: Wayne State University Press, 1996.
Gillingham, Susan. *Psalms Through the Centuries*. Vol. 1. Oxford: Blackwell, 2012.
Godfrey, Sheldon, and Judy Godfrey. *Search Out the Land: The Jews and the Growth of Equality in British Colonial America, 1740–1867*. Montreal and Kingston: McGill-Queen's University Press, 1995.
Goldsmid, Francis Henry. *Remarks on the Civil Disabilities of British Jews*. London: Henry Colburn and Richard Bentley, 1830.
Gray, Alyssa M. "Jewish Ethics of Speech." *The Oxford Handbook of Jewish Ethics and Morality*. Ed. Elliot N. Dorff and Jonathan K. Crane. Oxford: Oxford University Press, 2013, pp. 433–444.
Hadlow, Janice. *A Royal Experiment: The Private Lives of King George III*. New York: Henry Holt, 2014.
Hamlin, Hannibal. *Psalm Culture and Early Modern English Literature*. Cambridge: Cambridge University Press, 2004.
Hannay, Margaret. "'Wisdome the Wordes': Psalm Translation and Elizabethan Women's Spirituality." *Religion and Literature* 23, 3 (1991), 65–82.
Harris, Daniel. "Hagar in Christian Britain: Grace Aguilar's 'the Wanderers.'" *Victorian Literature and Culture* 27, 1 (1999), 143–169.
Hartog, Marion Moss. "Song of the Expatriated." *The Occident and American Jewish Advocate* 5, 7 (Oct. 1847), 338–339.
Hasan-Rokem, Galit, and Dundes, Alan, eds. *The Wandering Jew: Essays in the Interpretation of a Christian Legend*. Bloomington: Indiana University Press, 1986.
Hazlitt, William. *The Complete Works of William Hazlitt*. Ed. A. P. Waller and Arnold Glover. London: J. M. Dent, 1904.
HC Deb. *1 March 1833*, Vol. 16, cc 10–7.

———. *17 May 1830, Vol. 24, cc 784–814*.
Hemans, Felicia. *Selected Poems, Prose and Letters by Felicia Hemans*. Ed. Gary Kelly. Peterborough, ON: Broadview Press, 2002.
Heschel, Abraham Joshua. *The Prophets*. New York: Harper and Row, 1962.
Hill, Geoffrey. *The Collected Poems of Geoffrey Hill*. New York: Oxford University Press, 1986.
Hurwitz, Hyman. *A Grammar of the Hebrew Language*. 2nd ed., rev. and enlarged. London: John Taylor, 1835.
———. *An Introductory Lecture Delivered in the University of London on Tuesday, November 11, 1828*. London: John Taylor, 1828.
———. *[Kinat Yeshurun]: A Hebrew Dirge, Chaunted . . . on the Day of the Funeral of Princess Charlotte*. Trans. S. T. Coleridge. London: H. Barnett, 1817. Reprint, Cincinnati: Society of Jewish Bibliophiles, 1962.
———. *A Letter to Isaac L. Goldsmid, Esq. F.R.S., Chairman of the Association for Obtaining for British Jews Civil Rights and Privileges, on Certain Recent Mis-Statements Respecting the Jewish Religion*. London: Effingham Wilson; Royal Exchange, 1833.
Hyman, Leonard. "Hyman Hurwitz: The First Anglo-English Professor." *Transactions of the Jewish Historical Society of England, 1962–67*. Vol. 21. London: Jewish Historical Society of England, 1968, pp. 232–241.
The Jewish Bible. Philadelphia: Jewish Publication Society, 2003.
Johnson, Samuel. *The Lives of the Most Eminent English Poets; With Critical Observations on Their Works*. Ed. Roger Lonsdale. Oxford: Oxford University Press, 2006.
Katz, David. *God's Last Word: Reading the English Bible from the Reformation to Fundamentalism*. New Haven, CT: Yale University Press, 2004.
———. *The Jews in the History of England, 1485–1850*. Oxford: Oxford University Press, 1994.
Keats, John. *Complete Poems*. Ed. Jack Stillinger. Cambridge, MA: Harvard University Press, 1982.
Knowles, Melody D. "'Now English Denizened, Though Hebrue Borne': Did Mary Sidney Herbert, Countess of Pembroke, Read Hebrew?" *Studies in Philology* 109 (2012), 279–289.
Kugel, James. *The Idea of Biblical Poetry: Parallelism and Its History*. Baltimore: Johns Hopkins University Press, 1981.
Labbe, Jacqueline. *Charlotte Smith: Romanticism, Poetry and the Culture of Gender*. Manchester: Manchester University Press, 2001.
Lamb, Charles. *Essays of Elia*. London: E. P. Dutton, 1916.
Levi, David. *Letters to Dr. Priestley, in Answer to Those He Addressed to the Jews; Inviting them to an Amicable Discussion of the Evidences of Christianity. The third edition*. London: Printed for and by D. Levi; and sold by J. Johnson; J. Walker, and J. Parsons, 1793.
———. *A Succinct Account, of the Rites, and Ceremonies, of the Jews, as Observed by them . . . with a Chronological Summary,. . . .* London: Printed for J. Parsons, 1782(?).
Levin, Michael. *The Condition of England Question: Carlyle, Mill, Engels*. Houndmills, Basingstoke, Hampshire: Macmillan, 1998.

Levy, Amy. *The Complete Novels and Selected Writings of Amy Levy, 1861–1889*. Ed. Melvyn New. Gainesville: University Press of Florida, 1993.

———. *A London Plane Tree and Other Verse*. London: T. F. Unwin, 1889.

———. *Reuben Sachs: A Sketch*. Ed. Susan David Bernstein. Peterborough, ON: Broadview Press, 2006.

———. *The Romance of a Shop*. Ed. Susan David Bernstein. Peterborough, ON: Broadview Press, 2006.

Lindsay, Lord (Alexander Crawford Lindsay). *Letters on Egypt, Edom, and the Holy Land*. Vol. 1. London: Henry Colburn, 1838.

Lowth, Bishop, and Others. *Select Psalms in Verse, with Critical Remarks*. London: Printed for J. Hatchard, 1811. https://archive.org/details/seleinveoolond. Last accessed June 3, 2017.

Lyon, Emma. *Miscellaneous Poems*. Oxford: J. Bartlett, 1812.

Macaulay, Thomas Babington. *Critical and Historical Essays*. Ed. and arranged A. J. Grieve. London: Dent, 1961–1963.

Matthew, H. C. G. "Milman, Henry Hart (1791–1868)." *Oxford Dictionary of National Biography*. Oxford: Oxford University Press, 2004. http://www.oxforddnb.com/index/18/101018778. Last accessed June 30, 2017.

McCarthy, William. *Anna Letitia Barbauld: Voice of the Enlightenment*. Baltimore: Johns Hopkins University Press, 2008.

McCaul, Rev. Dr. "Sketches of Judaism and the Jews." *The Church of England Quarterly Review* 11: Article 7. 1840, 129–141. https://archive.org/details/churchenglandquo8unkngoog. Last accessed June 28, 2017.

Michie, Elsie B. "On the Sacramental Test Act, the Catholic Relief Act, the Slavery Abolition Act, and the Factory Act." *BRANCH: Britain, Representation and Nineteenth-Century History*, ed. Dino Franco Felluga. *Extension of Romanticism and Victorianism on the Net*. http://www.branchcollective.org/?ps_articles=elsie-b-michie-on-the-sacramental-test-act-the-catholic-relief-act-the-slavery-abolition-act-and-the-factory-act. Last accessed June 26, 2017.

Mill, John Stuart. "Thoughts on Poetry and Its Varieties." *Autobiography and Literary Essays*, ed. John M. Robson and Jack Stillinger, vol. 1. Toronto: University of Toronto Press, 1981, pp. 341–366.

Milman, Henry Hart. *The History of the Jews, From the Earliest Period Down to Modern Times*. Vol. 1. New York: A. C. Armstrong, 1893.

Milton, John. *The Complete Poetry and Essential Prose of John Milton*. Ed. William Kerrigan, John Rumrich, and Stephen M. Fallon. New York: Random House, 2007.

Moss, Celia, and Moss, Marion. *Early Efforts: A Volume of Poems by the Misses Moss, of the Hebrew Nation, Aged 18 and 16*. 2nd ed. London: Whittaker, 1839.

———. *The Romance of Jewish History, by the Misses C. and M. Moss*. 3 vols. London: Saunders and Otley, 1840.

———. *Tales of Jewish History*. London: Miller & Field. 1843.

Nance, Agnieszka. *Literary and Cultural Images of a Nation Without a State: The Case of Nineteenth Century Poland*. New York: Peter Lang, 2008.

Page, Judith W. "Hyman Hurwitz's *Hebrew Tales* (1826): Redeeming the Talmudic Garden." *British Romanticism and the Jews: History, Culture, Literature*, ed. Sheila A. Spector. New York: Palgrave Macmillan, 2002, pp. 197–213.

———. *Imperfect Sympathies: Jews and Judaism in British Romantic Literature and Culture*. New York: Palgrave Macmillan, 2004.

Paine, Thomas. *Thomas Paine: Political Writings*. Ed. Bruce Kuklick. Cambridge: Cambridge University Press, 2000.

Parens, Joshua. *Maimonides and Spinoza: Their Conflicting Views of Human Nature*. Chicago: University of Chicago Press, 2012.

Passover Hagaddah. Ed. Rabbi Nathan Goldberg. New York: KTAV Publishing House, 1949.

Perry, Thomas. *Public Opinion, Propaganda, and Politics in Eighteenth-Century England: A Study of the Jew Bill of 1753*. Cambridge, MA: Harvard University Press, 1962.

Porter, Brian. *When Nationalism Began to Hate*. Oxford: Oxford University Press, 2002.

Prazmowska, Anita, J. *A History of Poland*. New York: Palgrave Macmillan, 2011.

Robinson, Daniel. "Elegiac Sonnets: Charlotte Smith's Formal Paradoxy." *Papers on Language and Literature* 39, 2 (2003), 185–220.

Rosenfeld, Abraham. *Tisha B'Av Compendium*. New York: Judaica Press, 1965.

Roth, Cecil. *The Great Synagogue, London, 1690–1940*. London: Edward Goldston, 1950.

Ruderman, David. *Jewish Enlightenment in an English Key: Anglo-Jewry's Construction of Modern Jewish Thought*. Princeton, NJ: Princeton University Press, 2000.

"The Sabbath of the Jew." *Intellectual Repository and New Jerusalem Magazine* 128, 11 (Aug. 1850), 282.

Scheinberg, Cynthia. *Women's Poetry and Religion in Victorian England: Jewish Identity and Christian Culture*. Cambridge: Cambridge University Press, 2002.

The Scottish Collects from the Scottish Metrical Psalter. Ed. Millar Patrick. Edinburgh: Church of Scotland Committee on Publications, 193–?.

Scrivener, Michael. "British-Jewish Writing of the Romantic Era and the Problem of Modernity: The Example of David Levi." *British Romanticism and the Jews: History, Culture, Literature*, ed. Sheila A. Spector. New York: Macmillan, 2002, pp. 159–177.

———. "Following the Muse: Inspiration, Prophecy, and Deference in the Poetry of Emma Lyon (1788–1870), Anglo-Jewish Poet." *The Jews and British Romanticism: Politics, Religion, Culture*, ed. Sheila Spector. New York: Palgrave, 2005, pp. 105–126.

———. *Jewish Representation in British Literature 1780–1840: After Shylock*. New York: Palgrave Macmillan, 2011.

Seidman, Naomi. *Faithful Renderings: Jewish-Christian Difference and the Politics of Translation*. Chicago: University of Chicago Press, 2006.

Shakespeare, William. *Shakespeare's Sonnets*. Ed. Katherine Duncan-Jones. London: Methuen, 2010.

Shaw, David W. *Elegy and Paradox: Testing the Conventions*. Baltimore: Johns Hopkins University Press, 1994.

Shedlock, J. S. "Coronation Music." *Journal of the Royal Musical Association* 28 (1901), 141–160.

Shelley, Percy Bysshe. *Shelley's Poetry and Prose: Authoritative Texts, Criticism*. Ed. Donald H. Reiman and Neil Fraistat. New York: Norton, 2002.

Simpson, David. *Wordsworth's Historical Imagination: The Poetry of Displacement*. London: Methuen, 1987.

Singer, S. "Jews and Coronations." *Transactions of the Jewish Historical Society of England* (1908), 80–84.

Smith, Charlotte. *The Poems of Charlotte Smith*. Ed. Stuart Curran. Oxford: Oxford University Press, 1993.

The Spectator, May 8 1830, p. 8. http://archive.spectator.co.uk/page/8th-may-1830/8. Last accessed June 8, 2016.

Spector, Sheila A., ed. *British Romanticism and the Jews: History, Culture, Literature*. New York: Palgrave Macmillan, 2002.

———. *Byron and the Jews*. Detroit: Wayne State University Press, 2010.

———, ed. *Romanticism/Judaica: A Convergence of Cultures*. Farnham: Ashgate, 2011.

"State and Prospects of the Jews." *London Quarterly Review* 125 (1839), 93–107.

Steinsaltz, Adin. *A Guide to Jewish Prayer*. New York: Schocken, 2000.

Sternhold, Thomas, and John Hopkins et al. *The Whole Book of Psalmes / collected into English Meeter*. . . . London: Printed by G. M. for the Company of Stationers, 1638.

Telushkin, Joseph. *Hillel: If Not Now, When?* New York: Schocken, 2010.

Tennyson, Lord Alfred. *The Poems of Tennyson*. Ed. Christopher Ricks. Berkeley: University of California Press, 1987.

Trumpener, Katie. *Bardic Nationalism: The Romantic Novel and the British Empire*. Princeton, NJ: Princeton University Press, 1997.

Valman, Nadia. *The Jewess in Nineteenth Century British Literary Culture*. Cambridge: Cambridge University Press, 2007.

Vital, David. *A People Apart: The Jews in Europe, 1789–1939*. New York: Oxford University Press, 1999.

Watts, Isaac. *The Psalms of David / imitated in the language of the New Testament* . . . Exeter: C. Norris and Co., 1815.

Weisman, Karen A. "Anglo-Jewish Culture and the Condition of England: The Poetry of Marion and Celia Moss." *BRANCH: Britain, Representation, and Nineteenth-Century History*, ed. Dino Franco Felluga. *Extension of Romanticism and Victorianism on the Net*. http://www.branchcollective.org/?ps_articles=karen-weisman-anglo-jewish-culture-and-the-condition-of-england-the-poetry-of-marion-and-celia-moss. Last accessed July 21, 2017.

———. "Anglo-Jewish Romantic Poetry." *Blackwell Companion to British Romantic Poetry*, ed. Charles Mahoney. Oxford: Blackwell, 2011, 268–284.

———. "Mourning, Translation, Pastoral. Hyman Hurwitz and Literary Authority." *Romanticism/Judaica: A Convergence of Cultures*, ed. Sheila Spector. Farnham: Ashgate, 2011, pp. 45–55.

———, ed. *The Oxford Handbook of the Elegy*. Oxford: Oxford University Press, 2010.
White, Daniel. *Early Romanticism and Religious Dissent*. Cambridge: Cambridge University Press, 2007.
Wordsworth, William. *The Prelude 1799, 1805, 1850*. Ed. Jonathan Wordsworth, M. H. Abrams, and Stephen Gill. New York: Norton, 1979.
———. *William Wordsworth*. Ed. Stephen Gill. Oxford Authors. Oxford: Oxford University Press, 1984.

INDEX

Abendanon, Joseph Ben Jacob, 84–90
Abraham, 77–78, 208–9
Abrahams, I., 83
Acculturation and assimilation, 94–95, 99–105, 110, 190, 217–18
Addison, Joseph, 26–27, 32–33, 35–38, 40, 42, 45
Adler, Elkan, 84–88, 90
Adler, Nathan, 84
Aguilar, Grace, 2, 5, 7, 15, 167–214; and alienation, 171–72, 176, 197–98, 203; assertion of cultural authority by, 206; background of, 167–68, 175; on conversion of Jews, 179–83; and cultural values, 12; and exile, 174, 177, 196–99, 208–9; Hartog's (Moss's) tribute to, 222–23; helping as theme for, 188, 190–91, 194–200; and history, 169–72; on infants, 181–83; Jewish heritage of, 167–68, 174–85, 190, 193, 195–96, 204–5, 210–14; as Jewish Protestant, 5, 176, 232n8; and nature, 170–71, 177–80, 185–94, 206, 231n5; and pastoral, 171–72, 174–75, 191–93; religion and spirituality of, 193–98, 210–14; self-reflexivity of, 190–91; and Spain, 173–75; and subjectivity, 175, 200, 203; as a woman author, 12–13; on women in Judaism, 180–83; and Wordsworth's poetry, 169–72, 193, 194
Aguilar, Grace, writings by: "Autumn Leaves," 185–87; "Autumn Winds," 185–91, 194; "Dialogue Stanzas," 149, 168–73, 194; "The Evergreen," 177–80; "The Hebrew's Appeal, on Occasion of the Late Fearful Ukase Promulgated by the Emperor of Russia," 175–76; "History of the Jews in England," 10, 171, 176–77, 206; "I Never Loved a Flower," 191–94; "An Infant's Smile," 181–85; *The Jewish Faith*, 183; "The Rocks of Elim," 200–207; "Sabbath Thoughts," 195–96, 210–14; "Song of the Spanish Jews, During their 'Golden Age'," 173–74; *The Spirit of Judaism*, 184–85, 196–97, 211; "A Vision of Jerusalem," 195–200, 203; "The Wanderers," 207–9; *Women of Israel*, 180
Ahasuerus, 117–19, 168–69
Alienation: Aguilar and, 171–72, 176, 197–98, 203; of Anglo-Jewish poets, 2, 7, 79–80, 127; from expressive resources, 7, 11, 79, 174–76; Levy and, 218; Lyon and, 19; Moss sisters and, 134
Alpers, Paul, 225n2
Amelia (princess), 47–48
Amidah prayer, 86–87, 120–21, 194
Anderson, Benedict, 10
Anglo-Jewish identity: acculturation/assimilation and, 94–95, 99–105, 110, 190; Aguilar and, 176–77, 200, 212; Anglo-Jewish poets and, 11–12; contested nature of, 4–6, 9–12, 98–99, 104–6, 110–11, 116, 121–22, 126, 156–57, 200; Hurwitz and, 98–112, 115; Levy and, 217–18; monarchial elegies and, 85, 88, 90; Moss sisters and, 128–29, 137–42; York Massacre and, 137–40
Anglo-Jewish poets: alienation of, 2, 7; assertion of cultural authority by, 85; and the elegy, 71, 72; identity formation of, 4, 7; Moss sisters on, 142; and pastoral, 3, 218; subjectivity of, 2–3, 6–7, 91
Anne (queen), 84
Apion the Grammarian, 107
Arnold, Matthew, "Stanzas from the Grande Chartreuse," 215–18
Ashley, Anthony Ashley Cooper, Lord, 167, 200–201, 206–7
Assimilation. *See* Acculturation and assimilation
Aston, Walter Hutchinson, 27

INDEX

Backscheider, Paula, 28
Barbauld, Anna Letitia, 30–32
Bate, Julius, 34–35
BCP. *See* Book of Common Prayer
Beaumont, George Howland, 72
Beauty, 134–35
Behrendt, Stephen, 73
Benjamin, Walter, 150
Blake, William, 111
Blasphemy, 89–90
Blasphemy Act, 89
Boethius, 110
Bonaparte, Napoleon, 108–9
Bonivard, Francois, 139–40
Book of Common Prayer (BCP), 21, 26, 39–40, 42, 44–45, 49, 57–59, 66
Bridegroom imagery, 36
Britannia, 73, 77, 79, 105, 111
Bronson, Bertrand, 16, 23
Browning, Robert, "Home Thoughts from Abroad," 161
Bulwer-Lytton, Edward, 115–16
Byron, George Gordon, Lord, 159, 216; "From the Day of the Destruction of Jerusalem by Titus," 138; "The Isles of Greece," 159–60; "The Prisoner of Chillon: A Fable," 139–40; "The Vision of Judgment," 92, 119

Cambridge, Duke of, 91
Carlyle, Thomas, *Chartism*, 123–27, 131
Catherine the Great, 175
Catholic Relief Act, 9
Catholics, 8–9, 29
Charles III, Duke of Savoy, 139
Charlotte, Princess of Wales: brief history of, 73; as Britannia, 73, 77, 79; Hurwitz's elegy on, 14, 73–82, 102, 105, 109, 112–13, 158; Lyon's dedication to, 17–18, 32, 47
Chartists, 124
Child, as Romantic trope, 16, 181–83
Christian Hebraists, 32, 34, 46, 64, 83, 85
Christian Zionism, 200
Church of England, 8–9, 83, 91, 126
Church of England Quarterly Review, 179, 199
Civil and political disabilities, 8, 64, 88, 99, 117, 125, 153–54, 156, 177
Clark, Michael, 9
Cobbett, William, 70, 89, 106–7, 115–16
Coleridge, Samuel Taylor: "Dejection: an Ode," 97, 103, 112, 114–15, 150, 174; "The Eolian Harp," 41; "Frost at Midnight," 131–32; Hurwitz's friendship with, 73, 76; and the meaning of nature, 41–42; translations of Hurwitz by, 14, 74–78, 82, 93, 96, 100, 102–3, 105, 113–14, 119–21
Colley, Linda, 10
Consolation: disappearing sources of, 215–17; of elegy, 48, 70, 115; Jewish alienation from, 20, 218; landscape as source of, 20, 144; Lyon and, 19, 23, 25; lyric in relation to, 2, 3; Moss sisters and, 147; nature as source of, 147, 189; pastoral, 20, 115, 218
Conversion, 63–64, 179–83, 206–7
Cosmopolitanism, 1–2, 6, 111, 175, 220, 222
Cromwell, Oliver, 7
Crusades, 74
Crypto-Jews, 168
Cumberland, Duke of, 91

Deism, 101
Diana, Princess of Wales, 72
Dickens, Charles, *Hard Times*, 123
Dimock, Henry, 83–84
Disraeli, Benjamin, 230n20
Disraeli, Isaac, *The Genius of Judaism*, 8
Dissenters, 29–31
Donne, John, 27

Edict of Expulsion, 74
Edward I, 74
Elegies for British monarchs, 14
Elegy and elegies: Anglo-Jewish poets and, 3, 71, 72; for Charlotte, 73–82; connection to the deceased established by, 48–49, 74–75; for George III, 82, 91–104, 111–22; Hebrew, on English monarchs, 84–90, 94; Lyon's use of, 48–49; for Mary, 84–88; pastoral, 71; self-reflexivity as characteristic of, 96–97; themes and characteristics of, 70–71; for William III, 90
"Elements of Faith: for the use of Jewish Youth of Both Sexes," 109
"Eli Tzion Ve'areha" (medieval Hebrew poem), 74
Emancipation, for the Jews: controversy over, 4, 9–11, 89, 91; conversion as factor in support for, 63. *See also* Jewish Relief Bill
Endelman, Todd, 10, 63, 94
Enfield, William, 30
England: Christianity-based national identity of, 8–10, 90, 126, 138, 157; workers'

sociopolitical place in, 123–27, 131. *See also* Anglo-Jewish identity; Royalty
Esther, 117–19, 168–69, 172, 194
Evil, 59
Exile: Aguilar and, 174, 177, 196–99, 208–9; Jewish people characterized by, 7, 74, 79, 81, 106, 111–12, 127, 133, 135–36, 138, 153, 156–59, 164, 175, 177–79; Lyon and, 13; Moss sisters and, 15, 133, 135–36, 138, 153, 156–61, 164–65
Ezekiel, 195

Felsenstein, Frank, 179, 180
Flower, as Romantic trope, 135
French Revolution, 125

Galchinsky, Michael, 182, 195, 232n8
Gascoyne, Isaac, 9
Generalization, 16, 23
George III, 14, 48, 82, 87, 91–104, 111–22
George IV, 17, 72
Gillingham, Susan, 28
Gloucester, Duke of, 91
God, interpretation and knowledge of, 37–46
"God Save the King," 110
Goldsmid, Francis, 9
Gray, Thomas, "Elegy in a Country Churchyard," 20
Great Synagogue of London, 91

HaCohen, Abraham Ben Shabthi, 110
Hagar, 207–9
Haman, 117–19, 168–69, 171
Handel, George Frideric, "Zadok the Priest," 87
Hannay, Margaret, 27
Hartog, Alphonse, 128
Hartog, Numa, 125
Haskalah (Jewish Enlightenment), 11
Haydn, Franz Joseph, 26, 38–39
Hazlitt, William, 4–5, 116
Hebrew Bible: controversies over translation and interpretation of, 13–14, 21–23, 34, 36, 76, 80; misconceptions of vengeance's place in, 56–58
Hebrew language: Christians' knowledge of, 83–84; declining knowledge of, 11, 14, 94–95, 99; Hurwitz and, 14, 73, 76, 80, 98–101, 103–5, 110–11; Lyon and, 13, 17, 22, 28, 34–35; monarchs celebrated in, 83. *See also* translation

Hebrew Psalms, 13, 19, 22–64; Psalm 8, 110; Psalm 19, 26–46; Psalm 24, 78–79; Psalm 29, 133; Psalm 49, 46–54; Psalm 50, 65–69; Psalm 55, 97–98; Psalm 72, 55–56, 116–17; Psalm 73, 23–24; Psalm 137, 106, 111, 157, 159; translation into English of, 34
Heine, Heinrich, 1
Hemans, Felicia: "Casabianca," 153, 157; "England's Dead," 152
Hill, Geoffrey, "September Song," 71
Hillel, Rabbi, 209
Historicity, 4
History, Aguilar's "Dialogue Stanzas" and, 169–72
Hurwitz, Hyman, 7, 14, 70–122; assertion of cultural authority by, 14, 74, 80, 96; background of, 73; cosmopolitanism of, 111; and cultural values, 12; defense of Jews by, 107–10; on George III's death, 14, 82–83; and Hebrew language, 14, 73, 76, 80, 98–101, 103–5, 110–11; Jewish heritage of, 76, 83, 93–94, 98–105, 110–12; literary inheritance claimed by, 91, 104, and pastoral, 78, 114–15; self-reflexivity of, 96, 104
Hurwitz, Hyman, writings by: elegy on Charlotte, 14, 73–82, 102, 105, 109, 112–13, 158; *A Grammar of the Hebrew Language*, 110–11; *Hebrew Tales*, 73, 100, 229n46; "Israel's Lament," 75, 95–96; "A Letter to Isaac L. Goldsmid," 107–10; "The Tears of a Grateful People," 82–83, 91–104, 111–22
Hutchinson, John, 13, 34

Identity: British, 10; Jewish, 60, 103, 182; poets' construction of, 4, 7. *See also* Anglo-Jewish identity; Subjectivity
Inquisition, 7–8, 168, 175, 199
The Intellectual Repository and New Jerusalem Magazine, 213
Irony. *See* Romantic irony
Isaiah, 212
Ismael, 207–9

James II, 88
Jeremiah, 54–55, 102, 110, 112, 119
Jerusalem, 81, 106, 111–12, 135, 157–59, 163, 195–200. *See also* Temples of Jerusalem, destruction of
Jewish Naturalization Bill, 9–10
Jewish Publication Society (JPS), 23, 36, 40, 42, 44, 46, 49, 57–59, 61, 74

INDEX

Jewish Relief Bill, 4, 10, 153–54, 156, 161, 164. *See also* Emancipation, for the Jews

Jewish Sabbath Journal, 128

Jews and Judaism: acculturation/assimilation and, 217–18; conversion of, 63–64, 179–83, 206–7; crypto-, 168; defenses of, 4, 107–10, 115–16, 154; derogatory attitudes toward, 5, 9, 89, 106–8, 116, 156–57, 167, 179, 212; history of, in England, 7–8; identity of, 60, 103, 182; interpretive authority of, concerning the Bible, 13–14, 21–23, 34, 36, 46; loyalty of, to crown and country, 54–55, 82–85, 91, 93–94, 97–99, 105–6, 108–11, 117–19, 155–58, 200; Polish, 164; population of, in England, 8; Protestants linked with, 231n23; separateness/particularism of, 5, 93–95, 101, 103–5, 119, 123, 154, 176, 185, 213–14; universality of, 5, 11, 100–101; women's role, 180–83; York Massacre of, 74, 80, 133, 137–40. *See also* Acculturation and assimilation; Anglo-Jewish identity; Anglo-Jewish poets; Civil and political disabilities; Emancipation, for the Jews; Jewish Relief Bill; Subjectivity

Joel, 74–75, 112–14

Johnson, Samuel, 72

Joseph of Chartres, 74, 80

Josephus, Flavius, 107–8

JPS. *See* Jewish Publication Society

Judaism. *See* Jews and Judaism

Kaddish, 38

Katz, David, 21

Keats, John, "To Autumn," 147

Kennicott, Benjamin, 13, 21, 34, 83

King, Edward, 146

King James Bible (KJV), 21, 42, 43, 44–45, 49, 55–59, 65–66

KJV. *See* King James Bible

Lamb, Charles, 5, 93

Lamentations, 106, 111–12, 194

Leopold, Prince of Saxe-Coburg, 72, 77

Leshon hara (inappropriate speech), 88–89

Levi, David, 55, 64, 95, 99

Levin, Michael, 126

Levy, Amy, 1, 4, 6, 217–23; "London in July," 220; "A London Plane Tree," 219; *The London Plane Tree*, 218–19; "A March Day in London," 219–21; *Reuben Sachs*, 218; "The Village Garden," 221

Lindsay, Lord, 200–206

London Society for the Promotion of Christianity among the Jews, 63

London Working Men's Association, 124

Lowth, Robert, 26–27, 46–47, 54, 83

Luzzatto, Moses Chaim, "The Contented Shepherd," 110

Lyon, Emma, 2, 7, 16–69; assertion of cultural authority by, 17, 22, 24–26; background of, 17; and cultural values, 12; and exile, 13; and Hebrew language, 13, 17, 22, 28, 34–35; and identity, 16–17; Jewish heritage of, 17, 21, 23, 27–28, 37–38, 43–44, 51–52, 54, 62–63; literary inheritance claimed by, 19, 27–32, 38–41, 43, 45, 67; Neoclassical and Romantic aspects in work of, 22–23; and pastoral, 19–21; relation of, to royalty, 46–49, 54–56; self-conception of, 13; subjectivity of, 19, 23, 25; translations by, of Hebrew Psalms, 13, 19, 22–64; as a woman author, 12–13, 17

Lyon, Emma, writings by: "On the Death of Her Royal Highness, The Princess Amelia," 47–48; "Lines Addressed to the University of Cambridge," 20–21; "Lines to the Muse," 24; "Ode on Ambition," 50–53, 68; "An Ode on Death," 20; "Ode to Genius," 67–69; "An Ode to Honour," 53; "An Ode to Indifference," 53; Psalm 19, 26–46; Psalm 49, 46–54; Psalm 50, 65–69; Psalm 58, 56–63; Psalm 72, 55–56; Psalm 73, 23–24; "Revenge: An Ode," 62

Lyon, Solomon, 13, 17, 21, 84

Lyric, 3; Moss sisters and, 142–44; subjectivity as characteristic of, 130

Macaulay, Thomas, 153–54, 156

Maccabees, 140, 141

Maimonides, 67

Marx, Leo, 225n2

Mary (queen), 84–89

Mays, J. C. C., 96, 97, 102, 105, 112, 116–17, 120

McCarthy, William, 30

Metastasio, Pietro, 110

Mill, John Stuart, 130

Milman, Henry, 137–39, 141, 157, 173

Milton, John, 18, 43–45, 52–54, 72, 90; "Lycidas," 20, 52–53, 70–71, 145–47, 152, 155

Miriam, 88, 202, 205–6

Monarchs. *See* Royalty

Monotheism, 184
Moses, 88, 202, 204, 205
Moss, Celia and Marion, 2, 7, 123–66; assertion of cultural authority by, 127; background of, 128; on beauty, 134–35; context for poetry of, 123–27; and English national identity, 137–40; exile as theme of, 15, 133, 135–36, 138, 153, 156–61, 164–65; father of, 128–30, 132; Jewish heritage of, 137–42, 151; literary careers of, 127–28, 165; literary inheritance claimed by, 12, 15; and lyric, 142–44; and national identity, 133, 138–40, 157, 159–61, 230n19; and nature, 141–50; and pastoral, 134; on Poland, 161–64; self-reflexivity of, 127, 136, 147–48, 152; speech and listening as themes of, 129–33; subjectivity of, 130, 133, 141, 145, 164–66; woman as theme for, 134–36, 144–45; as women authors, 12–13, 128–29; York Massacre as subject of, 133, 137–40
Moss, Celia and Marion, writings by: "Autumn Is Coming," 145–52; *Early Efforts*, 15, 123, 128, 130; "Emigrant's Song," 160–61; "The Fadeless Flower," 134–35; "Father's Lament," 132–33; "The Feast of Trumpets," 129; "The Fortunes of Herod Agrippa," 151; "The Jewish Girl's Song," 135–36; "Lament for Poland," 162; "The Massacre of the Jews at York: A Historical Poem," 133, 137–40; "The Moss Rose," 142–44; "Polander's Song," 162–64; *The Romance of Jewish History*, 141, 151, 159; "Song of the Expatriated," 165; *Tales of Jewish History*, 151; "Thou Sittest Alone, Like a Widow'd Bride," 157–58; "To a Young Mother," 129, 131, 133; tribute to Aguilar, 222–23; "Up, Up with the Anchor," 166; "Weep No More," 152–58

Nature: Aguilar and, 170–71, 177–80, 185–94, 206, 231n5; ambivalent meanings of, for Anglo-Jewish poets, 79; Moss sisters and, 141–50; signifying capacity of, 39–42
Naylor, James, 89
Neoclassicism: in Lyon's work, 22–23; Romanticism compared to, 16
New Criticism, 16
Nicholas I, 175
Nonconformists, 8–9
November Uprising (Poland, 1830–1831), 161, 164

The Occident and American Jewish Advocate (journal), 165, 190, 193, 207–8

Page, Judith, 100, 173, 229n46
Paine, Thomas, 40
Pale, 175
Palestine, 200–201
Passover Haggadah, 60
Pastoral: absence of, 216; Aguilar and, 171–72, 174–75, 191–93; Anglo-Jewish poets and, 3, 218; concept of, 225n2; expressive resources of, 79–80; Hurwitz and, 78, 114–15; Lyon and, 19–21; Moss sisters and, 134; original biblical, 80
Peripatetic. *See* Romantic peripatetic
Perry, Thomas, 10
Pitt, William, 98
Pogroms, 83
Poland, 161–64
Priestley, Joseph, 64
Prophets, 66–67
Protestantism, 231n23. *See also* Dissenters; Nonconformists
Psalms. *See* Hebrew Psalms
Purim, 118, 168–69, 172

Reform Bill (1832), 106, 124
Resettlement (1656), 83, 89
Return, as Jewish theme, 110–11, 193–94, 200–201
Richard I, 82, 139
Romantic irony, 2–3, 20, 71, 79–80, 130, 136, 171–76, 215
Romanticism, 2–3
Romantic peripatetic, 20, 79, 175
Rosenfeld, Abraham, 75, 81
Rothschild, Lionel de, 125
Royalty: Jews' loyalty to country and, 54–55, 82–85, 91, 93–94, 97–99, 105–6, 108–11, 117–19, 155–58, 200; Lyon's relationship to, 46–49, 54–56
Ruderman, David, 13, 21, 46, 64, 95, 100

Sabbath observance, 212–14
Sacramental Test Act, 9
Sanhedrin conference (1807), 108–9
Scheinberg, Cynthia, 179, 210, 231n5, 233n5
Scottish Psalter, 57
Scrivener, Michael, 22, 64
Sensibility poems, 51–53
Sephardim, 94, 168

Shakespeare, William, 134
Shelley, Percy Bysshe, 39, 216; "Adonais," 70, 147, 152; "England in 1819," 91; *Hellas*, 6; "Lines Written among the Euganean Hills," 174; "Ode to the West Wind," 145, 147–50, 186–91, 219, 220; "Ozymandias," 154, 156
Shema prayer, 184
Sidney, Mary, 27
Slavery, 175
Smith, Charlotte, 51–53, 68–69, 137
Song of Songs, 81
Soul, 192–93
Southey, Robert, "A Vision of Judgement," 92, 119
Spain, 7, 74, 94, 173–75
Speech, ethical codes governing, 58–61, 88–90
Sternhold-Hopkins translation of the Psalms, 25, 57
Subjectivity: Aguilar and, 175, 200, 203; Anglo-Jewish, 104, 110, 112, 121–22, 142; of Anglo-Jewish poets, 2–3, 6–7, 91; as characteristic of Romanticism, 130; generalization in relation to, 16; Lyon and, 19, 23, 25; Moss sisters and, 130, 133, 141, 145, 164–66. *See also* Anglo-Jewish identity; Identity
Syncellus, Michael, 203

Temples of Jerusalem, destruction of, 14, 74, 106, 111–12, 135, 138, 163
Tennyson, Alfred, Lord, 161–63
Test and Corporation Acts for Nonconformists, 9
Tisha B'Av, 14, 73–74, 76, 80–81, 111–13, 194
Translation: debates over biblical, 13–14, 21, 23, 34, 76; as means of preserving Jewish heritage, 95, 100; of the psalms, 22; women and, 27

Trumpener, Katie, 138

Ukases, 175
Universality: of children, 182; in Hurwitz's elegy on Charlotte, 76–79; of Judaism, 5, 11, 100–101
Universities Tests Act, 8, 125

Valman, Nadia, 11, 135, 230n19, 230n21, 231n23, 232n8
Vengeance, 56–57, 62
Victorianism, 215–18
Vital, David, 8

Wandering Jew, 6, 20, 84, 169, 175–76
Watts, Isaac, 25, 57
Wessely, Hartwig, 110
White, Daniel, 30
William, Prince of Orange, 73
William II, 87
William III, 84, 90
Women and women authors: Aguilar as, 12–13; Judaism and, 180–83; Lyon as, 12–13, 17; Moss sisters as, 12–13, 128–29; religious writings and translations by, 27–30; societal place of, 233n5
Wordsworth, William, 3, 25, 26, 43, 79–80, 134–35, 143–45, 169–72, 181–83, 190, 194, 221; "Dialogue Stanzas," 15; "Expostulation and Reply," 170–71, 194; "Immortality Ode," 181, 183, 193; "A Jewish Family," 172–73; "Peele Castle," 71–72; "She Dwelt Among the Untrodden Ways," 144; "A Slumber Did my Spirit Seal," 143; "The Tables Turned," 170, 194; "Tintern Abbey," 135, 174, 175, 183
Workers, condition of England for, 123–27

York Massacre (1190), 74, 80, 133, 137–40

ACKNOWLEDGMENTS

This book has been the labor of many years, and it is a daunting and delightful task to express my gratitude to the many individuals who have supported, encouraged, and helped me along the way: Susan David Bernstein, Alan Bewell, Mark Canuel, Brian Corman, Harry Fox, Michael Galchinsky, Marjorie Garson, Sol Goldberg, Sarah Gracombe, Heather Jackson, the late J.R. de J. Jackson, Heidi Kaufman, Jacques Khalip, Mark Knight, Amir Lavie, Deidre Lynch, Michael Macovski, Charles Mahoney, Tirzah Meacham, Kate Merriman, Michael Morgan, Timothy Morton, Andrea Most, David Novak, Judith Page, Thomas Pfau, Arkady Plotnitsky, Arthur Ripstein, Terry Robinson, Meri-Jane Rochelson, Jonathan Sachs, Cynthia Scheinberg, Esther Schor, Michael Scrivener, Naomi Seidman, Anna Shternshis, Sheila Spector, Paul Stevens, and Daniel White.

The two anonymous readers for the University of Pennsylvania Press offered astute and carefully considered comments that helped me improve the final product. Jerry Singerman has been a most patient and astute editor, and I am grateful for his wisdom and guidance.

Conferences have provided valuable forums for discussion, debate, and critique. I am especially grateful to audiences of the Association for Jewish Studies, North American Society for the Study of Romanticism, and North American Victorian Studies Association conferences for valuable feedback and discussion that have shaped the development of my ideas.

Some of this material has appeared elsewhere in earlier versions: "Anglo-Jewish Culture and the Condition of England: The Poetry of Marion and Celia Moss," in *BRANCH: Britain, Representation, and Nineteenth-Century History*, ed. Dino Franco Felluga, *Extension of Romanticism and Victorianism on the Net*, 2013, http://www.branchcollective.org/?ps_articles=karen-weisman-anglo-jewish-culture-and-the-condition-of-england-the-poetry-of-marion-and-celia-moss; "Anglo-Jewish Romantic Poetry," in *The Blackwell Companion to British Romantic Poetry*, ed. Charles Mahoney (Oxford: Blackwell, 2011), pp. 268–284;

and "Mourning, Translation, Pastoral: Hyman Hurwitz and Literary Authority," in *A Convergence of Cultures*, ed. Sheila Spector (Farnham: Ashgate, 2011), pp. 45–55.

My husband, Arthur Ripstein, has been my most astute reader and the most resolute source of encouragement. Arthur and our children, Aviva and Noah, have ensured that our home is always filled with love, understanding, and wisdom. In the context of a book about the complexities of inheritance, nothing could be more deeply cherished.